# Turning the Solomon Key

## George Washington, the Bright Morning Star, and the Secrets of Masonic Astrology

### Robert Lomas

www.RobertLomas.com
www.Bradford.ac.uk/webofhiram/
www.TurningtheSolomonKey.com

Foreword by Katherine Neville

**FAIR WINDS**
PRESS
BEVERLY, MASSACHUSETTS

First published in the USA in 2006 by
Fair Winds Press, a member of
Quayside Publishing Group
100 Cummings Center, Suite 406-L
Beverly, MA 01915-0610
www.fairwindspress.com

11 10 09 08 07      1 2 3 4 5

ISBN-13: 978-1-59233-284-7
ISBN-10: 1-59233-284-6

Library of Congress Cataloging-in-Publication Data available


Cover design by TracingBoards.com
Book design by *tabula rasa* graphic design

Printed and bound in USA

Dedicated to my wife Ann.

# Contents

# Acknowledgments

Firstly, I would like to thank Holly Schmidt, my publisher at Fair Winds Press, for inspiring me to tackle this subject.

As I was putting the book together I discussed it with thriller writer Katherine Neville, who is married to the well-known brain scientist, Karl H. Pribram. She lives in Washington, D.C., and is knowledgeable about the city. Katherine kindly offered to write a foreword, although she was busy working on a new novel as well as editing a new European edition of *The Eight*. I would like to thank both Holly and Katherine for encouraging me.

I was delighted when Karl took time out from editing his forthcoming book on the history of brain research to look through my ideas on neuron growth and, as will become apparent later on, generously pointed my research in a remarkably useful direction.

Ellen Phillips has proved a delightful editor. She has guided me with a light touch and helpful suggestions, positively yet unobtrusively, so that it is only with hindsight that I see how much she has helped me shape my thoughts and stopped me drifting too far into jargon and "nerd-speak." Thank you, Ellen, for your support, amusing asides and for sharing your addiction to Sherlock Holmes, wet muddy dogs, and the use of myths in storytelling.

John Wheelwright, who did the copy-editing, could not fairly be described as delightful, but he is a witty fount of knowledge and a stern guardian of clarity of expression. He has proved a trusted partner, quick to spot oversights and ambiguity. I thank him for his efforts too.

John Gettings has been a steady hand coordinating the production and a center of calm in the middle of the chaotic publishing process. He has the calm voice and unflusterable attitude of a NASA mission controller, and I am grateful for his help and advice.

Martin and Trevor Jackson of www.tracingboards.com have done a wonderful job on the cover and illustrations. My agent Bill Hamilton and his assistant Corinne Chabert have been their usual professional selves and have encouraged and guided me throughout the writing process.

Finally I want to thank my wife Ann, and children, Rhisiart, Delyth and Geraint for their continual help and encouragement.

# Foreword

"It was a dark and stormy night . . ." That may sound like the traditional opening of a thriller novel—but it is also a very accurate description of the meteorological setting on the night when Karl Pribram and I first met Robert Lomas. Ensconced in a comfy booth at the restaurant of the Hotel Kirkwall in Orkney, and undaunted by the pounding rain and wild waves crashing against the sea wall just outside, we passed four hours over dinner in scintillating conversation, along with our companions— old friend Andrej Detela, a fascinating Slovenian physicist, and Robert's erstwhile coauthor of his early books, Christopher Knight.

All five of us had been invited to speak at the Orkney Science Festival by our equally fascinating host, festival director Howie Firth (who graciously swept in from the deluge long enough to pay for our elaborate three-course meal!) Professor Firth's great strength and mission is to bring together, for one week each year, the widest possible potpourri of scientists and craftspersons to present their recent discoveries in both ancient and futuristic sciences.

In our lectures, Karl—with his more than sixty years of research into the workings of the brain—was able to cover both ends of the time spectrum. As a crafter of novels, I had volunteered to speak about the ancient legends of these North Sea isles, tales that were mined by my fiction-writing predecessors like Sir Walter Scott: pirates, Norsemen, Egyptians, Druids. And of course, Prince Henry Sinclair, the "First Earl of Orkney," whose grandson William would one day construct the famous Roslin Chapel, which has once more, recently, inspired so much fiction and furor.

Over our lengthy meal that night, we quickly learned that we had much in common: for instance, Andrej and Robert had both written books about the great scientist and inventor, Nikola Tesla—who also appears as a pivotal character in my novel, *The Magic Circle*. I had read the two books Robert and Chris had published to-date—*The Hiram Key* and *The Second Messiah*—and found that these overlapped greatly with my own researches into ancient esoteric practices. And Robert—both as a Freemason and a scientist—was deeply interested in Karl's decades of research on memory and consciousness, and how these research findings might help us understand the ancient roots of initiatory rituals of which, today, Robert believed we could still perhaps see as vestiges in Masonic ceremonies. (Some years later, Robert would develop this idea into the seminal spark of his book, *Turning the Hiram Key*.)

In Orkney, we were still lingering over our desserts, dialogues, and digestifs, until it was nearly midnight: the storm outside had dissipated, all other diners had departed, and the waiters were becoming palpably restless over our extended stay.

"Well," announced Robert at last, "I think we had better get on. The place we're headed might not let us in, if we arrive with such a large group after midnight."

Andrej wondered what place could possibly still be open, so late at night on such a tiny island: in Ljubljana, he pointed out, everything closes by 10 p.m.

Chris explained: "It may be one of the oldest extant Lodges in the world, not far from here, containing what some believe is the oldest Lodge artifact . . . "

No one needed to ask what sort of "Lodge" they were referring to, since both authors are high-level Freemasons. I was excited at the prospect of seeing something few had ever seen—and I was privately thanking heaven that Karl had had the tact *not* to point out that our little group included a female—someone who would likely not have been permitted to go on a private midnight tour of the "inner sanctum" of any American Masonic lodge.

So this merry band of scientists set out in the midnight hour through a dense funnel of fog. We scaled the narrow cobbled streets of Kirkwall—to a place whose location I am still forbidden to reveal—three knocks on a secret door, trooping up a flight of thirty-three steps to a hidden room . . . and I found myself, quite by accident, to be one of the few people ever permitted (and perhaps one of the last—since it is now locked away in a vault!) to lay eyes upon the rare and ancient Kirkwall Scroll.

This midnight visit would be destined, as the screenwriter said, to be "the beginning of a beautiful friendship." Robert Lomas describes the event in *Turning the Hiram Key*, where he discusses (and shows pictures of!) the mysterious Kirkwall Scroll, and speculates upon its age and significance.

Shortly after receiving my presentation copy of *Turning the Hiram Key*—but before I had the chance to read it—a matter of some urgency arose. I had agreed, along with thirty other invited authors, to contribute to the first anthology of Thriller stories, launching the new British-American organization, International Thriller Writers.

My story, *The Tuesday Club*, takes place on the very first day that Benjamin Franklin, John Adams, and Thomas Jefferson met in Paris on the French diplomatic mission and something mysterious is about to take place. I knew that Ben Franklin—a Freemason who'd been Worshipful Master of the French Loge des Neuf Soeurs—had received his honorary doctorate from St. Andrews in Scotland, a place believed to have been a bastion of pre-English masonry.

Early Scottish masonry is a subject few have written of and is therefore hard to research—even now its very existence is hotly contested by "western" masons here in America. I was aware of this, for I had recently attended a series of lectures on Washington, D.C. Masonic history organized by the capital's lodges, which included an all-day bus tour of Masonic sites here in Washington, and a visit to Alexandria, Virginia, Lodge #22 ("The Lighthouse"), of which George Washington had been first Worshipful Master. Furthermore, these lectures and tours in modern-day Washington—many set amid bus fumes and air conditioning noises—were somehow lacking the immediate, evocative sense of history that we had experienced in our midnight Kirkwall sojourn.

I realized that I knew someone who had more recently written the definitive book on early Scottish Freemasonry: *Freemasonry and the Birth of Modern Science*. It was packed with little known facts in the background of Christopher Wren, Robert Boyle, and the creation of the Royal Society. The publication of that book had made my friend Robert Lomas the best-selling Masonic author of all time.

I knew that the research in Robert's earlier books had often influenced my fellow novelists: my friend Steve Berry has acknowledged *The Second Messiah* for a pivotal idea involving the Shroud of Turin in his novel, *The Templar Legacy*—a book which, as of this writing, has spent many months on the bestseller lists. And Dan Brown has gone on record stating that he was inspired by secrets of Roslin Chapel revealed in *The Hiram Key*, in his research for *The Da Vinci Code*. (Indeed, in British esoteric circles, the joke is that "symbologist" Dr. Robert Langdon is actually Freemason Dr. Robert Lomas in disguise!) So I hoped that Robert would pull some little known Masonic trivia from his sleeve for my story, regarding Ben Franklin's secret role in early Scottish Masonry. But when I phoned Robert in England to query him, I was in for a big surprise.

"My new project," Robert told me, "is to unveil the true Masonic meaning hidden within Washington, D.C., as seen through the eyes of its Founding Freemason Father: George Washington."

Nothing could have made me happier. Everyone already knows the Masonic sagas of Washington laying the cornerstone of the Capitol building wearing his Masonic apron designed by Lafayette's wife. And Robert and I had often discussed the esoteric aspects of the layout of our nation's capital, the square of the altar, the four North-East-South-West directions of the Masonic initiation, and so forth. But few people recall that George Washington was not only our first president and a famous general: he was also a master surveyor. Indeed, before inheriting his property at Mt.Vernon, he had made his living by surveying the Ohio River Valley. As a surveyor, he needed a grasp of the relationship between geography and astronomy: the Earth and its relation to the movements of stars and planets.

I was in for an even bigger surprise when I read the first draft of Robert's manuscript. The book itself is nothing short of an initiation into the mind of a trained surveyor who was also our most famous Freemason.

If you were a person with such skills, knowledge, and authority—and you were in the position to create a pristine city that would be the headquarters of a new civilization, a "Great Experiment," as our Founding Fathers termed it— where would you begin?

From the moment Robert Lomas, a scientist himself, reveals to us that Washington had clipped the pages of his almanacs, tracking the helical (predawn) risings of the Masonic icon—the Bright Morning Star—and had pasted these almanac pages into his diary for fourteen years — we are hooked by the intimate insight into the mind that was guided by that morning star.

I had made my own journey up the thirty-three steps and into the hidden room in Kirkwall. I leave the voyage of discovery hidden within this book to you!

—Katherine Neville
Best-selling author of *The Eight* and *The Magic Circle*

# Introduction

# In Pursuit of a Mystery: Washington, D.C.

George Washington, the first president of the United States, was a Freemason. This book is the story of my personal quest to understand George Washington and the Masonic sources of his inspiration. It is a journey through unexpected and seemingly unrelated aspects of superstition, the human condition, and modern science. But tying the whole quest together are the unlikely linkages of Freemasonic ideas.

When I first started looking closely at Washington's life, I was intrigued to discover that for the first fifteen years of his married life, while he was living and working around his estate of Mount Vernon, he pasted a table of the rising times of all the bright planets into the front of each of his personal diaries, alongside some astrological charts. When I later discovered that he took a lot of trouble to lay out the two most important sites of the Federal City of Washington, D.C., to point to a rising of Venus that was important in Masonic myth, I had to find out why.

It took many years of research to uncover Washington's motive. When I finally did, I found that he had an awesome purpose—a purpose that I was able to trace back to the earliest buildings and symbols known to the human race. George Washington learned a powerful secret from Masonic ritual, which he used to help establish the United States.

I came to see that George Washington became a great leader because he learned the Masonic art of self-knowledge as a young man of twenty-one. For the rest of his life, he practiced the Masonic virtues of Brotherly Love, Relief, and Truth, and these working tools of the Freemasons' Craft helped him become the Father of his Nation.

Washington's virtues of patriotism, compassion, and truthfulness have been covered many times by other writers. But his knowledge and his application of the principles of Freemasonry to inspire later generations through the layout of the Federal City of Washington, D.C., is little understood.

I set myself to study the practical Masonic heritage that George Washington created in Washington, D.C. And I uncovered an ancient truth within the rituals of Freemasonry that encourages an understanding of the effect of environment on human achievement and creativity. I found that this teaching of the Craft has a sensible scientific basis that cries out for further study. Once its teachings are understood, Masonic geomancy can help all people to manifest a better reality. This is the American dream that Bro. George Washington built into the Federal center of the United States Government.

In his study of achieving societies throughout the world, Harvard psychologist David McClelland pointed out that 1800 marked the beginning of a great surge of achievement among the citizens of the United States, which eventually culminated in its present superpower status.[1] Other countries with similar natural resources did not manage to achieve anything like the U.S. did. As I researched the motivational effect of Masonic ritual, I came to realize that George Washington had used these teachings to benefit and inspire his country.

One secret, little known outside the Craft, is that one of the purposes of Masonic Initiation is to teach you how to dream better dreams. George Washington went on to use this knowledge throughout his career. Masonry taught him that people become great not by what they do with their bodies, but by what they are inspired to do with their minds.

The rituals of Freemasonry say there is a hidden power at the center of the human mind. But this truth can be revealed only to an Initiate who is properly prepared. The Masonic system uses allegory and symbols to work its magic on the human spirit, by showing you that both your own motivations and the "benign rays" of the Bright Morning Star influence what you can become.

The roots of the United States' success at building a high-achieving society can be traced directly back to the period when Washington was its founding president. His actions during this time produced vast benefits, but my initial study of Washington's early diaries revealed that this success was driven by a deep and abiding interest in the movements of the planets. The dramatic ritual that made George Washington a Master Mason also taught him about the importance of the Masonic Bright Morning Star, and it is a lesson he used when creating the focal points of the new Federal City, as it was then called, of Washington, D.C. (The fact that the seat of government moved from Philadelphia to the newly created city of Washington in the pivotal year of 1800 strikes me as no coincidence.)

At first, I expected to uncover a simple tale of psychological and political motivation, drawing on the spiritual myths of Freemasonry: a heritage that Washington shared with so many of the Founding Fathers of the American Constitution. But I found much more.

It soon became clear that Washington was drawing on an ancient tradition of building inspiring landscapes, which dated back thousands of years and which had been adopted by his brother Freemasons in Europe as important for the laying out of new cities. The early Freemasons who did this work, based on what I came to call Masonic geomancy, combined early experimental science and hoary vestiges of superstition. They worked on the boundary of science and magic, in a realm poised between astrology and astronomy, and in a Masonic environment that encouraged them to study the hidden mysteries of nature and science in order to make themselves better members of society.

David McClelland's studies of achieving societies showed that their ideas had worked, but he was unable to explain why. They had applied ideas from Masonic ritual which seemed to have no scientific basis whatsoever. Yet, when I investigated these claims using modern science and statistics, I found a real force of nature that helped shape high-achieving individuals. As I traced this idea back through a range of different disciplines, a pattern emerged.

Brother George Washington incorporated his Masonic knowledge into the layout of the Federal City he founded. As I will show, he placed the President's House (the White House) and the Capitol to take advantage of the real inspirational force of Masonic geomancy. But, as I investigated his legacy of symbolism, I uncovered an unexpected and startling scientific truth about the Masonic science of human achievement, a truth that left me awestruck. Masonic geomancy is far more than ritual mumbo-jumbo: it provides the key to the development of civilization.

This book is the story of my quest to understand the mind of a great leader. I have used my knowledge of Masonic ritual to understand what inspired Bro. George. I have used my researcher's patience to uncover the sequence of his actions. And I have used my skill as a scientist (I was trained as a physicist) to arrive at a rational explanation for the enormous success he achieved. Join me in uncovering the real story of Bro. George Washington, Past Master of the Craft and the Father of the United States of America.

—Robert Lomas

# Prologue

# George Washington:
# A Most Famous Freemason

George Washington was an inspiring general in the American War of Independence, an inspiring leader of the young United States of America, and an inspiring human being. He is famous for three virtues: a great love for the people of his country, a great concern for their welfare, and a great love of the truth. He is also the most inspiring example of the application of the three great principles of Freemasonry: Brotherly Love, Relief, and Truth.

Though most Americans remain unaware of it to this day, George Washington was a very passionate Freemason. And he was fascinated by a Masonic symbol known as the Bright Morning Star. As a young man of twenty-one he became a Master Mason in the Fredericksburg Lodge, in Fredricksburg, Virginia and this involved a dramatic ritual that ended with a bright five-pointed star (representing Venus) shining from high on the Eastern wall of the blacked-out lodge room down onto him.

But how did George Washington come into contact with Freemasonry? The story lies with his family history.

Washington's father Augustine died when George was eleven years old. The boy and his mother Mary Bell Washington went to live at Mount Vernon, by the Potomac River in the colony of Virginia. Mount Vernon was a plantation owned by George's half-brother Lawrence.

As a young man of sixteen, George got a job as a surveyor working for a Freemason, Thomas, Lord Fairfax, formerly of Denton Hall in Yorkshire, but at that time a major landowner in Virginia. For the next three years, young

*Figure 1: Brother George Washington, Master Mason.*

George surveyed Lord Fairfax's lands in the Shenandoah Valley in the company of Fairfax's younger brother Robert. The Fairfax family were active Freemasons, being patrons of the Grand Lodge of York, and it is highly likely that the young Washington first came to hear about the Craft during the period he worked as a surveyor for Lord Fairfax.

In 1751 Washington sailed to Barbados with his brother Lawrence to try to find a climate that would improve Lawrence's poor health. The Fairfaxes also owned land in Barbados. George returned to Mount Vernon, leaving Lawrence there to stay with members of the Fairfax family. On the way back he dined at Williamsburg with a friend of the Fairfax family, Governor Robert Dinwiddie. On April 6, 1752, Lawrence wrote saying that he felt his health was failing and he was returning to Mount Vernon. He died at home on July 26, 1752.

At the age of twenty, George was master of Mount Vernon. Three months later, on Saturday, November 4, 1752, he was initiated into Fredericksburg Lodge No. 4, and immediately afterwards was appointed a military adjutant by Governor Dinwiddie. During the French and Indian War, Washington served as a messenger between the French and English forces then fighting along what is now the eastern part on the U.S.-Canadian border, and was described by Dinwiddie as "a person of distinction."

On the first Saturday of March 1753, George was allowed leave from his military duties to be passed to the second Freemasonic degree, that of a Fellowcraft, in Fredericksburg. And on Saturday, August 4, 1753, the Fredericksburg Lodge raised him to the third, and sublime, degree of Master Mason. Four months later, he was chosen to lead a Virginia military expedition to challenge French claims to the Allegheny River Valley.

Washington's Masonic career then remains undocumented until two years after the signing of the Declaration of Independence (1776), by which time he was Commander in Chief of the Revolutionary Army. Towards the end of 1778 he celebrated the Masonic Feast of St. John the Evangelist and took part in a Masonic parade held at White Plains in New York State. The following June, he celebrated the other Feast of St. John, that of the Baptist, at a Masonic Festival held by the American Union Military Lodge at West Point. Later in 1779 he was offered the Office of General Grand Master Mason of the United States, but was unable to accept because of his military commitments.

In 1789 George Washington was inaugurated as the first President of the United States. He took his oath of office on a Volume of the Sacred Law borrowed from St. John's Lodge No. 1, New York, in the City's new hall, built by a Frenchman who had joined the American army, Major Pierre Charles L'Enfant.

On September 18, 1793, Washington laid the cornerstone for the United States Capitol in Washington, D.C., taking office as Presiding Master at the Masonic ceremony. This ceremony was conducted in full Masonic regalia and used the complete Masonic ritual for laying a cornerstone.

When he was buried at Mount Vernon on December 18, 1799, his Lodge brethren from Alexandria Lodge No. 22 carried out a full Masonic funeral ceremony in addition to the rites of the Church. Bro. George was a Past Master of Alexandria Lodge, having been installed in the Chair of King Solomon (i.e., made Master of the Lodge) by No. 22 on April 22, 1788.

These facts are well established, but George Washington's important Masonic legacy remains confused, misunderstood, and largely misrepresented. As I will show, Masonic teaching influenced the way Bro. George created the city of Washington, which is his enduring monument.

The dialogue below is part of a Masonic lecture, given as a ritual series of questions and answers, that would have been given to Bro. Washington, to help him understand the significance of the Masonic message. It was an early clue in my struggle to understand him.

*Q: Why were you made a Mason?*
*A: For the sake of obtaining the Secrets of Masonry,*
   *and to be brought from darkness.*
*Q: Have Masons Secrets?*
*A: They have many invaluable ones.*
*Q: Where do they keep them?*
*A: In their Hearts.*
*Q: To whom do they reveal them?*
*A: None but Brothers and Freemasons*
*Q: How do they reveal them?*
*A: By Signs, Tokens, and particular Words.*
*Q: As Masons, how do we hope to get at them?*
*A: By the help of a key.*

The ritual goes on to explain that once there were three mythical Grand Masters of Freemasonry, each of whom held a different part of the secret key. The complete secret was lost when one of them was killed, and it is the task of each individual Freemason to search for this lost knowledge. The ritual lecture explains:

*Q: What inducement have you to leave the East and go to the West?*
*A: To seek for that which was lost, which, by your instruction and our own industry, we hope to find.*
*Q: What is that which was lost?*
*A: The genuine secrets of a Master Mason.*

When Washington became Master of his lodge, he was entrusted with the key of King Solomon, and that key inspired him when he came to build the Federal City. As I studied the actions and writing of Washington, I realized he had systematically used his Masonic knowledge to benefit the newly formed United States.

My long and surprising investigations took me into areas ranging from theories of eighteenth-century politics to modern radar research, but the convoluted thread of Washington's inspiration finally led to a hard science of creativity and the development of achievement. Yet it all started and ended in Freemasonry's obsession with the faint rays of the Bright Morning Star.

This surprising and unusual intellectual journey ends with the truth at the center of Washington, D.C. However, our starting point is not in Washington but at one of the oldest buildings in the world.

# Chapter One

# The Secret of the Solomon Key

## A Sense of Place

There are some places in the world where it is impossible not to feel a sense of history. This is usually because some dedicated person in the past decided to create a marker to draw later generations to the site. The famous stone circle of Stonehenge, in the south of Britain, is one such place, but there is another, lesser-known example far to the north: a place called Brodgar, in Orkney, an island to the north of Scotland.

Anyone who stands within the stone circle of Brodgar, in the cool light of a pre-dawn sky cannot fail to be impressed and inspired by that great construction. It poses many questions:

- Why did the ancients who built it dig a ditch 12 feet deep and 375 feet in diameter into solid bedrock?
- Why did they laboriously remove some three-and-a-half million wheelbarrows full of stone (not that they had wheelbarrows, they carried all 80,000 tons in rough baskets), with no better tools than deer-antler picks?
- If that wasn't enough work, why quarry and shape sixty stones, each weighing around 10 tons, from a rock outcrop twenty miles away in Sandwick, and then drag them to the site?
- Why cut deep sockets in the rock to hold the stones secure for the next 5,000 years?

The answer to all these questions is that they wanted to link a sacred center on the ground to the movement of the heavens. A retired Oxford Professor of

Engineering, Alexander Thom, showed that the stones of Brodgar provide sight lines to spectacular astronomical events. Go there at the right time, and you will see the sun rise in the west.[2]

As a sight to impress the population and inspire the leaders who controlled the site, this spectacle takes some beating. But surely it is nothing more than a device that unscrupulous pagan priests used to impress superstitious Stone Age savages. Such astral alignments can't have any role in the modern world, can they? Certainly such tricks of the landscape couldn't play any role in a modern capital city such as Washington, D.C. Or could they?

Robin Heath, Course Director for the Master's degree in Archeoastronomy at the University of Wales in Lampeter, thinks the study of astral alignments is important and relevant to understanding why humans build where they do. He says:

*The study of the landscape's effect on Man, a subject which has preoccupied some of our best poets, writers and artists since time immemorial, has only quite recently demanded scientific attention. We now live on a planet which is teaching us a kind of environmental Newton's Law—that for every action there is an equal and opposite environmental reaction. Our effect on the landscape incurs a natural reaction as the landscape brings noticeable new effects on Mankind. Modern concerns have made this an urgent study . . .*

*We read in history books that the choice of siting for ancient settlements depended on a water supply, a non-exposed site which attracted winter sunshine, and a defendable place against the onslaughts of uncivilised savages eager to ransack, rape and pillage . . .*

*We may pick out a natural landmark, a mountain peak, waterfall or a single Scots pine; we are unlikely to do more than write a poem about it, enjoy a picnic within view of it or capture its image on a digital camera. What that mark on the land may be doing to the local occupants or to ourselves remains wholly unclear. It appears that our forebears understood such things rather better than ourselves. There are important clues concealed within the ancient built landscape of Britain which will shed light on geomantic arts.[3]*

He goes on to speak of many improbable alignments that occur in ancient human settlements, drawing attention to the fact that, from the earliest public structures, the builders of enduring artifacts have chosen to incorporate straight sight lines into them. Heath points out that city of Edinburgh is built around two points of civil power, connected by a sight line.

*The Castle and Holyrood Palace are ancient buildings which occupy two unique locations separated by a street called The Royal Mile. The Edinburgh tourist guide informs us that both Holyrood and the Castle were built on much older, prehistoric sites. Although we know very little about these, whatever form they may have taken, they were built on the same locations and thereby always separated by that umbilical straight line connecting them, now called the Royal Mile. Without archaeologically exploring the ground underneath the Castle and Holyrood, we can know little of the form or function of these earlier buildings—they and their meaning elude us. They are obscured from us by a covering of modern overlays, the present Castle and Palace, yet to measure the connecting distance between them, all that is required is a ruler.[4]*

After the great fire of London, the great architect and Freemason Sir Christopher Wren put forward to the Stuart king, Charles II, a plan that would have created a similar alignment in London. Historian Harold Hutchinson, in his biography of Sir Christopher Wren, describes how it happened.

*On 11 September, 1666, less than a week after the fire was under control, Dr Wren presented his plan for a new City of London . . .*

*Wren's plan was theoretically attractive. His logical approach made the Exchange and the Cathedral the two major focal piazzas in a rebuilt commercial capital. With the old City gates and London's only bridge determining the approaches, he planned three major arterial roads linking Newgate with the Exchange, the Exchange with St. Paul's [Cathedral], and St. Paul's with the Tower. The Cathedral ended the vista of the Fleet Street and Ludgate approach— the Ludgate itself was to be replaced by a triumphal arch to Charles II—and the City's churches "with useful Porticos and lofty ornamental Towers and Steeples" were to be re-sited on the main highways. His ideal City of London was to be a city, and not a compromise between town and country.[5]*

*Figure 2: Brother Sir Christopher Wren.*

In his essay "Discourse on Architecture," Wren argued that the buildings of a city have a political as well as a functional significance. He said they should inspire in people a love of their country, but their architecture should also "aim at Eternity."[6] This essay paints a picture of the development of building that draws on Wren's knowledge of the Old Testament, Josephus, Pliny, Herodotus, and Masonic legend. He discusses Cain's City of Enos, the two columns of Enoch, and Noah's Ark. He describes the Tower of Babel and the Pyramids of Egypt, and tells of the walls of Babylon, the Pillar of Absalom, and the Temple of Solomon. It is a virtual tour of the Masonic myths of the Craft.

Wren drew on this Masonic background when he proposed to create two focal points for his new plan for London. He wanted to build an avenue that pointed to Eternity, and he arranged it to align with a key Sunrise in the Masonic calendar. Wren's plan for London was not used, for reasons I will explain later, but (importantly for our story) it had a strong influence on the ideas of the French architect Pierre Charles L'Enfant when he drew up a plan for the city of Washington D.C.

It may be only coincidence, but one of the key focal points of the Royal Mile in Edinburgh, Holyrood Palace, had been destroyed by Oliver Cromwell's troops during the English Civil War. Interestingly, Charles II, the king who had earlier commissioned Wren's plan for rebuilding London, restored the Scottish palace:

*King Charles commanded Sir William Bruce, The Grand Master Mason of Scotland, to rebuild the palace of Holyrood House at Edinburgh; which was accordingly executed in the best Augustan style.*[7]

This took place a few years after Charles had had to turn down Wren's plan for a similar alignment in London. Perhaps Wren's Masonic message was not lost on that Freemason king, because the alignment that Charles II restored, between Edinburgh Castle and Holyrood Palace, points to the same key Masonic Sunrise that Wren wanted to commemorate in his proposed layout for the city of London.

But why should these alignments matter?

## The Ancient Art of Geomancy

Robin Heath suggests why people through the ages have gone to such great trouble to align structures on the ground with the rising and setting points of bright astral objects:

> *If the land stores memories of ancient powerful ritual practices undertaken along alignments, inducing these memories within later cultures, this could explain the continued siting of important human powerpoints along much older alignments . . . perhaps some of the most ancient sacred sites identified themselves. They were said to be places where the gods were actually seen. But who or what are these gods? . . . What generated the alignments? Does the land itself generate them, or form geometric shapes upon itself? The gods aside, there is presently no mechanism to account for such a thing to have occurred without human intervention.*[8]

Heath thinks that these alignments are created by traditional ideas resurfacing in the minds of the builders, and he also notes that some key alignments seem to incorporate a right-angled triangle, which can be constructed from rods of 5, 12, and 13 units long. Robin is not a Mason, so he was unaware that the knowledge of the right-angled triangle is a key part of the ritual of making a Freemason and is a symbol of the Master of a Lodge of Freemasons. But he speculates about the Masonic origins of these right-angled alignments, saying:

> *The Freemasons adopted another symbol of solar power [the five-pointed star of Venus], and thereby became a brotherhood. Whatever geomantic secrets they once possessed would have required high levels of responsibility and personal integrity in application. But modern masons appear to know nothing of these alignments nor of this triangle. They may, however, draw the energies of such things to them.*[9]

Robin uses the term geomancy to describe the secrets that Freemasons may have once possessed but have since lost. Geomancy means intentionally to use astronomy to incorporate the energies of the sky, the planets, and the cosmos into sacred sites, and into the lives of people who live in them. The geomancer thereby aligns the observers with points in time as well as space. Robin's comments reminded me of the writings of nineteenth-century republican activist and chronicler of Freemasonry, Richard Carlile, and what he said was the purpose of Freemasonry:

*The proper business of a Mason is astronomical, chemical, geological, and moral science, and more particularly that of the ancients, with all the mysteries and fables founded upon it. A good Mason . . . is able to build Solomon's Temple, in the allegorical sense.*[10]

Carlile goes on to mention a key to the mysteries of Freemasonry:

*The Key to the mysteries of Freemasonry . . . is the worship of the Sun as God, under a variety of personifications, in all its Zodiacal transits, in the personification of the year, of the seasons, of the months, of time generally, and of all the divisions of time, and as the source of all physical and all moral phenomena. The Masonic building of Solomon's temple is the getting of a knowledge of the celestial globe, knowing the mysteries of all the figures and groupings of stars on that globe; knowing, further, that this globe is the foundation of all religion, knowing how to calculate the precession of the equinoxes, the return of comets and eclipses, and all the planetary motions and astronomical relations of time.*[11]

Heath, who is an experienced scientist and engineer, suggests that the right-angled triangle and the whole art of celestial alignments can be described using the mathematics of chaos theory. He says that the largely unconscious secrets of these sites act as a "strange attractor" to influence human states of mind. He believes that this may be an emotional response in the individuals concerned, but points out this does not make it any less real. He closes his book on geomancy by quoting William Blake's poem about building a new Jerusalem:

*And did those feet in ancient time,*
*Walk upon England's mountains green*
*And was the Holy Lamb of God*
*On England's pleasant pastures seen?*
*And did the Countenance Divine,*
*Shine forth upon our clouded hills?*

*And was Jerusalem builded here*
*Among these dark Satanic Mills?…*

*Bring me my bow of burning gold!*
*Bring me my arrows of desire!*
*Bring me my spear; O clouds unfold!*
*Bring me my chariot of fire!*
*I will not cease from mental fight,*
*Nor shall my sword sleep in my hand,*
*Till we have built Jerusalem*
*In England's green and pleasant land.*

This well-known hymn gave me a link to George Washington. "Jerusalem" was written in 1800, just after George Washington died. Seven years earlier, Blake had written an illustrated book entitled *America: A Prophecy* to celebrate Washington's election to a second term as President of the United States. It was printed in a limited edition of seventeen hand-printed copies, eleven of which went to America, with the rest selling in Britain. Its theme is liberty and the overthrow of long-established repressive religious and political systems. It celebrates the American Revolution and George Washington's role in it, portraying a great and glorious future for the young United States. It is an inspirational book and appeared in America just as Washington became deeply involved in the work of establishing a capital city for the new republic.

In the text of the book, Blake portrays Washington as looking to the East and seeking inspiration to found a new way of life. A bright fiery angel arises in the dawn sky who inspires the Americans to fight on and win. The text, also a poem, is full of Masonic symbolism, which Washington would have recognized instantly. Blake tells how the thirteen angels of the Masonic Council of Truth appear to Washington, Paine, and Warren as a succession of bright flaming stars in the East. He tells how Washington prevails against the forces of Albion (England) and how "the five gates are consumed, and the bolts and hinges melted. And the fierce flames burn round the heavens and round the abodes of men."[12]

This poem, with its skillful use of Masonic imagery, could not have failed to inspire Bro. George Washington. And it may well have influenced his decision

Figure 3: *William Blake's* America: A Prophecy.

to utilize key parts of the symbolism in the layout of the Federal City, as Washington himself and the Founding Fathers referred to the city that was to become Washington. D.C.

Robin Heath says of Blake:

> *Like all mystics, Blake was highly receptive to messages from the unconscious. A highly skilled geometer, painter, poet and Freemason, his most famous poem ["Jerusalem"] picks up the time-line that has been revealed. In verse two, the implications are of Jerusalem having already been built, "among these dark Satanic Mills." Then, in verse four, he vows that it must be built again. The counter-point between these verses creates a timeless quality to its relevance, and expresses perfectly the way cosmic order will continually manifest—as self—similar forms in time and space. The poem is not Blake's Masonic secret, it is his inspirational and intuitive understanding of the link between Jerusalem and Britain, with instructions on what one must do in order to align with spiritual power.[13]*

## The Keys to the Secrets of Masonry

In *America: A Prophecy*, William Blake speaks of a voice coming forth and shaking the Temple. Traditionally there were three Grand Masters who conducted the rituals of the Masonic Temple, and each knew a different part of the secret of Freemasonry. They were Hiram, King of Tyre; Hiram Abif; and Solomon, King of Israel. Each held one of three keys to the mystery. Hiram of Tyre held the key to the secrets of where and what to build; Hiram Abif held the key to the secrets of death and rebirth; but Solomon alone held the key to understanding the purpose of the Temple and the import of the Bright Morning Star, known to Masonic legend as the Shekinah, which shines into the Temple once it is consecrated. King Solomon's task, which is now the responsibility of the Master of the lodge, was to continually build the new Jerusalem within the minds of the Brethren as a sacred place for the Divine Shekinah to shine its benign rays over all the human race.

Blake casts George Washington in the role of Grand Master Solomon, and he maps out for him a threefold task: to loosen the chains that bind his people, to unlock the dungeon doors to the light of the Bright Morning Star, and to build a new Jerusalem on the plains of America. Blake sets Washington the duty of embedding the secrets of the Solomon Key into the new Republic. And, as I will show you, Bro. George used the concept of Masonic astrology to create an enduring muse for his people.

*America: A Prophecy* was inspired by Washington's successful first presidency. The year after Washington died, Blake wrote "Jerusalem," and I cannot help but wonder if this poem was in turn inspired by Washington's success in establishing a new home for the Divine Shekinah in the Federal City and Blake's urge to emulate that success in England.

But even more startling, as I began to investigate the Masonic Solomon Key of ritual, I started to uncover an enduring and totally unexpected science of human consciousness within the Federal City that Washington created.

## Conclusions

There is an ancient tradition of astral alignments which seems to capture the imagination and inspire the human spirit. Freemasons possess some knowledge of this, and Richard Carlile claimed that it should be the heritage of every Mason. Archaeoastronomer Robin Heath thinks that Freemasonry shows indications of having once possessed this knowledge, but that modern Freemasons have lost the key to understanding what he calls geomancy.

In the illustrated poem *America: A Prophecy*, William Blake attributes knowledge of Masonic geomancy to George Washington, and predicts that Washington will use the power of a bright angel arising in the East as a key to unlock the dungeon in which the people of the American colonies are enslaved.

This all seems grand and noble but, apart from Robin Heath's ideas that astral alignments and associated rituals could influence people's ideas, it at first seemed to me to be largely myth. There did not seem to be much science involved in geomancy. Perhaps George Washington was simply inspired by the ritual of Freemasonry to produce a layout for his Federal City that would create Masonic resonances in the minds of future generations in the same way that Blake used Masonic symbolism to capture inspiring ideas. Or was there more?

I decided to review Masonic ritual to see just what inspiration Bro. George could have found in the rays of the Bright Morning Star. In the next chapter, we'll explore the rituals of Freemasonry and see what we find out.

# Chapter Two

# Ritual Keys and Bright Morning Stars

## What Is Freemasonry?

To understand George Washington, you must first understand the Freemasonry that inspired him. Ask a Freemason "What is Freemasonry?" and the answer you will get comes straight from the ritual: "A peculiar system of morality, illustrated by symbols and illuminated by allegory." But this doesn't tell you much. Let's explore Freemasonry and find out what it is, and why Bro. George found it so valuable.

### The Three Degrees

Freemasonry consists of three degrees, each teaching a different spiritual lesson.

The First degree, known as the Entered Apprentice degree, equips you to develop a rational mind and bring your intellect into balance with the irrational urges of the flesh. To aid you in this task, Freemasonry teaches you postures, provides a lodge structure to focus your thinking, and gives you a set of symbols and spiritual tools. Only when you have balanced your rational mind against your bodily urges, learned how to adopt and use postures, learned to comprehend symbolism, and gained proficiency in the use of spiritual tools are you ready to move on to the Second degree.

The Second degree, known as the Fellowcraft degree, helps you to balance your intellect and your emotions so that you learn how to recognize truth and discriminate between irrational urges of the flesh and the true voice of the spirit. You are given further postures, tools, and symbols to help you to strengthen your rational mind and learn to handle your emotions so that you are prepared for the discovery of the blazing star of truth, which is as yet only visible as darkness at your center. Here you meet the spiral symbol, which can teach you how to approach the center. The postures affect your body and feed hormonal responses back into your rational mind to help you learn how to subdue emotion. But before you can proceed to the Third degree, you must learn to let go of your ego and self-regard.

In the Third degree, the sublime degree of Master Mason, you must learn how to allow your ego and rational mind to die. That may sound extreme, but it is necessary so that your spirit may be reborn as the keystone of your being and support your quest to attain the vision of light which emanates from the center. The ritual of death and rebirth stills the urges of your body, your intellect, and your emotion and brings forth your suppressed spirit. In this degree, the circle of your being is rendered complete and perfect as you acquire mastery over its four component parts (body, intellect, emotion, spirit). When this mastery is fully achieved, a master of the Craft has undergone a radical transformation of the mind and a regeneration of his entire nature. Now you are ready to allow the light of the center to flow through fresh channels in the brain so that the true secret of the Craft is fully internalized.

This is a summary of the ritual teaching that every Freemason goes through while "working" the three degrees of the Craft. But in my experience the main impact of the teaching of Masonry is to be found in the symbols, which are summarized in diagrams called tracing boards.

### Tracing Boards

In a modern lodge, the tracing boards are a series of formal symbolic pictures that are displayed according the degree the lodge is working at the time. But in George Washington's day, the tracing board was the most revered symbol in the Lodge. The diagrams were not bought from Masonic specialty shops, as they are today, but each Brother was taught to draw them individually. At each lodge meeting the Board of the Degree about to be worked was drawn from memory with chalk and charcoal on the floor of the Lodge by the Master, who from previous practice was able to do this quickly and accurately.

*Figure 4: Tracing boards (reproduced by permission of www.tracingboards.com).*

During the ceremony, the candidate would make a ritual journey from West to East across the floor of the lodge. The steps of the degree would be shown on the diagram, and the Candidate would walk the steps. In the early days of Freemasonry, some lodges used floor cloths—cloths on which the diagram was drawn. The floor-cloths were then rolled out like carpets. The diagram would be explained as part of the Ceremony.

However, the symbols themselves are not explained in the ritual. Instead, the interpretation of their meaning is left to each individual to work out through reflection and contemplation of the symbolic essence of the secret Masonic instruction. One thing is certain: The meanings absorbed by Brethren who work the ritual cannot easily be put into words.

When the tracing board was hand-drawn on the floor of the lodge in chalk and charcoal, the Candidate would be required to clean it away with a mop and pail of water at the end of the ceremony, to preserve its secrets from uninitiated eyes. The Masonic lectures explain the symbolic value of chalk, charcoal, and clay:

*Chalk, an ancient deposit, pure in its whiteness, abundantly free to the service of man and leaving a mark on whatever it touches, was taken as an emblem of the Masonic secret wisdom, which is an ancient doctrine revealed and deposited from heavenly sources for the spiritual uplift of man; pure in its teaching; free to whoever seeks it, and such as cannot fail to leave a mark upon his mind. Charcoal, an emblem of fervent heat, meant that that doctrine must become burned into the fabric of our being, mingled with our personal clay and inscribed on the fleshy tablets of the heart, just as with chalk and charcoal the diagram is personally imprinted upon the earthy flooring of the Lodge.*

But what is the ritual purpose of the tracing boards? To understand them, bear in mind that masons were originally builders; the word "stonemason" is still used to describe a skilled builder who works with stone. The Freemasons adopted the terminology of building when they established their Order, and the tracing boards show different aspects of the art of building and the rituals connected with it. The Masonic lectures say that the tracing boards have three purposes, which are outlined here.

- First, an operative Mason (one who actually works in stone and creates new buildings), should be able to draw and read plans of his work. Speculative Masons (who work on spiritual rituals using themselves as living stones) work on spiritual architecture, so they should understand the structural principles of a temple not made with hands, and be able to draw and read plans for the mystical building upon which they are to work. (This mystical building is the spirit of the individual Freemason.)

- Second, Masonry teaches that the Great Architect has a plan and purpose for us and with us, and we may assume that this plan and purpose are sufficiently revealed that we may know what they are and co-operate with them. The tracing board acts as an image and reminder of the Divine Plan.

- Third, the Candidate, when taking certain steps over the Board as he travels from West to East, should identify with the significance of the diagram and sacramentally pledge to pursue a path of life that leads from temporal darkness to the light of the Bright Morning Star in the East.

During George Washington's time, the practice of drawing the diagram on the floor of the lodge from memory was in general use, but toward the end of the eighteenth century, drawing was superseded first by painted floor-cloths, and later by wooden boards, resting on trestles, on which the diagram was permanently painted. It was not until 1846 that a set of printed boards, designed by Bro. John Harris, was approved for general use.

W. L. Wilmshurst, the well-known Masonic writer, noted in one of his unpublished lodge talks that:

*The present employment of a painted floor cloth or a board is no doubt a convenience, but to the machine-made substitute there never attaches the same worth as the product of one's personal handiwork; and as we little value that which has cost us nothing, the Boards, which once were symbols of prime importance, are to-day the subject of deplorable neglect. Were each new Candidate trained, as formerly, both to draw them for himself and to understand the details of their symbolism, the complaints we hear of lack of instruction in our system would quickly disappear . . .*

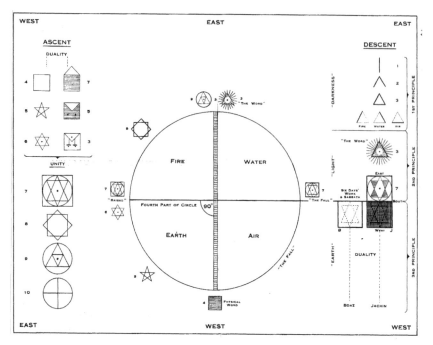

*Figure 5: The Tracing Board of the Center by W. L. Wilmshurst.*

>   *Their composition has been inspired by a master-mind; they are packed with meaning for those who have the eyes to read it, but—as was also their intention— they are sealed figures to those who have not; they enshrine and perpetuate certain esoteric teaching common to all ages and lying behind the public doctrine of all religions. Their concealed ideas are as true to-day as in antiquity, nor can they ever cease to be true, since they testify to certain immutable truths of our being. Hence they are called with us "immovable jewels" and "landmarks" and are given conspicuous prominence in our Lodges for our earnest and continual contemplation.*

In his private writings Wilmshurst says that tracing boards are "symbolic prescriptions of a world-old science taught and practiced in secret in all ages by the few spiritually ripe and courageous enough for following a higher path of life than is possible as yet to the popular world." He says that the interpretation of their symbolism is always difficult, because symbols convey much more than can be put into words. Masonic symbols use the language of ancient esoterica.

Wilmshurst drew his own tracing board to summarize the whole teaching of the Craft and the Royal Arch (which I reproduced in *Turning the Hiram Key*). As I will explain, I came to believe that this board helps explain just what George Washington would have learned about the ancient science of geomancy by working the rituals of Masonry.

### The Four Symbolic Directions

The tracing board shows the boundaries of the lodge, and its purpose is to draw attention to Masonry's symbolic interpretation of the cardinal directions that are in everyday use. These are East, West, South, and North. Their (symbolic) explanation is an important theme in Masonic ritual and offers a key to understanding Masonic geomancy.

The main direction of the tracing board runs from East at the top to West at the bottom. This is because, in Masonry, transitions between West and East are vitally important. The ritual of the third degree says "Masonry finally teaches you how to die." This involves something deep. The Craft is a technique of *living*, yet its ritual speaks of a way of *dying*. But this is not physical death, it is a secret process of mystical death and resurrection, which helps candidates learn about the inner creative resources of their minds.

The ritual lectures warn that unenlightened people dread death in any form and wish to hear as little about it as they can, but a mystical dying results in the raising and rebirth that turns a Candidate into an Initiate. During this process, the aspirant experiences an inward renewing of the mind. And, importantly for understanding the layout of the Federal City, this ritual is carried out by the faint light of a bright star rising in the east of the darkened Lodge.

The faint rays of this Bright Morning Star are said to raise your whole being to a higher level, which the ritual calls being made perfect. "To be perfect is to be initiated" is an old Masonic saying.

Each of the four quarters of the Lodge, and by inference the points of the compass, has particular properties. The North is a place of darkness and stands for unenlightenment. It symbolizes exertion in the teeth of opposition, while its darkness and difficulty call forth the energy of the spirit. The North is a place of imperfection and undevelopment. (This idea also appears in religious culture: in the past, the bodies of suicides, reprobates, and unbaptized children were buried outside the churchyard on the north, or sunless, side of the church.) The junior members of the Lodge are seated in the North, to represent the fact they are spiritually unenlightened. The ritual says they are novices whose latent spiritual light has not yet risen above the horizon of their consciousness; they have still to learn how to curb their material interests and control their sensual impulses.

The East of the Lodge represents spirituality, which Freemasonry says is the highest and most mystical mode of consciousness. In people who have not been initiated this is underdeveloped, but it becomes active in moments of stress or deep emotion, which the ritual has evolved to induce.

The West, the polar opposite of the East, represents normal rational understanding, the commonsense consciousness we employ in everyday affairs. Midway between East and West is the South. Masonic ritual teaches that this is the meeting place of spiritual intuition and rational understanding, denoting abstract thought and intellectual power at its highest. It lies opposite the North, the place of ignorance, sense-reactions, and impressions received from our physical senses.

Thus the four sides of the Lodge point to four progressive modes of consciousness. These are sense-impression (North), reason (West), intellectual thought (South), and spiritual intuition (East), making up four possible ways to know yourself. This Masonic perception of the meaning of directions is a key factor in understanding why George Washington choose to lay out the Federal City of Washington, D.C., as he did.

Masonic ritual teaches its members to employ all of these modes of awareness. Most people use only the first two (or perhaps three). Without the use of all the perceptions, your outlook on life and knowledge of truth is restricted and imperfect. Freemasonry teaches that full and perfect knowledge is possible only when all four methods of knowledge are in perfect balance and adjusted like the four sides of the Lodge. George Washington incorporated this principle into his decisions about the layout of the Federal City.

Washington knew from his own experience that Freemasonry is a well-tried system that seeks to improve the mental and spiritual condition of its followers. Its rituals can be understood and its ideas can be explained, but its secrets cannot be given away. They can be experienced and understood only by enacting and internalizing them, as you live them out. This, too, is something Bro. George learned as a young man. He understood that Freemasons practice ritual to learn about themselves and the world they live in.

Freemasonry is an ancient science that has shaped human ambition, achievement, and well-being. It may yet offer greater insights into the mystery of the inner self that will enhance rather than conflict with modern science. But if it is to do so, we must learn to understand what it is and how our generation may best teach it to our successors. And we need to study what great practitioners of the past, such as George Washington, did with it.

### The Ritual, the Solstices, and the Compass Points

Each of the three degrees of Freemasonry is carried out at a different point of the compass, as represented by the different corners of the Lodge. These corners are boundaries between the various qualities represented by the cardinal points of the compass. The First degree, which teaches how to control your emotions, is carried out in the Northeast corner of the lodge. This represents the direction of the sunrise on the longest day. You are most aware of your body and its needs during the hours of daylight, and so, at the point of sunrise on this longest day, Freemasonry plants the foundation stone for the living temple that a new Candidate represents. As you stand at the point of the summer solstice sunrise, you are told:

*When beginning the work on all imposing and superior buildings, it is traditional to lay the first, or foundation stone, in the Northeast corner of the building. You, being newly initiated into Freemasonry are placed in the Northeast corner of the lodge, symbolically to exemplify that stone, and, from the foundation laid this evening, may you raise a superstructure, perfect in all its parts, a living stone honorable to the builder.*

When you move on to Second degree, you are placed in the Southeast corner, at the point of the rising Sun on the shortest day of the year, the day with most darkness. As you stand there, you are told:

*When you were transformed into a Masonic Apprentice, you stood in the Northeast corner of the lodge, marking the rising of the Sun on the day of most light.*

*Now, as an aspirant to greater knowledge of yourself, you mark the rising of the Sun at the time of winter darkness. As the beautiful floor of the lodge is made of light and dark squares, so is the progress of the year made up of days of light and days of darkness. As you learn to enjoy light so you must learn to withstand darkness; in this way you mark the progress you have made in our Craft.*

*When you stood at the point of high summer you were likened to a foundation stone of a great temple. You were encouraged to become aware of your ethical and moral nature, exposed as it was to the light of high summer. Now, as you stand at point of greatest winter darkness, look around and above you to see the more hidden mysteries of nature and science. They will be your next great area of study, to develop your rational nature.*

Finally in the Third degree, which teaches you how to live with the reality of your personal death, you are placed on the East-West line of the sunrise at the vernal equinox and the ritual says to you:

*You joined our Order in a state of darkness and spiritual poverty. You were allowed to bring nothing in to the lodge but your own spirit, stripped to a state of naked indigence. As an Apprentice Freemason you were told there was a spiritual light at the center and how to prepare your spirit to perceive it. You were shown how to use the working tools of an Apprentice to equip you to develop a rational mind and bring your intellect into balance with the irrational urges of the flesh. To aid you in this you were equipped with postures, a lodge structure to focus your thinking, and a set of symbols and spiritual tools. Only when you had balanced your rational mind against your bodily urges, learned how to use posture, symbolism, and gained proficiency in the use of spiritual tools were you ready to move on the Second degree.*

*When you passed the test of merit that lifted you to the spiritual level of a Fellow of our Craft you were exhorted to develop your intellect and to study the more hidden ways of nature and science in order to better understand the rule of the Sacred Law and to begin to contemplate the mind of the Grand Geometrician of the Cosmos. The Second degree helps you to balance your intellect and your emotions, so that you learned how to recognize truth and discriminate between irrational urges of the flesh and the truth of the spirit. You were given further postures, tools, and symbols to help you strengthen your rational mind and learn to handle your emotions, so that you were prepared for the discovery of the blazing star of truth, which was as yet only visible as darkness at the center. Here you met the spiral symbol, which can teach you how to approach the center. The postures affect your body and feed back hormonal responses into your rational mind, so helping you learn how to subdue emotion. But before you can proceed to the Third degree you must be prepare yourself to let go of your ego and self-regard.*

*Now your mind has been shaped by morality and logic, creation has a further noble and functional insight to offer the prepared mind and body. The knowledge of yourself. As you ponder and anticipate your own demise you must face the final challenge of personal extinction.*

*This, my dear brother, is the singular aim of this sublime degree of Freemasonry. It invites you to meditate upon this somber subject and seeks to show you that to the true Mason death has no horror that matches that of being false and dishonorable.*

This final ceremony is conducted in darkness until the final few moments, when the faint light from a five-pointed star is shown in the East of the lodge. You are turned to face it and following ritual is delivered to you:

*Let me now beg of you to observe, that the light of a Master Mason is but as darkness visible, serving only to express that gloom which hangs over the prospect of futurity.*

*It is that mysterious veil of darkness that the eye of human reason cannot penetrate, unless assisted by that Divine Light which is from above. Yet even, by this glimmering ray you will perceive that you stand on the very brink of the grave into which you have just figuratively descended, and which, when this transitory life shall have passed away, will again receive you into its cold bosom. Let those emblems of mortality which now lie before you, lead you to contemplate your inevitable destiny and guide your reflections into that most interesting and useful of all human studies the knowledge of yourself.*

*Be careful to perform your allotted task while it is yet day; listen to the voice of nature which bears witness that, even in this perishable frame, there resides a vital and immortal principle, which inspires a holy confidence, that the Lord of Life will enable us to trample the King of Terrors beneath our feet, and lift our eyes to that Bright Morning Star whose rising brings peace and tranquility to the faithful and obedient of the human race.*

This is the dramatic high point of the ritual, when the importance of the rising of the Bright Morning Star in the East is pointed out as important in forming the character of the newly made Master Mason. The diaries of Bro. George Washington show he was impressed by this powerful symbolism.

## Washington's Diaries

In 1759 Washington resigned his commission with the Virginian Colonial Forces and returned to Mount Vernon, where he married Martha Custis and settled down to manage the estate. During the early 1770s Washington bought more lands near Mount Vernon and along the Ohio Valley. He spread his risks into different types of farming, growing wheat as well as tobacco. He also expanded and remodeled Mount Vernon.[14]

Washington kept a regular diary, heading each handwritten page with the title "Where and how my time is spent." For this entire period, until 1775 when he was finally called away to the War of Independence, he pasted into the relevant pages of his diary star charts from the *Virginia Almanack*. These showed the rising and setting of all the bright planets. The almanac not only showed the risings of the Bright Morning Star, it also incorporated advice about the astrological effect the stars were supposed to have on the people whose rays they shine upon. Almost all of the almanacs of this period have near their beginning a chart that they describe as showing "The Anatomy of the Human Body," as governed by the Twelve Constellations. The fact that Washington took the trouble to preserve these astrological notes, along with a timetable of the appearances of the Bright Morning Star, suggests that he was taking an interest in the movements of the stars and their effect on humanity.

Of course, all Freemasons are inspired by the dramatic message of the Third degree of Freemasonry. But did the teachings of Masonry influence Washington's plans for the new Federal City of Washington, D.C.? Let us take a closer look.

*Figure 6: "The Anatomy of the Human Body" as governed by the Twelve Constellations. George Washington took this image from the* Virginia Almanack *and pasted it into his diary.*

## Tracing out a Capital City

Because he had a distinguished and well-documented Masonic career, there is no doubt at all about Bro. Washington's Masonic credentials. But what of the Federal City that bears his name, and the men who designed and built it? Could they have been Masonic occultists with a hidden agenda? And did they incorporate Satanic symbols into the city, as so many conspiracy theorists claim?

The siting of a capital city for a new state is an important matter. Douglas Freeman, in his biography of George Washington, notes:

> *The House of Representatives entered vehemently into a debate over the permanent seat of government, which was proposed at one time or another for almost every town of any size between Trenton and Georgetown. Washington wished that the decision of Congress would be for a site on the stream that separated his own state from Maryland.*[15]

Freeman goes on to add that working out a deal over the siting of the city of Washington was the result of political opportunism on the part of Thomas Jefferson:

> *Jefferson saw no reason why he should not use his influence with members of Congress in what he considered good causes, such as seating the government on the Potomac. Morris was desperately anxious to have the government moved temporarily to Philadelphia, doubtless in the hope the choice might be* in perpetuo. *Out of these interests came agreement whereby the advocates of assumption of state debts were to effect conversion of a few doubters, in return for which Philadelphia was to be the seat of government until 1800. After that the capital was to be near Georgetown, on the Potomac. The bill "for establishing the temporary and permanent seat of the Government of the United States" was passed and presented to the President July 12, 1790. Those who favored New York as the capital and those who opposed assumption of state debts were furious.*
>
> *The President signed the bill on July 16. For this action Washington received the first direct newspaper censure that had been leveled at him since he had taken office. It was mild, guarded intimation that Washington lacked gratitude to New*

*York. Doubtless conversation of disappointed members of Congress was sharp, but there is no record of any rebuke from the floor, nor does any letter by Senator or Representative allege that Washington was party to the bargain. Washington had hoped the valley of the Potomac would be chosen as the site of the capital, but if any member's vote was affected by the President, it was because the individual wished to do what Washington desired and not because the General asked him to do it.[16]*

Washington's choice for the site of the Federal City has long been the subject of speculation. Elizabeth van Buren's thoughts on Washington's motives are typical of a whole class of speculative literature about the Federal City:

*Sir Francis Bacon had formed with the aid of his secret society . . . the plans for the colonization of the Western Hemisphere . . . There is a secret and immutable destiny planned for mankind, one not recognized by or dreamt of by the mass of humanity. The northern continent of America had been decreed to be the land of a democratic commonwealth of states thousands of years before Columbus ever sailed to its shores. There can be no doubt that the Enlightened Ones had a hand in the formation of the new nation. Thomas Paine, George Washington, Benjamin Franklin, Thomas Jefferson, John Adams, and countless others who were involved in signing the Declaration of Independence were all Freemasons or members of some other sect. The designs for both the Great Seal of the United States and earlier, the flag of the colony, indicate that they were inspired by those with esoteric knowledge.[17]*

I reasoned that, if this esoteric knowledge was Masonic, I should be able to find its purpose in the ritual. Washington may well have been inspired by Masonic ritual to build a new Temple of humanity, but what exactly motivated him, and what did he do about it? The idea that the spiritual teachings of Freemasonry have practical implications for political actions is now gaining more academic credibility. Andrew Prescott, Professor for Freemasonry at the University of Sheffield, says:

*An interest in the spiritual traditions of Freemasonry is a thread connecting much of the secularist counter-culture of the nineteenth century. In studying the history of Freemasonry, an important dimension is lost if this complex relationship with radical traditions is neglected.[18]*

And David Stevenson, Professor of History at the University of St. Andrews, said in the introduction to his book *The First Freemasons: Scotland's Early Lodges and Their Members*:

*Sometimes a historian is lucky enough to stumble on a significant subject totally neglected by fellow historians, yet with copious surviving evidence. That's how I came to the history of Freemasonry. Following up an isolated lead, I found that the records of many early Scottish lodges survived. They were unknown to, or ignored by other academic historians, who shared the common British perception that Freemasonry was disreputable and, illogically, extended this to the history of the movement. Some colleagues were worried that being known to be researching Masonic history would damage my career. Somehow, it was respectable to research Hitler or Stalin, but not Freemasonry. The contrast with Europe and America was striking. There, Masonic history was seen as an integral part of social and cultural history, while in Britain, where the movement began, academics chose to pretend it did not exist. Things are now changing. Masonic history is taken more seriously.[19]*

The two main inspirational messages of Masonic ritual that might have influenced Bro. George Washington are the importance of ritual journeys and the influence of the Bright Morning Star. I have mentioned that there are Masonic implications to the directions of the compass, but what of the Bright Morning Star?

A key aspect of Masonic lore says that the rising of the Bright Morning Star just before dawn is a good omen. As you may recall from our discussion of the Third degree, the words of the ritual say:

*Lift your eyes to that Bright Morning Star whose rising brings peace and tranquility to the faithful and obedient of the human race.*

Freemasonry preserves an ancient belief that all true Freemasons are made special by being reborn when "the Bright Morning Star" is on the horizon, just before dawn. Freemasonry and science have long since drifted apart. But is this concept a remnant of a lost science, or just meaningless ritual?

Masonry also clearly states in its ritual that certain sunrises are important, so I decided to review the ideas about stars and sunrises contained in that ritual.

## The Sun and the Bright Morning Star

There are a lot of reference to stars in Masonic ritual. The following extracts from William Preston's lectures are typical:

*The Universe is the Temple of the Deity whom we serve; Wisdom, Strength and Beauty are about His throne as pillars of His works, for His Wisdom is infinite His Strength omnipotent, and Beauty shines through the whole of the creation in symmetry and order. The Heavens He has stretched forth as a canopy; the earth He has planted as a footstool; He crowns His Temple with Stars as with a diadem, and with his hand He extends the power and glory. The Sun and Moon are messengers of His will, and all His law is concord. The three great pillars supporting a Freemason's Lodge are emblematic of those Divine attributes.*

*Those two grand luminaries, the Sun and Moon, were created one to rule the day, and the other to govern the night. The sacred historian further informs us they were ordained for signs and for seasons, for days and years. Besides the Sun and Moon, the Almighty was pleased to bespangle the ethereal concave with a multitude of Stars, that man, who He intended to make, might contemplate thereon, and justly admire the majesty and glory of His creator.*

*Almighty and Eternal God, Architect and Ruler of the Universe, at whose creative fiat all things first were made, we, the frail creatures of Thy providence, humbly implore Thee to pour down on this convocation assembled in Thy Holy Name the continual dew of Thy blessing. Especially we beseech Thee to impart Thy grace to this Thy servant, who offers himself a candidate to partake with us the mysterious Secrets of a Master Mason. Endue him with such fortitude that in the hour of trial he fail not, but that passing safely under Thy protection, through the valley of the shadow of death, he may finally rise from the tomb of transgression, to shine as the stars for ever and ever.*[20]

As I have already noted, Masonic ritual says this about the rays of the Bright Morning Star:

*Be careful to perform your allotted task while it is yet day; listen to the voice of nature which bears witness that, even in this perishable frame, there resides a vital and immortal principle, which inspires a holy confidence, that the Lord of Life will enable us to trample the King of Terrors beneath our feet, and lift our eyes to that Bright Morning Star whose rising brings peace and tranquility to the faithful and obedient of the human race.*

Further information is given in a formal exchange of question and answer between the chief officers of the Lodge. These are the Master, who sits in the East and his two Wardens: the Junior Warden, who sits in the South, and the Senior Warden, who sits in the West. As the Lodge is closed these officers carry out a ritual of question and answer.

*Q: Brother Junior Warden in your situation what have you discovered?*
*A: A sacred symbol, Master.*
*Q: Brother Senior Warden Where situated?*
*A: In the center of the temple, Master.*
*Q: Brother Junior Warden. How is it delineated?*
*A: By the letter "G" in the center of a blazing star, Master.*
*Q: Brother Senior Warden to whom does that allude?*
*A: To the Grand Geometrician of the Universe, to whom you, I, and all must bow, Master.*
*Then, Brethren, let us remember, wherever we are, whatever we do, He is with us. His all-seeing eye ever beholds us, and whilst we continue to act as faithful Fellowcrafts, may we never forget to serve him with fervency and zeal.*

Elias Ashmole is among the earliest documented of English Freemasons. He was initiated into The Lodge of Lights in Warrington on October 20, 1645. After his Masonic initiation, he took a keen interest in the stars and went on to become a well-known astrologer. He said this about the astrology he studied:

*Astrology is a profound science. The depth this art lies obscured in, is not to be reached by every vulgar plummet that attempts to sound it . . . and eclipse the glory of that light, which if judiciously dispensed to the world would cause admiration, but unskilfully exposed becomes the scorne and contempt of the vulgar.*[21]

As a Freemason, Ashmole would have known of the legendary effect of the Bright Morning Star. He would have known that the symbol is introduced to the newly raised Master Mason as a mark of his rebirth as a balanced and rational being. During the ritual Ashmole would have submitted to the assaults on his emotional nature, then been called to attack the forces of his rational mind, and finally he would have been taught to allow his ego to die so that his spirit could rise freely.

But why is this symbol of the Bright Morning Star given such an important place in the powerful ritual of the Third degree? (See *Turning the Hiram Key* for a fuller discussion and a description of this ritual and how it works.) As the Candidate turns away from fear of death, the sign of hope and the symbol of future success is the Bright Morning Star that rises in the darkness of the East as a forerunner of the Sun. The ritual is powerful and motivating. But does it have any real meaning behind it? Freemasonry describes itself as the Royal Art, the secret science of self-knowledge. Is the Bright Morning Star simply a powerful emotional symbol, or is it something more? While researching *The Book of Hiram* I came across an unexpected correlation between the appearance of bright stars in the dawn sky (which turned out to be rare conjunctions of Mercury and Venus appearing as a single bright star), and these coincided with the rise of high-achieving societies. Masonic astrology appeared to work, but I could find no explanation for why it did.

The United States of America is a high-achieving society by any standards. Did its level of achievement have anything to do with the influence of the Bright Morning Star on its seat of government? And did George Washington lay out a tracing board in the ground plan of the Federal City to apply his Masonic knowledge to support the fledgling United States? If he did, does this mean there is some measurable effect caused by the interaction between the alignment of the city with the sun and stars? Do the benign rays of the Bright Morning Star really bring peace and salvation to the faithful and obedient of the human race, as the ritual suggests?

All these questions seem to revolve around what is called natural, judicial, or mundane astrology. Astrologer Nicholas Campion defines mundane astrology as:

*That branch of astrology that deals with society, or with the world as a whole. The original astrology of the Babylonians from c. 2000 to 500 BC was mundane in that it was concerned solely with the success and survival of the community. Predictions were made in relation to political events, such as the prospects for peace or war, or climatic factors such as the imminence of drought or flood . . .*

*A mundane astrologer had two tasks, to analyse short-term political trends and to shed light on the nature of long-term historical cycles. The latter were interpreted and measured with reference primarily to the Jupiter-Saturn cycles . . .*

*Mundane astrology was widely used as a result of its natural appeal to political leaders, whether spiritual or secular, for it promised a glimpse into the political future. The holder of this knowledge thus possessed a natural advantage in any conflict.*[22]

Deborah Houlding, another astrologer, and writer on the history of astrology, says this field of mundane, or judicial, astrology was pioneered by Francis Bacon, whose works were the key inspiration for the group of Masonic astrologers who surrounded Christopher Wren:

*Success in judicial astrology largely depends on the skill and interpretative judgement of the astrologer. Natural astrology, however, offered unlimited scope for improvement, a barely trodden field, which through research and investigation might possibly offer some kind of scientific "proof" or breakthrough. Fresh observation appeared to be the key and attempts were made to collect data to support a positive statement of astrology's validity. Francis Bacon, back in the 1620s, had been one of the first to advocate experiment and testing of astrology in order to support its effect upon weather, agriculture and plagues. His view, like that of Kepler before him, was that astrology offered tremendous potential for reliable prediction in such matters, but that it needed to be purified and filtered of all that was superstitious and frivolous. Traditional theories needed verification and proof, rather than acceptance at face value. Like Kepler, Bacon dismissed the use of "houses" as unscientific, and placed the emphasis on the use of aspects, eclipses, and fixed stars.*

*The technical advances of astronomy, which had been pioneered by the work of Galileo and Copernicus, provided fertile ground and encouragement for such ideas, and argued that the works of men like Ptolemy, now "incorrect" in their astronomical basis, need no longer be relied upon for their astrological theories. "Though astronomy be corrected, astrology remains yet uncorrected" stated Joshua Childrey, a great admirer of Bacon, who set out to verify astrology through his own experiments.*[23]

## A Ritual Key

To help me understand what George Washington could have learned about the astral mysteries of Freemasonry and their key to the secrets of Solomon's wisdom, I decided to look at what popular writers about Freemasonry were saying in the eighteenth century. I have already pointed out the works of William Blake. They were not about Masonry, but simply drew on its symbolism. The most popular Masonic writer of the eighteenth century was William Preston, so I began my research with him.

Preston was a printer who lived in London, and he was a fanatical and inspired documenter of the rituals and history of Freemasonry. His biographer, Colin Dyer, says of him:

*His life was Freemasonry, and he spent over fifty years in active, involved, and often stormy, membership of that institution, gaining a wealth of experience and knowledge in the study and practice of it. He was by nature impetuous and in his younger days given to physical expression of his feelings; he was proud and stubborn, especially in matters involving what he considered as principle; these characteristics made him a controversial figure in the Freemasonry of his times.*[24]

Preston wrote a seminal book on Masonic thinking called *Illustrations of Masonry,*[25] the first edition of which was published in 1772. In it, he set out to collect, preserve, and publish as many of the traditional rituals as he could. His ideas were well known in the American colonies, as Dyer explains:

Illustrations of Masonry *was popular, and each succeeding edition was brought up to date with a commentary on what he saw as the major masonic events since the last edition. As a result it went through a number of editions in his lifetime (nine English editions) and it continued to be published and read for more than fifty years after his death . . . [it] was sufficiently widely read . . . [and] ultimately influenced the development of Freemasonry over the whole of the United States . . . there can be no doubt that his thoughts on, and arrangement of, masonic ritual, procedure and symbolism represent the major contribution by any one man to the practice of Freemasonry.*[26]

Preston said this of his life's work, in the introduction to the 1795 edition of *Illustrations of Masonry*:

*I was encouraged to examine the contents of our various lectures. The rude and imperfect state in which I found them, the variety of modes established in our lodges, and the difficulties which I encountered in my researches, rather discouraged my first attempts; persevering, however, in the design, I continued the pursuit; and assisted by a few friends, who had carefully preserved what ignorance and degeneracy had rejected as unintelligible and absurd, I diligently sought for, and at length happily acquired, some ancient and venerable landmarks of the Order.*

*I continued my industry till I had prevailed on a sufficient number to join in an attempt to correct the irregularities which had crept into our assemblies, and to exemplify the beauty and utility of the masonic system.*[27]

Looking at the text of his lecture in the First degree, it contains this exchange of information about an important key in Freemasonry.

*Q: How do we hope to obtain the Secrets of Masonry?*
*A: By the help of a key.*
*Q: Does that key hang or lie?*
*A: It hangs.*
*Q: Why is the preference given to hanging?*
*A: It should always hang in a Brother's defense, and never lie to his prejudice.*
*Q: What does it hang by?*
*A: The thread of life, in the passage of utterance.*
*Q: Why is it so nearly connected with the heart?*

*A: Being an index of the mind, it should utter nothing but what the heart truly dictates.*

The ritual use of the phrase "the mind should utter nothing but what the heart truly dictates" was one of my first clues as to why George Washington may have chosen to create an inspirational Masonic symbol at the heart of the Federal City.

Some symbols have a deep impact on our consciousness. In *Turning the Hiram Key*, I discussed how certain ancient symbols have an emotional impact on minds that can be measured with a technique used in lie detectors called galvanic skin response. I discovered that many Masonic symbols provoke an unconscious emotional response in everyone who sees them. When I first realized this, I posed a question:

*Did these symbols survive because they were instinctively appealing? Or were they shapes which some evolutionary force had shaped our brains to like? And if human brains are hard-wired to like particular symbols, what is the evolutionary pay-off for this? Could this explain the peculiar appeal of Masonic symbolism? The square and compasses form a lozenge shape, and that, I had found, both evokes a galvanic skin response and is perceived as attractive and pleasurable.[28]*

Three major symbols used in the tracing boards are the sun, the moon, and the stars. The opening ceremonies of lodges that work variations of Old York ritual include this phrase, "Let us give thanks to Him that made great lights, the Sun to rule the day, the Moon and the Stars to govern the night; for His mercy endureth forever." As I was eventually to discover, the layout of Washington, D.C., creates a massive Masonic symbol, which involves the Bright Morning Star and Holy Royal Arch of Jerusalem. (The Holy Royal Arch of Jerusalem is a Masonic term for the great astral arch of the Zodiac.) The key to understanding the positioning of these great lights is geometry, as William Preston explained:

*Geometry is the first and noblest of sciences, and the basis on which the super-structure of free-masonry is erected . . . When the Geometrician exalts his view to the more noble and elevated parts of Nature, and surveys the celestial orbs, how*

# THE
# VIRGINIA
# ALMANACK

### FOR THE

## YEAR of our LORD GOD 1773,
### BEING THE FIRST AFTER
## BISSEXTILE, or LEAP YEAR.

### WHEREIN ARE CONTAINED

The LUNATIONS, CONJUNCTIONS, ECLIPSES, the SUN and
MOON's Rifing and Setting, the Rifing, Setting, and Southing,
of the HEAVENLY BODIES, true Places and Afpects of the
PLANETS, WEATHER, &c. Calculated according to Art,
and referred to the HORIZON of 38 Degrees North Latitude,
and a Meridian of five Hours weft from the City of *London*;
fitting VIRGINIA, MARYLAND, NORTH CAROLINA, &c.—
but more efpecially thofe that have got a BIT to fpare to buy an
Almanack: Wherein the Reader may fee (if he have any Eyes,
and be neither drunk nor afleep) many very remarkable Things,
worthy his Obfervation.

Alfo a Table of COURT DAYS; a Lift of his Majefty's COUNCIL,
and of the Houfe of BURGESSES, with the NUMBER of
TITHABLES in each County; a Lift of PARISHES, and the
MINISTERS in them; the GOVERNOURS and VISITERS of
WILLIAM & MARY College; a Defcription of the FOUR QUAR-
TERS of the YEAR; humorous Obfervations for each Month;
an Effay on TRIFLES, fhowing that Half the Actions of Life
are Nothing elfe, and how by flow and imperceptible Degrees
they often fap the Foundation of a Man's Fortune, and bring
him to a Morfel of Bread; CONTENTMENT and COVETOUS-
NESS, TEMPERANCE and GLUTTONY, SOBRIETY and
DRUNKENNESS, compared, fhowing their refpective Effects on
our Happinefs and Mifery, &c. &c.

*All this, and much more Benefit you reap,*
*For the fmall Price of a BIT——very cheap;*
*and if the Book fell well, you need not fear*
*To have an Almanack another Year.*

## WILLIAMSBURG:
## Printed and Sold by PURDIE & DIXON.

*Figure 7: The Frontispiece of the* Virginia Almanack, *which George Washington pasted into his dairy for 1773.*

*much greater is his astonishment, if, on the principles of geometry and true phi-losophy, he contemplate the Sun, the moon, the stars, the whole concave of heaven . . . By geometry . . . we may discover the power, the wisdom, and the goodness of the grand Artificer of the universe . . . By it, we may discover how the planets move in their different orbits, and demonstrate their various revolutions.*

*A survey of Nature, and the observation of her beautiful proportions, first determined man to imitate the divine plan, and study symmetry and order. This gave rise to societies, and birth to every useful art, the architect began to design, and the plans which he laid down, improved by experience and time, produced works which have been the admiration of every age.*[29]

Within eighteen months of the publication of this ritual explanation, George Washington took the trouble to paste into the front of his diary the pages of his local almanac that allowed him to work out the movements of the great lights, so he could understand "the whole concave of heaven."

In February 1773, a year after the publication of Preston's *Illustrations of Freemasonry*, as Washington stood on the banks of the Potomac near Foggy Bottom, he would have seen the Bright Morning Star rise above Jenkins Heights. Did the view of this Masonic symbol in the dawn sky inspire him to study the "lunations, conjunctions, eclipses, the Sun's and moon's rising and settings and southings of the heavenly bodies, true places and aspects of the planets," as the *Virginia Almanack* offered to explain?

Did George Washington take up the challenge to carry the Solomon key forward and build his Federal City as a new Temple to propagate the light of knowledge? I believe he did, and I felt it should be possible to discover from the ritual how he did it. To move forward, I decided to look at the whole question of the layout of the Federal City of Washington D.C.

## Conclusions

There are in the Masonic ritual three possible sources of inspiration that George Washington could have drawn on:

1. The marking of the various sunrises of the changing seasons of the year, which is described by the placing of the Candidate at key

compass points that highlight important turning points of the year: the Northeast Sunrise of the summer solstice, marking the lightest day, the Southeast Sunrise of the winter solstice, marking the darkest day, and finally the East-West alignment marking the Vernal Equinox.

2. The tracing boards, which lay out ritual journeys for the Candidate to travel and which, in Bro. George's time, were drawn on the floor of the lodge for the candidates to walk the steps during the ceremony.

3. Finally, there was the legendary influence of the benign rays of the Bright Morning Star on the welfare of the population and on the motivation of the individual Mason.

But did George Washington know more about Masonic geomancy than modern Freemasons do? He certainly took an interest in astrology, so much so that while he was living full time at Mount Vernon he pasted pages of the local almanac in his diary so he would be ready for the appearance of the Bright Morning Star. But how did Washington use this Masonic ritual to design an inspirational city? Now it was time to look at the theories of how Washington, D.C., is laid out. In the next chapter, you'll see what I discovered.

# Chapter Three

# The Layout of Solomon's Key

## The Streets of Washington

Type "New York Street Layout" into Google and you get a guide to the streets of New York. Type "London Street Layout" and you get a discussion of "Street Management-Initiatives & Project, Road Safety" in London. The same search for Paris, Rome, Milan, Edinburgh, Detroit, Chicago, or Delhi takes you to sites that help visitors find their way about the cities. But type "Washington Street Layout" into the same search engine, and it's not a mapping program or a tourist guide that's the top hit, but a Web site site that claims:

*You are about to learn that the U.S. Government is linked to Satanism. The street design in Washington, D.C., has been laid out in such a manner that certain Luciferic symbols are depicted by the streets, cul-de-sacs and rotaries. This design was created in 1791, a few years after Freemasonry assumed the leadership of the New World Order in 1782 . . .*

*Once they are hidden, these occultic symbols are thought to possess great power. The Snake Basilisk is "said to have the power to destroy all upon whom it looks." To a person who is not an occultist, they will have no concept of the true hidden meaning contained within the symbol. And that hidden purpose is to communicate certain meanings to other occultists while hiding this meaning from all non-occultists.*

*The symbols that were interwoven into the design of the Governmental Center, communicate tremendous power to the occultist while at the same time they hide the true meaning from the non-occultist. These symbols take on a life of their own, in the mind of the occultist, possessing great inherent power to accomplish the plans of the occultist . . .*

*The Washington Monument was constructed to honor the first Masonic President, was designed so that both the White House and the Capitol face toward it so that the leaders of both branches have to face the spirit of Lucifer thought to be residing in it.*[30]

The Web site where I found this startling "information" is popular. When I checked its traffic ranking, it was at 151,000 in the World-Wide-Web ranking, which means a lot of people look at it. Whoever runs this site hides behind an anonymous Post Office box in Tucson, Arizona. However, being afraid to admit your name does not necessarily make your message invalid. Is there any truth in the claims this Web site makes? Is there a deep Masonic conspiracy behind the layout of Washington?

When I investigated, I found that the Masonic truth behind the layout of Washington, D.C., involves matters far more startling than anything claimed by the massed ranks of conspiracy theorists. Most writers about the Masonic symbolism of George Washington's Federal City are not Freemasons, and so they fail to understand the symbolism and Masonic inspirations which Brother George Washington experienced and bequeathed to the USA.

As I began to investigate the facts, I found a whole pile of unsupported misinformation and inaccurate assertions, which, when seen for what they are, destroy the whole basis for the satanic claims. But they do touch on a deeper truth about Masonic astrology that few modern Masons suspect.

Did Freemasons design Washington according to some secret Masonic plan? (The claim that Masons lay out cities in the form of Masonic symbols is a popular urban myth.) I decided to check the evidence for myself. One Web site makes this claim:

*In 1791, Pierre Charles L'Enfante [sic] (the designer, who was a Freemason), laid out the Governmental Center of Washington, D.C., he planned more than just streets, roads, and buildings. He hid certain occultic magical symbols in the layout of U.S. Governmental Center. When these symbols are united they become one large Luciferic, or occultic, symbol.*

*He intended to show that Governmental Center was planned to be ruled by Satan. Further, the Goathead Pentagram was placed so the Southernmost point, the spiritual point, is precisely centered on the White House. The White House is the precise point where the two lines formed by Connecticut Avenue flowing from Dupont Circle, and by Vermont Avenue flowing from Logan Circle, intersect. The meaning is all too clear. Occultists planned for the White House to be controlled by Lucifer in accordance with his occultic power and doctrine.*

*Everything was deliberately planned to stamp the power of Freemasonry and the symbols of its plans for America indelibly upon Government Center in Washington, D.C.*[31]

Then I checked out the U.S. Government's National Parks Web site. It agreed in part, although it seems to have overlooked the Satanic influence:

*The plan of the city of Washington was designed in 1791 by Pierre L'Enfant, and mapped the following year; a design which remains largely in place.*[32]

It was clear that if I wanted to understand the city of Washington, I needed to look at the timeline of who did what and when. Fortunately, this was relatively easy to do, as all George Washington's diaries and letters are now available online.[33]

## Building the Federal City

As I've already mentioned, the story of the Federal City of Washington, D.C., formally begins on July 12, 1790, when the Congress of the United States of America entrusted President Washington with the task of choosing a site for a capital city for the new Union. He was instructed to select land on the river Potomac to become a Federal territory and the permanent seat of U.S. government.

Washington had spent his youth surveying the area and knew it well. He wanted to position Washington, D.C., at a site "central to the United States"—a statement that reminds us what a small conglomeration of Eastern Seaboard ex-colonies the USA then was.

The President announced the place for the new city on January 24, 1791. He reported that the Federal City would be built on a diamond-shaped area of land, measuring about ten miles per side, situated where the flows of the Potomac and the Eastern Branch came together.

The next problem Washington faced was to find builders. His diary for March 28, 1791, says:

> *Andrew Ellicott was appointed to survey the district lines . . . Appointed L'Enfant to design a Federal City to be built within the district.[34]*

Benjamin Banneker was appointed to assist Ellicott, and Washington instructed them personally, as his diary entry of March 30, 1791, shows:

> *Some directions given to the Commissioners, the Surveyor [Ellicott] and Engineer [L'Enfant] with respect to the mode of laying out the district—Surveying the grounds for the City & forming them into lots—I left Georgetown—dined in Alexandria & reached Mount Vernon in the evening.[35]*

On March 31, 1791, Washington, who was still at Mount Vernon, wrote to Thomas Jefferson:

> *The terms agreed on between me, on the part of the United States, with the Land holders of Georgetown and Carrollsburg are. That all the land from Rock creek along the river to the Eastern-branch and so upwards to or above the Ferry including a breadth of about a mile and a half, the whole containing from three to five thousand acres is ceded to the public, on condition That, when the whole shall be surveyed and laid off as a city, (which Major L'Enfant is now directed to do) the present Proprietors shall retain every other lot; and, for such part of the land as may be taken for public use, for squares, walks, &ca., they shall be allowed at the rate of Twenty five pounds per acre. The Public having the right to reserve such parts of the wood on the land as may be thought necessary to be preserved for ornament &ca. The Land holders to have the use and profits of all their ground until the city is laid off into lots, and sale is made of those lots which, by this agreement, become public property. No compensation is to be made for the ground that may be occupied as streets or alleys.[36]*

In this letter, Washington reserved his right to have a say in the placing of the key buildings. He said:

> *The enlarged plan of this agreement having done away the necessity and indeed postponed the propriety, of designating the particular spot, on which the public buildings should be placed, until an accurate survey and sub-division of the whole ground is made, I have left out that paragraph of the proclamation.*[37]

Ellicott laid out forty boundary marker stones at one-mile intervals to set the bounds of the city. The astral observations to decide where they were to be placed were carried out by Ben Banneker, a self-taught astronomer. Banneker was a free black man, and Washington's choice to employ him shows a surprising lack of prejudice for that period of history.

The boundary stones marked out a 100-square-mile diamond. This became the District of Columbia, and the city of Washington was positioned within it.

## The President and the President's House

Historian Jean Jules Jusserand thinks that George Washington played a key part in the positioning of the Capitol and the White House (or the Federal House and the Palace for the President, as they were then known). He quotes L'Enfant as reporting to Washington:

> *After much menutial [sic] search for an eligible situation, prompted, as I may say, from a fear of being prejudiced in favor of a first opinion, I could discover no one [situation in which] so advantageously to [position] the congressional building as that on the west end of Jenkins heights, which stand as a pedestal waiting for a monument. ... Some might, perhaps, require less labor to be made agreeable, but, after all assistance of arts, none ever would be made so grand.*[38]

Jusserand goes on to comment that Washington suggested the spot for the siting of the President's Palace as one he had already noted as a convenient location.[39]

Washington said that he wanted distant views and prospects to be used to the best advantage. The "Observations Explanatory of the Plan" that L'Enfant added on the back of the plan confirm this:

*Attention has been paid to the passing of those leading avenues over the most favorable ground for prospect and convenience.*[40]

The consensus view seems to be that L'Enfant insisted that the grandeur of his plan must not be limited. He wanted it to be a symbol of the greatness of the United States for future times, saying he "must leave to posterity a grand idea of the patriotic interest which promoted it."[41] But L'Enfant did not see the project through to completion. He acted as though he was responsible to no one, and eventually provoked a crisis by demolishing a dwelling which was not owned by the Commissioners.

On December 2, 1791, George Washington wrote to L'Enfant:

*Dear Sir:*

*I have received with sincere concern the information from yourself as well as others, that you have proceeded to demolish the house of Mr. Carroll of Duddington, against his consent, and without authority from the Commissioners or any other person. In this you have laid yourself open to the Laws, and in a Country where they will have their course. To their animadversion will belong the present case.*

*In future I must strictly enjoin you to touch no man's property without his consent, or the previous order of the Commissioners. I wished you to be employed in the arrangements of the Federal City: I still wish it, but only on condition that you tend to—some of which, perhaps, may be unknown to you—Commissioners (to whom by law the business is entrusted, and who stand between you and the President of the United States), to the laws of the land, and to the rights of its citizens.*

*Your precipitate conduct will, it is to be apprehended, give serious alarm and produce disagreeable consequences. Having the beauty, and regularity of your Plan only in view, you pursue it as if every person, and thing was obliged to yield to it; whereas the Commissioners have many circumstances to attend to, some of which, perhaps, may be unknown to you; which evinces in a strong point of view the propriety, the necessity and even the safety of your acting by their directions.*

*I have said, and I repeat it to you again, that it is my firm belief that the Gentlemen now in Office have favorable dispositions towards you, and in all things reasonable and proper, will receive, and give full weight to your opinions; and ascribing to your Zeal the mistakes that have happened, I persuade myself, under*

*this explanation of matters, that nothing in future will intervene to disturb the
harmony which ought to prevail in so interesting a work. With sincere esteem, etc.*[42]

This was only the beginning of L'Enfant's defiance of the Commissioners. In
a letter to Commissioner David Stuart, dated November 30, 1792, Washington said:

*Major L'Enfant, if he could have been restrained within proper bounds, and his
temper was less untoward, is the only person . . . I am acquainted, that I think fit for
it. There may, notwithstanding, be many others although they are unknown to me.*

L'Enfant refused to accept that he was answerable to the Commissioners for
the design of the city and refused to take instruction from them. On February
28, 1792, Washington lost patience with him and in his own hand wrote him the
following letter, drafting and redrafting it to maintain a polite tone while showing a firm resolve to control L'Enfant. (It remains untranscribed, as a photo
image, among the George Washington Papers at the Library of Congress.)

*Sir*

*Your final resolution being taken I can delay no longer to give my ideas to the
Commissioners for carrying into effect for the plan for the Federal City.*

*The continuance of your services as I have often assured you, would have been
pleasing to me could they have been retained on terms compatible with the Law.
Every mode has been tried to accommodate your wishes on this principle except
changing the Commissioners. For Commissioners there must be, and under their
directions the public buildings must be carried on, or the Law will be violated; this
is the opinion of the Attorney General of the United States, and other competent
judges. To change the Commissioners cannot be done on the grounds of propriety,
justice or policy.*

*Many weeks have been lost since you came to Philadelphia in obtaining a plan
for engraving, notwithstanding the earnestness with which I requested it might be
prepared on your first arrival, further delay in this business is inadmissible. In like
manner five months have elapsed and are lost, by the compliment which was
intended to be paid you in depending alone upon your plans for public buildings*

*instead of advertising a premium to the person who should present the best, which would have included yourself equally. These are unpleasant things to the friends of the measure and are very much regretted.*

*I know not what kind of certificate to give that will suffice the purpose of Mr. Roberdeau. My conversations with and letters to you have uniformly conveyed the idea that the Commissioners stood between you and the President of the United States; that it lay with them to draw the line of demarcation between themselves and you; and that it was from them alone you were to secure your directions. A reference to my letters of the 2nd and 13th of December will show you the light in which I have considered this subject. With sincere wishes for your happiness and prosperity.*

*I am Sir, your most obedient servant.*

*—G Washington* [43]

Two previous letters from Washington had both turned down pleas from L'Enfant for the President to overrule the Commissioners in favor of L'Enfant's ideas. On March 6, 1792, Thomas Jefferson wrote to the Commissioners: "It having been found impracticable to employ Major L'Enfant in that degree of subordination which was lawful and proper, he has been notified that his services are at an end."

On March 8, Washington wrote to Commissioner David Stuart, presenting his ideas for the building of the Federal City. His main concern addressed the position of the President's House relative to the Capitol:

*I see no necessity for diminishing the Square allotted for the Presidents House, &ca. at this time. It is easier at all times to retrench, than it is to enlarge a square; and a diviation from the plan in this instance would open the door to other applications, which might perplex, embarrass and delay business exceedingly; and end, more than probably, in violent discontents.* [44]

If Washington was constructing a vast, diabolical ground layout with the active assistance of L'Enfant, then it is hard to explain why he sacked L'Enfant and only showed concern for the placing of the President's House and the Capitol. In a letter to the Federal City Commissioners, dated March 3, 1793,

Washington repeats that the site of the President's House should remain as fixed on the original plans:

> *It was always my idea that the building should be so arranged that only a part of it should be erected at present; but upon such a plan as to make the part so erected an entire building, and to admit of an addition in future, as circumstances might render proper; without hurting, but rather adding to the beauty and magnificence of the whole as an original plan. . . . to avoid the inconvenience which might arise hereafter on that subject, I wish the building to be upon the plan I have mentioned.[45]*

But Washington is unconcerned about major changes to the city layout, as this comment written to the Commissioners of the Federal City on October 21, 1796, shows:

> *I have no hesitation in giving it as my opinion, that all the Squares (except those of the Capitol and President's) designated for public purposes, are subject to such appropriations as will best accommodate its views, yet it is, and always has been my belief, that it would impair the confidence which ought to be had in the Public, to convert them to private uses, or to dispose of them (otherwise than temporarily) to individuals.[46]*

In this letter Washington is talking about map squares. Only the relative positioning of the Capitol and President's House are non-negotiable. Anything else can be moved. These are not the words of a fanatical Freemason intent on making sure he imposes a five-pointed star and a square and compass on the layout of the new city.

In a later letter to the Commissioners, Washington makes it clear that most of L'Enfant's original plan can easily be changed. On December 1, 1796, he wrote from Philadelphia:

> *It is a well known fact, or to say the least, it has been always understood by me, that the establishment of a University in the Federal City depended upon several contingencies; one of which, and a material one too, was donations for the purpose*

*. . . What would have been the answer of the Commissioners if he had previously applied to them, to know if a University would be placed where he is now contending for? . . . A University was not even contemplated by Majr. L'Enfant in the plan of the City which was laid before Congress .[47]*

So why has this myth of a Masonic plot to lay out the city of Washington on diabolical lines arisen? As you recall, the claim is:

*In 1791, Pierre Charles L'Enfante [sic] (the designer, who was a Freemason), laid out the Governmental Center of Washington, D.C., he planned more than just streets, roads, and buildings. He hid certain occultic magical symbols in the layout of U.S. Governmental Center. When these symbols are united they become one large Luciferic, or occultic, symbol.[48]*

But after consulting the correspondence in the Washington Archive of the Library of Congress, I find that L'Enfant was not allowed to do as he wished, and that when he continued to appeal to Washington to overrule the Commissioners, he was dismissed. So what *is* the real story of Pierre Charles L'Enfant?

### The Man Who Designed Washington

Born in Paris on August 2, 1754, Pierre (or Peter, as he came to call himself) Charles L'Enfant was not a Frenchman who did brilliant work in America, but a brilliant American who was born in France. So says historian Kenneth R. Bowling, author of one of the few biographies of L'Enfant.[49]

Bowling says L'Enfant used the name "Peter" on documents, certifying his purchase of a plot of land in the new federal district, in October 1791. This is confirmed by his signature on the manuscript map of the plan owned by the Library of Congress (the only extant copy of the map in his own hand), which reads "Peter Charles L'Enfant." L'Enfant stopped using his French first name in 1777, soon after he arrived in America to serve in the Revolutionary Army at the age of 22. At the end of the Revolutionary War he decided to stay in America and commit his talents to the service of the United States.

L'Enfant had traveled to America as one of a band of French adventurers headed by General Lafayette. Marie Joseph Paul Yves Roch Gilbert du Montier,

*Figure 8: Peter Charles L'Enfant.*

the Marquis de Lafayette, became a Major General in the American Revolutionary Army and a firm friend of George Washington. In 1784, to celebrate Washington's victory in the War of Independence, Bro. Lafayette presented Bro. Washington with a Masonic apron. However, although Lafayette is well documented as a Freemason, that says nothing about L'Enfant's Masonic status. L'Enfant came to America as a soldier, serving under Lafayette and he remained a soldier for many years.

In 1784 L'Enfant wrote to Congress suggesting a corps of engineers in the American military. This shows him to have been well ahead of his time as an engineer, but he was quite out of touch with the realities of American politics, as his later actions confirm. He got into trouble with his commanding officer when he wrote a letter that was published in the *New York Gazette* of September 4 that year to complain that he had been overlooked when acclaim was apportioned for some military engineering work. Typically, he appealed directly to Washington, his supreme commander at that time, in his own defense. He ends his letter thus:

*And as your Excellency's esteem is infinitely precious to me I beg you will accept my justification and render justice to my statements.*

*I have the honor to be with great regard Sir, your Excellency's obedient and most humble servant,*

*—P. C. L'Enfant.*[50]

Washington did not reply.

On February 18, 1782, L'Enfant again wrote to Washington. A prickly man who did not accept orders easily, he felt he had been overlooked for field promotion in favor of a junior officer, He complained directly to Washington, bypassing his line officer, General Duportail. Washington replied on March 1.

*I am sensible how disagreeable it is to have an inferior officer promoted over your head and am sorry it is not in my power to remedy it . . . Your zeal and fervour are such as to reflect the highest honour on yourself and are extremely pleasing to me, and I have no doubt that they will have their due weight with considering any future promotion in your Corps.*[51]

On March 7, 1783, Washington wrote to Congress:

*Repeated applications have been made to me, in favor of Major Villefranche, and Capt L'Enfant, of the Corps of Engineers, for their individual promotion; and being again pressed upon me, by Major Genl Duportail, I take the Liberty, thro your Excellency, to submit to Congress, whether some general principles of promotion, applicable to this Corps, as well as others in the Army, might not be established, which may prevent the necessity of particular applications, and the Embarrassment of giving promotion out of its common course.*[52]

During his time in the army, L'Enfant wrote at least three more letters to Washington, all seeking promotion. Clearly he was ambitious and not afraid of making a case for his own advancement.

When Congress announced that a new Federal City was to be built to house the government of the new nation, L'Enfant approached Washington and put himself forward as engineer for the new project. His opportunity occurred when Washington invited L'Enfant to Mount Vernon in 1787 to discuss business concerning the funding of the Society of the Cincinnati.[53] (The Society of the Cincinnati was founded in New York during 1783 by Continental Army officers who fought in the American Revolution. L'Enfant, as a member of Lafayette's original contingent of French soldiers, became a founding member, and Washington had been elected the society's honorary president.) After the War of Independence L'Enfant had moved in 1787 to New York, where he designed the New York City Hall. This building, in which Washington would later be sworn in as the First President of the United States, became a temporary home for the new government of the United States, and formed part of the bid by New York to become the seat of Government. Washington was widely reported to be impressed with the beauty of the building.

I wondered if L'Enfant took the opportunity of this meeting to plant ideas about the new Federal City in Washington's mind. Whether he did or not, he certainly got the job of planning it. It is widely maintained that L'Enfant requested the honor of designing a plan for the national capital, although no copy of any letter making such a request can be found in the Library of Congress, where the many other letters he wrote to George Washington are stored.

After surveying the site, L'Enfant put forward a plan featuring ceremonial spaces and grand radial avenues within the natural contours of the land. He created a system of intersecting diagonal roadways superimposed over a grid system. The avenues radiated from the two most significant building sites, which were to be occupied by the Capitol and the President's House. But where did he get his inspiration?

L'Enfant is on record as saying that Christopher Wren's unexecuted plans for London (which also featured two focal points, the Royal Exchange and St. Paul's Cathedral) inspired him.[54] The focus of L'Enfant's design was to be the Capitol and the President's House (the White House), which were to act as hubs for broad avenues that would radiate like spokes of a wheel over the regular north-south grid pattern. However, the deciding factor in the positioning of major buildings was the geography of the land. L'Enfant chose the site for the Capitol first, locating it on Jenkins Hill, which, as I have already noted, he saw as "a pedestal waiting for a monument."

It got that monument on September 18, 1793, when the cornerstone of the Capitol Building of the United Stated of America was laid with full Masonic honors by Worshipful Brother and President George Washington, supported by Rt. Wor. Joseph Clark, Grand Master *pro tem* of Georgia; Rt. Wor. Brother Clark of Maryland; Wor. Brother Elisha C. Dick, Master of Alexandria Lodge No. 22 of Virginia; as well as Wor. Brother Valentine Reintzel, Master of Lodge No. 9 of Maryland.

Brother John Duffey, a silversmith of Alexandria who was a member of Fredericksburg Lodge No. 4, where Bro. Washington was initiated, made a silver trowel, a gavel, and full set of Masonic working tools for this ceremony. The trowel has a silver blade, silver shank, ivory handle, and a silver cap on the end of the handle. At the end of the ceremony, Brother Washington presented the Gavel to the Master of Lodge No. 9 and the Trowel to the Master of Alexandria Lodge No. 22. (An inscription, engraved on the underside of the trowel blade sometime after 1805, reads: "This Trowell, the property of Alexandria-Washington Lodge No. 22 A.F.& A.M. was used by General George Washington September 18, 1793, to lay the corner stone of the Capitol of the United States of America at Washington, D.C."[55])

The Capitol was the first Federal building in the gigantic Federal Triangle. This triangle—marked out by the Capitol, the White House, and the Washington

Monument—is the foundation of the L'Enfant plan and all subsequent modifications. But Washington himself fixed the upper end of its hypotenuse, the President's House.

A letter from George Washington dated June 22, 1791, says that he accepts L'Enfant's suggestions for placing the Capitol "on the west end of Jenkins heights." Washington argued that the President's House would provide an answering vista to the Capitol with a great diagonal avenue linking the two buildings to "add to the sumptuousness of a palace, the convenience of a house and the agreeableness of a country seat." Once the President's House was positioned relative to the Capitol, Washington would not allow any further changes to be made. Indeed, as we saw from his letters, he tried to defend L'Enfant when the engineer demolished a new house which had been built on one of the chosen spots by Mr. Carroll of Duddington.

As I was studying this material, I discussed my views on Washington's attitude toward the placement of the President's House with the writer Katherine Neville. Katherine lives in Washington with her scientist husband Karl Pribram, and she has a large collection of material about the setting up of the city. She pointed out to me that recently published evidence confirmed that George Washington had taken a close interest in the exact siting of the President's House. She drew my attention to an article by historian William Seale in *White House History*, the journal of the White House Historical Association. It adds this telling detail about Washington's personal interest in the siting of the President's House:

*Washington's engineer, Major Pierre Charles L'Enfant first sited the White House northeast of where it is, but the president shifted it, driving stakes to locate the building where it is today.*[56]

I now knew that the public record of state correspondence does not support the myth of L'Enfant as a determined Masonic occultist, enlisted by a Masonic President and a Masonic surveyor to build a Federal City based on demonic symbols. Not only was L'Enfant unable to carry out such a task, he was not a Freemason. No record exists of his membership in any Masonic lodge, or of his attendance at any of the Masonic ceremonies associated with the founding of the city. In his copious correspondence, mainly seeking favors from Washington, he never once uses any Masonic phrases. Washington, on the other hand, was quite free in his use of Masonic phrases to brother Masons, as examples from his letters show:

*I shall always feel pleasure when it may be in my power to render Service to lodge No 39, and in every act of brotherly kindness to the Members of it; being with great truth your Affect. Brother, etc.*[57]

*I am much obliged by your good wishes and appreciate them with sincerity assuring you fraternally of my esteem . . . I shall always be ambitious of being considered a deserving Brother.*[58]

*Permit me to reciprocate your prayers for my temporal happiness and to supplicate that we may all meet much hereafter in that eternal temple, whose builder is the Great Architect of the Universe.*[59]

The Web site of the Grand Lodge of British Columbia and Yukon, which has access to lodge membership lists of early American lodges, confirms my view that L'Enfant was never a Freemason, but it goes further and suggests where this odd idea first arose. They say:

*Although Freemason George Washington commissioned Pierre Charles L'Enfant and approved the streetplan of Andrew Ellicott and Benjamin Bannaker, they were not Freemasons.*

*The first of these unfounded theories seems to have appeared in 1989 with Michael Baigent and Richard Leigh's* The Temple and the Lodge *in which, without documentation, they assert that George Washington and Thomas Jefferson interfered with Pierre L'Enfant's work to impose a pair of octagonal shapes around the Capitol and the White House.*

*The claims took an anti-masonic turn the following year and many professional anti-masons quickly became promoters. The assumptions required to believe that the position of a number of streets and buildings reveal a secret political or occult agenda have no foundation.*[60]

My own investigation confirms this view. But there is another theory to consider. I now needed to look at the claims put forward by an astrologer that Washington used traditional astrology to lay out the Federal City.

## Sunrise, Sunset

Astrologer David Ovason is not an anti-Mason, and when he wrote *The Secret Zodiacs of Washington*, he was not a Mason. He joined the Craft after that book was published. Hence the views propounded in the book are not drawn from any knowledge of Masonic ritual.

Ovason's claim is that L'Enfant and Ellicott (both of whom he erroneously asserts were Freemasons) intended Pennsylvania Avenue to point from the Capitol building towards the setting sun at a time when Sirius was due to appear in the sky. On the basis of this alignment, he claims "the city was intended to celebrate the mystery of Virgo, the Egyptian Isis, the Grecian Ceres and the Christian Virgin."[61]

This strange idea of a supposed Masonic obsession with the star Sirius and the constellation of Virgo was picked up by Graham Hancock and Robert Bauval in their book *Talisman*. As non-Freemasons, they accepted without question a statement they quoted from a popular magazine, *Freemasonry Today*. This is not an official Masonic publication, and in this case it was simply repeating urban myths from conspiracy theory Web sites, without checking the facts. The quote reads:

> *Washington, D.C., can fairly be described as the world's foremost "Masonic City." Its centre was laid out according to a plan drawn up by the French Freemason Pierre L'Enfant.*[62]

Ovason's lack of knowledge of Freemasonry at the time he wrote his book leads him to make some odd claims. For example, he says that the Year of Masonry is "symbolically denoting the era following the supposed foundation of the Temple of Solomon."[63] And he says later that the Masonic calendar is dated from the supposed creation date of the world, known as the Year of Light and abbreviated A.L. He says that "higher degrees" are somehow more powerful or important than the Craft degrees.[64] (The latter is not an idea supported by any Masonic organization I have studied.)

Ovason was also unaware of the Masonic significance of an ear of corn, particularly if it is standing by a pool of water. (Although since joining the Craft and having been raised to the Third Degree, he might now understand it.) He makes the bizarre interpretation that the symbol is a ritual reference to the goddess Virgo, whom he calls the "Beautiful Virgin," although there is no use of such a symbol in Masonic ritual. And his decision to equate the cornerstone-laying ceremony and the Bright Morning Star with Sirius, the dog star, has no basis in Masonic ritual at all.[65]

Does this all mean that there was no Masonic influence at all on the design of Washington, D.C.? I had noticed two facts that *do* indicate Masonic influence. The first is that L'Enfant drew his inspiration from a new layout for London proposed by Freemason Sir Christopher Wren, and the second, that Freemason George Washington influenced the position of the President's House relative to the Capitol.

Despite his lack of Masonic knowledge, David Ovason identified an important geomantic sun alignment between the Capitol and the White House. Hancock and Bauval confirmed that this alignment is accurate with a photograph of the August 10 sunset in their book *Talisman*.[66] However, they all overlook that fact that sunsets have little significance in Masonic ritual, but sunrises are extremely important. For example, the Third degree is conducted in pre-dawn darkness as the Bright Morning Star rises in the East just before the Sun.

An alignment towards a sunrise always holds critical significance for Freemasons. And there was one special sunrise alignment that George Washington found particularly inspiring. The possibility that he used Masonic geomancy to build the Federal City of the United States remained. And I now knew from his correspondence how small were his contributions to the layout of the city, but that the small points he insisted on were vital. I had to investigate why!

## Conclusions

Despite a prolific body of conspiracy literature suggesting that the layout of the city of Washington is a massive Masonic plot to build Satanic symbols into the fabric of the USA, there is no evidence to support such claims. The only factor in the layout of the city that seems to have been important to George Washington was the positioning of the President's House relative to the Capitol.

The claims that L'Enfant and Ellicott were Freemasonic Occultists who connived with Washington to manipulate the Federal Commissioners and Congress to force a Masonic ground plan onto the city just do not withstand close investigation. Likewise, the claim that L'Enfant and Ellicott imposed an agenda of Masonic geomancy to align the White House and the Capitol to point at a summer sunset that favored viewing the star Sirius has no Masonic basis either.

Just two facts stand out: L'Enfant admitted that he was inspired by the plan of London produced by Freemason Sir Christopher Wren after the Great Fire, and Bro. George Washington took a close interest in the exact positioning of the President's House once the site of the Capitol had been fixed.

The question of whether George Washington used Masonic geomancy to decide the relative positioning of the Capitol and President's House remained open. Bro. Washington certainly had been exposed to considerable Masonic teaching on the matter. My next task was to investigate how he could have used Masonic geomancy to lay out the city. I'll tell you about what I found out in the next chapter.

# Chapter Four

# Washington and the Streets of London

## Washington, Freemasonry, and Ritual

The three degrees of Freemasonry link to the movement of the sun through the seasons of the year. In the First degree, the candidate is placed in the Northeast corner, where the sun rises on the longest day of the year. In the Second degree, the candidate stands in the Southeast corner, where the sun rises on the shortest day of the year. And in the Third degree, the candidate is placed on the East-West line of the equinox, when day and night are of equal length, so darkness and light are brought into balance.

Masonic ritual says that the positions of the officers of a Masonic Lodge represent the movements of the Sun. The Junior Warden is placed in the South and said to "mark the Sun at its meridian." The Senior Warden sits in the West "to mark the setting Sun. As the Sun sets in the West to close the day, so is the Senior Warden placed in the West to close the Lodge." This is one of the few references to a sunset anywhere in the Masonic ritual, but the importance of the sunrise shows in the placing of the Master. His seat is in the East, because "as the Sun rises in the East to open and enliven the day, so is the Master placed in the East to open the Lodge and to employ and instruct his Brethren in Freemasonry."

The movements of the Sun during the day, and during the year, are built into the rituals of Freemasonry. As we've seen, George Washington's diaries from 1760 through to 1775 contain detailed astrological information, and, despite the looming prospect of war with England, he continued this interest in the movements of the heavenly bodies. In the opening pages of his diary for 1774, he again pastes sections from "The *Virginia Almanack* for the year of our LORD GOD 1774," as he had done for so many years after becoming a Mason, so that he was informed about the astronomical events of each day. Washington took the trouble to preserve some detailed comments from the *Almanack* that might help explain how he may have interpreted Masonic astrology. Page 17 of his 1774 diary contains this statement, copied from the *Almanack:*

*Is it possible to conceive that Chance, at the Birth of Time, could have balanced, in the Firmament those enormous Masses, those Globes of Fire, that pass through the immense Spaces? Could Chance direct them in their majestically rapid Courses? Could Chance fix the circle of the Revolutions, prevent their Collisions, and so hinder their being reduced into elementary Parts, as imperceptible as the Atoms out of which they have been formed?[67]*

And page 26 of this diary has an even more interesting quote from the same *Almanack*. Its Masonic overtones could not have been lost on Bro. George. Perhaps that is why he chose to preserve it.

*What must be our notions of the Grandeur and Power of a King, who, to make high Roads commodious for travelling, should level Mountains and fill up Vallies, who should adorn all the Cities of his Kingdom with Temples and Magnificent Palaces, and who should make Gold and Silver as plentiful everywhere as they were at Jerusalem in the Time of Solomon! Yet, what new Thing does this great King produce? His noble works are but the displacing of what is already made. He may form a Plan, but the Execution is not in his Power. He is under a Necessity of calling to his Assistance the Hand and Genius of a Number of Men, and these can do nothing without the Help of Instruments, he cannot, by the Force of his World and Authority of his Command, move even a Straw.*

In his later Masonic career, despite holding high office in the new Republic, Bro. Washington made a point of attending the feasts of the solstices, which in Freemasonry are known as the Feasts of St. John: St. John the Baptist for the summer solstice and St. John the Evangelist for the winter solstice. The Christian Church celebrates the Feast of St. John the Baptist on June 24 and St. John the Evangelist on December 27; but, as Masonic lodges meet on a fixed day of the week each month, the nearest day between the church festival and the solstice would be used for the Masonic celebration.

Operative Freemasons (Masons who actually work in stone and create new buildings, as opposed to speculative Masons, who work on spiritual rituals using themselves as living stones) have traditionally used an alignment with the rising Sun to fix the foundation stone of a building. Here is the ritual which was followed by Scottish Operative lodges to set up the alignment of a new church.

*The site of the Altar having been decided upon, a pole was thrust in to the ground and a day appointed for the building to be commenced. On the evening previous, the Patrons, Ecclesiastics, and Masons assembled, and spent the night in devotional exercises; one being placed to watch the rising of the Sun gave notice when his rays appeared above the horizon. When fully in view, the Master Mason sent out a man with a rod, which he ranged in line between the altar and the Sun, and thus fixed the line of orientation.*[68]

These men with rods are known as Deacons, and in a modern speculative lodge they always carry their poles of office.

In choosing the site of the President's House and then ritually consecrating the cornerstone of the Capitol, George Washington seems to have carried out this procedure not just for a building but for the whole city. As we've discussed, his papers say that he suggested the site for the President's House, and, once that was agreed, the alignment of the avenue to connect the two sites was fixed. David Ovason suggested that this alignment points to a sunset on August 10. But, as we've seen, sunsets have no ritual meaning in Freemasonry. In ritual terms, it is the sun*rise* which marks the beginning of the new life of the Master Mason, and the clues to the real meaning of the alignment must lie there.

In 1753, when George Washington was raised to the sublime degree of a Master Mason, the Master of Fredericksburg Lodge would have taken him by the arm, turned him towards the darkness of the lodge, and said these words to him:

*Thus, my dear Brother, have all Master Masons been raised from a figurative death, to a reunion with the companions of their former toil.*

In the East of the lodge a small, five-pointed star would be illuminated above the Master's chair, and while directing Bro. George's attention to this, the Master would say:

*Let me now beg of you to observe, that the Light of a Master is but as darkness visible, serving only to express that gloom which hangs over the prospect of futurity. It is that mysterious veil of darkness which the eye of human reason cannot penetrate, unless assisted by that Divine Light which is from above.*

He would then have turned Brother Washington towards the symbols of mortality (a skull and a pair of crossed thigh bones) and the grave, saying:

*Yet even, by this glimmering ray you will perceive that you stand on the very brink of the grave into which you have just figuratively descended, and which, when this transitory life shall have passed away, will again receive you into its cold bosom, let those emblems of mortality which now lie before you, lead you to contemplate your inevitable destiny and guide your reflections into that most interesting and useful of all human studies the knowledge of yourself.*

So the light of that star, rising before the Sun in the East, is the inspiration for the future lifework of the newly raised Master Mason.

In the late eighteenth century, when Washington was building his Federal City, the concept of Freemasonry was broader than it is assumed to be today. As I've mentioned, the radical republican writer, Richard Carlile, published a *Manual of Freemasonry* in his magazine *The Republican*. (At the time when Carlile was writing, America was a Crown Colony ruled by the King of England, and the idea that people could elect a President to rule them, instead of submitting to the hereditary rights of king, was an extreme concept.) Carlile later produced this manual as a separate volume, which remains in print today. In its introduction he says:

*The Key to the mysteries of Freemasonry . . . is the getting knowledge of the celestial globe, knowing the mysteries of all the figures and grouping of stars on that globe; knowing further, that this globe is the foundation of all religion, knowing how to calculate the precession of the equinoxes, the return of comets and eclipses, and all the planetary motions and astronomical relations of time.*[69]

Andrew Prescott, Professor of Freemasonic Studies at the University of Sheffield, says that Carlile "evidently thought that his *Manual of Freemasonry* represented an important contribution to radical ideology," and reports Carlile as saying that it would be the only correct history of Masonry and an important blow to superstition.[70]

Carlile said of his revelations:

*Astrology, gipsy fortune telling, Modern Freemasonry, Mahometanism, Christianity, and Judaism, have sprung from, and are so many corruptions of, the ancient mysteries of the Pagans . . .*[71]

*I sum up these observations, with the conclusion that the Key Stone of the Royal Arch of Freemasonry is the ancient science of the Zodiac.*[72]

This idea was popular in the nineteenth century in America, and was stated by the American Masonic Astrologer Robert Hewitt Brown, who said:

*The whole account of the building of King Solomon's Temple, given in Masonic myth is an astronomical myth.*[73]

Brown draws extensively on earlier work of English Masonic writer the Reverend Dr. George Oliver,[74] but puts the ideas into an astrological context. He asks where the Masonic tradition of aligning the cornerstone came from, and answers:

*The ancients believed that the movements, conjunctions and positions of the heavenly bodies influenced not only the destiny of nations but of individuals and regulated the affairs of life. Their temples were dedicated to the worship of the*

*Sun, and the whole process of their erection from the laying of the first stone, up to their completion had special reference to astrological conditions and the movement of the Sun in the zodiac . . . The temples always faced East to catch the first rays of the rising Sun . . . the cornerstone would be laid in line with the rising Sun.*[75]

Brown says the Royal Arch of Freemasonry can be defined in the same words as the Lodge. The Lodge is defined in the ritual lecture of the First degree in a series of questions and answers:

*Q: When placed at the Northeast part of the Lodge, assisted by the three lesser lights, what were you enabled to discover?*
*A: The form of the Lodge.*
*Q: What form?*
*A: A parallelepipedon.*
*Q: Describe its dimensions.*
*A: In length from East to West, in breadth between North and South, in depth from the surface of the earth to the center, and even as high as the Heavens.*

Brown notes that this definition includes the starry vault of heaven.[76] He develops the point, saying that Masonic myth maintains:

*At the time of building King Solomon's Temple, the celestial equator cut the ecliptic at about 10 degrees of the constellation Aries. At that period the constellation of Leo was therefore near the summit of the zodiacal arch.*[77]

Finally, he asks what the most favorable time to observe the Royal Arch is, and answers:

*If we wish to observe the constellations as they were at the summer solstice at the time of the completion of King Solomon's temple, we should view the heavens about the 1st of August, but as the Sun in the south at high twelve, by its overpowering light, prevents the proper stars being seen, it will be necessary to defer our observations for six months, or until about the 5th of February, at which time the same*

*stars are visible at midnight. "Low twelve," around the 5th of February, is, there-*
*fore, the best time to view the Royal Arch.*

*If we then take our station, looking south, and lift our eyes to the vast arch of*
*heaven, the spectacle will be one of unsurpassed magnificence, and to an intelligent*
*Mason, eloquent with the truths of his profession.*[78]

But did the suggestion that George Washington might have chosen to align the principal axis of Washington to point at some particular astral event make any sense in terms of what I knew about the inspiration of the layout of the city? I have mentioned that Peter L'Enfant claimed as his inspiration the plan for the layout of London that Sir Christopher Wren presented to King Charles II immediately after the Great Fire of London, and I knew that this included an alignment that was intended to point to a key sunrise in the Masonic Calendar. Let's look more closely at Bro. Christopher Wren and his plan to rebuild London, and see what we find out.

## Wren's Masonic Plan for London

Sir Christopher Wren was a skilled scientist, the best architect of his genera-tion, and a Freemason. He was also a founder member of the Royal Society of London. In an copy of the *Natural History of Wiltshire* by John Aubrey, held in the Bodleian Library, a note had been added in Aubrey's own hand:

*This day (May the 18th. being Munday 1691 after Rogation Sunday) is a great*
*Convention at St. Paul's—Church of the Fraternity of the Adopted Masons where*
*Sr. Christopher Wren is to be adopted as a Brother: and Sr. Henry Goodric . . . of*
*the Tower & divers others. There have been kings, that have been of this Sodality.*[79]

The Lodge minutes of Lodge Original, No. 1, now the Lodge of Antiquity No. 2 (United Grand Lodge of England) also mention Wren as being Master of the Lodge.[80]

Christopher Wren was born on October 20, 1632, near Salisbury. When he was only two years old his mother died. Soon after, his father was appointed Dean of Windsor and Registrar of the Order of the Garter. When Windsor was seized by Parliamentary troops, during the English Civil War that resulted in the execution of King Charles I and the establishment of Oliver Cromwell as Lord Protector, the young Christopher fled to London, where he went to school, and then in 1650 went to Wadham College at Oxford University to study under John Wilkins, the man who chaired the first formal meeting of the Royal Society.

When the post of Professor of Astronomy at Gresham College, in Bishopsgate, London, became vacant in 1657, Christopher Wren was appointed. In 1661 he left Gresham to become Savilian Professor of Astronomy at Oxford.

Wren played a key role in the aftermath of the Great Fire of London. This fire started during the night, and at three in the morning of Sunday, September 2, 1666, the famous diarist Samuel Pepys was awakened by his maid, who said that she could see a great fire in the City. Pepys went to her window to look at the blaze. The next day, as Pepys wrote, "the wind was great behind the fire," and it continued to spread. By four o'clock the following morning, the fire was getting closer to Pepys' house, so he loaded his valuables onto a cart and set off to the home of a friend in Bethnal Green, well away from the fire.

King Charles II was personally involved in fighting the fire. He helped to pull down houses to create firebreaks to try to stop it spreading. But, driven by a freshening wind, the fire jumped the gaps and continued to burn. It burned for almost five days, and destroyed an area half a mile wide and one-and-a-half miles long. Three-quarters of a square mile in the center of London were completely destroyed and its inhabitants made homeless. An estimated 13,000 homes were lost.

Christopher Wren came forward with a plan for the City of London on September 11, just a week after the fire had started. He was convinced that, out of the ashes of the old capital, a new city could be built that would reflect his understanding of architecture and Masonry. I have already noted that L'Enfant was partly inspired by Versailles. Wren, too, was inspired by France. He had visited that country in 1665 and returned fascinated by the natural beauty that could be derived from placing nature in the context of geometry. His biographer Harold Hutchison says of Wren at this time:

*Of geometrical figures he prefers the square and the circle, and straight lines are preferable to curves . . . Wren's future practice was based on more than a casual study of the achievements of the past—as always he was a scientist and theorist before he allowed himself to become a practitioner.*[81]

William Preston, writing in 1772, tells a Masonic version of the story of the great fire and Brother Wren's plan for a new London:

*The year 1666 afforded a singular and awful occasion for the utmost exertion of Masonic abilities. The city of London, which had been visited in the preceding year by the plague, to whose ravages, it is computed, above 100,000 of its inhabitants fell a sacrifice, had scarcely recovered from the alarm of that dreadful contagion, when a general conflagration reduced the greatest part of the city within the walls to ashes, This dreadful fire broke out on the 2d of September, at the house of a baker in Pudding-lane, a wooden building, pitched on the outside, as were also all the rest of the houses in that narrow lane. The house being filled with faggots and brush-wood, soon added to the rapidity of the flames, which raged with such fury, as to spread four ways at once.*

*Jonas Moore and Ralph Gatrix, who were appointed surveyors on this occasion to examine the ruins, reported, that the fire over-ran 373 acres within the walls, and burnt 13,000 houses, 89 parish churches, besides chapels, leaving only 11 parishes standing. The Royal Exchange, Custom-house, Guildhall, Blackwell-hall, St. Paul's Cathedral, Bridewell, the two compters, fifty-two city companies halls, and three city gates, were all demolished. The damage was computed at 10,000,000 £ sterling.*

*After so sudden and extensive a calamity, it became necessary to adopt some regulations to guard against any such catastrophe in future. It was therefore determined, that in all the new buildings to be erected, stone and brick should be substituted in the room of timber. The King and the Grand Master immediately ordered deputy Wren to draw up the plan of a new city, with broad and regular streets. Dr. Christopher Wren was appointed surveyor general and principle architect for rebuilding the city, the cathedral of St. Paul, and all the parochial churches enacted by parliament, in lieu of those that were destroyed, with other public structures. This gentleman, conceiving the charge too important for a single person, selected Mr. Robert Hook, professor of geometry in Gresham college, to assist him; who was immediately employed in measuring, adjusting, and setting out the grounds of the private streets to the several proprietors. Dr. Wren's model and plan were laid before the king and the house of commons, and the practicability of the whole scheme, without the infringement of property, clearly demonstrated: it unfortunately happened, however, that the greater part of the citizens were absolutely averse to alter their old possessions, and to recede from building their houses again on the old foundations. Many were unwilling to give up their properties into the hands of public trustees, till they should receive an equivalent of more advantage; while others expressed distrust. Every means were tried to convince the citizens, that by removing all the church-yards, gardens &c. to the out-skirts of the city, sufficient room would be given to augment the streets, and properly to dispose of the churches, halls, and other public buildings, to the perfect satisfaction of every proprietor; but the representation of all these improvements had no weight.*

*The citizens chose to have their old city again, under all its disadvantages, rather than a new one, the principles of which they were unwilling to understand, and considered as innovations. Thus an opportunity was lost, of making the new city the most magnificent, as well as the most commodious for health and trade, of any in Europe. The architect, cramped in the execution of his plan, was obliged to abridge his scheme, and exert his utmost labour, skill, and ingenuity, to model the city in the manner in which it has since appeared.*

*On the 23d of October 1667, the king in person levelled in Masonic form the foundation stone of the new Royal Exchange, now allowed to be the finest in Europe; and on the 28th September 1669, it was opened by the lord mayor and aldermen.*[82]

Wren's logical approach to rebuilding London made the Royal Exchange and St. Paul's Cathedral two major foci of the rebuilt city. He intended to have three major arterial roads forming a triangle to link Newgate with the Exchange, the Exchange with St. Paul's, and St. Paul's with Newgate. These roads were to be 90 feet wide, providing great vistas.

I already knew from my previous studies of Wren's work[83] that he chose the orientation of the great avenue between the Royal Exchange so that it pointed to a key Masonic sunrise. If Wren had ever built his great city, you would have

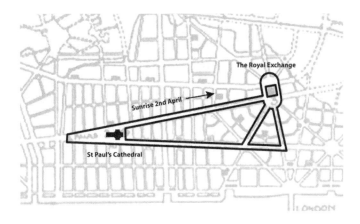

*Figure 9: This plan shows how the great architect and Freemason Sir Christopher Wren planned a great avenue to link London's new Cathedral to the Royal Exchange. The avenue points to the rising sun on April 2, the day on which Freemasons believe the building of Solomon's Temple was begun.*

been able to stand in front of St. Paul's Cathedral at dawn on the 2nd of April, look up the great avenue, and see the sun rise over the Royal Exchange.

Why did Bro. Wren choose April 2? The reason lies in Masonic lore, and a clue can be found in the inscription on the front of King's College, Aberdeen. Translated from the Latin, this says:

> *By the grace of the most serene, illustrious and ever-victorious King James IV: On the fourth before the nones of April in the year one-thousand five hundred the Masons began to built this excellent college.*

Historian David Stevenson of St. Andrews University puts forward an explanation for the meaning of this inscription:

> *The significance of the date, 2 April, is almost certainly that it was the date on which it was calculated, by reference to the Bible, that the building of Solomon's Temple had begun. It was, therefore, evidently chosen as a highly appropriate date*

*for a building project to be started. A written account of the building of the college makes clear references to the building of the temple, and it has been argued that the founder of the college, Bishop William Elphinstone, chose the starting date and commemorated it with the inscription. This, however, does not explain the peculiar wording of the inscription. It mentions the king as patron of the project, but states that 2 April was the date on which the masons started work. It is surprising that an inscription of this sort should specifically mention the craftsmen responsible for the work at all, yet here they are standing alongside the king. Is it possible that the masons were mentioned because it was they who, drawing on their traditions, pointed out that 2 April was a particularly appropriate day on which to start building?[84]*

Scottish Masons have long been fully aware of the emphasis the Craft legends put on Solomon's Temple as the greatest of all building projects, central to the development and dissemination of Masonry. Stevenson also found that the earliest written reference to a Masonic lodge in Scotland can be found in the minutes of Aberdeen Burgh Council:

*In Aberdeen in 1483 the burgh council was involved in the settlement of a dispute between the six "masownys of the luge," and fines were laid down for offences, with provision for the exclusion of masons from the lodge (presumably thus incurring loss of employment) in case of repeated offences. This Aberdeen lodge was under the supervision of the master of kirkworks, being a permanent or semi-permanent institution attached to the burgh church of St. Nicholas, and these late fifteenth-century references to the lodge coincide with a period of building activity when the choir of St. Nicholas was rebuilt.[85]*

The alignment of the main avenue of Wren's new London points to a key sunrise in the Masonic Calendar. It would have been a giant sundial marking the date that Masonic tradition assigned to the beginning of work on Solomon's Temple. But did George Washington also align the main avenue of his Federal City to a Masonic sunrise? The direction of the sunrise on any date varies with the latitude it is viewed from, so simply comparing the compass directions of L'Enfant's and Wren's plans would not tell me much.

Since George Washington was an active and interested Mason, he would certainly have read William Preston's famous work, in which case he would be aware of Wren's role in Freemasonry. Washington was also aware of the ritual teaching of Freemasonry, as he had worked the three degrees.

When L'Enfant proposed a layout for the Federal City based on Wren's ideas, he suggested building around a central triangle of avenues. Washington could easily have seen an opportunity to commemorate a suitable Masonic date in the alignment of the main avenue, linking the President's House with the Capitol. As we saw in Chapter 3, once L'Enfant had produced a layout based on two focal points, which he said was inspired by Wren's Masonic plan for London, the only influence Washington exerted was in the positioning of the President's House. But once Washington fixed that alignment by personally adjusting the position of the marking posts, he went to great lengths to make sure it was not changed.

As we know from Washington's diaries, he had taken a great interest in the horizon movement of the sun and planets, and had pasted key pages from the *Virginia Almanack* into the front of some of his diaries over the whole period he spent developing the estate at Mount Vernon before he was called away to serve in the War of Independence. As a practicing Mason and a trained surveyor, he had the skill to work out the date of the sunrise alignment that would occur when the President's House was placed where it was in relation to the Capitol.

We also saw in Chapter 3 that David Ovason identified an August 10 sunset alignment. However, there is a symmetry about sunrises and sunsets that Ovason overlooked. This date gives an azimuth for the sun of 290 degrees, which, if reversed, points to a sunrise on February 5. And I already knew from the writing of Bro. Robert Hewitt Brown that this sunrise marks a day whose evening will reveal the Zodiac in exactly the position that Masonic tradition says it was at the time of the completion of Solomon's Temple. So the layout of the Federal City echoes exactly the layout Wren tried to commemorate in his discarded plan, but it points to the date of the consecration of the Temple, not the start of its building work.

Not only does the layout of the city of Washington incorporate the features of Wren's design for London, but George Washington carried the similarity through to the laying of the cornerstone of the Capitol at the Autumnal

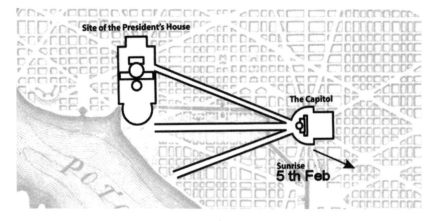

*Figure 10: Pennsylvania Avenue was originally planned as a straight avenue between the Capitol and the President's House (the White House). It points directly at the rising sun on February 5, the day when the Royal Arch of the Zodiac appears in the night sky as it was when Solomon's Temple in Jerusalem was consecrated.*

Equinox in 1793. Did he have in mind the Masonic ceremony that Preston reported Charles II to have carried out on the 23d of October, 1667, when "the king in person leveled in Masonic form the foundation stone of the new Royal Exchange"?

But there is an additional Masonic element in Wren's choice of alignment in his plan. In two out of every eight years, the Bright Morning Star of Venus, the third brightest object in the sky, would rise above the Royal Exchange, as viewed from St. Paul's. When I checked out the alignment in Washington, D.C., exactly the same happened there.

Here was another feature of Bro. Washington's choice of alignment which sent a shiver down my spine. Venus follows an eight-year cycle of changes between appearing as a morning and an evening star, and as it does so its point of rising moves relative to the sun. The alignment of the site of the President's House and the center of the Capitol is such that at the beginning of an eight-year Venus cycle, the Bright Morning Star will rise above the Capitol, about one hour and forty-five minutes before the sun. Then five years later in the cycle, Venus will again appear in the dawn sky above the

Capitol, this time forty minutes before the sun. Was this simply coincidence, or did Washington choose it because of its Masonic significance? Certainly, if you stand outside the house Washington planned for the President and look along the line of Pennsylvania Avenue at dawn, then once every eight years the Bright Morning Star of Venus will rise above the Capitol, one hour and forty-five minutes before the sun on February 5th.

In fact, there are two Masonic principles driving the alignments chosen by Bros. Wren and Washington. One is an annual solar event that marks a key date in Masonic tradition. This solar alignment acts like a great sundial, which acts as a reminder of a Masonic date, but the Bright Morning Star is seen as something different. That is an additional source of Masonic inspiration which calls for further investigation.

David Ovason was right about the solar alignment between the President's House and Capitol, even if he mistook its Masonic symbolism. So could some of his other claims be worth taking a second look at? He said of the creator of the Federal City:

*The designer intended this union of earth and skies to remain a secret. He knew how mysteries work. He recognized that it did not matter a great deal whether anyone who lived in his city discovered the meaning of his mystery: it was suffi-cient that he had bridged the material with the spiritual. He knew that the power born of this connection between earth and skies would continue to beneficially influence the souls of those who lived in the city, even if they did not know, with their conscious minds, whence this power came. His whole city was a Mystery, and he felt no need to explain it. He had taken for granted that the planner of a city should ensure that it was well designed on the earth, and that it was harmoniously linked with the skies.*

*A city which is laid out in such a way that it is in harmony with the heavens is a city in perpetual prayer. It is a city built on the recognition that every human activity is in need of the sanctification of the spiritual world, of which the symbol is the light of the living stars.*[86]

By now, I was sure that Bro. Washington was responsible for the alignment the Masonic Bright Morning Star, but I needed to investigate Ovason's claim about the beneficial effects that astrology confers on the city and see if there is any real effect, or if it's just astrological nonsense. Is there any scientific truth in Masonic astrology? To find out, I would have to review Masonic teaching about the Bright Morning Star.

## Conclusions

George Washington's diaries show that when he settled down at Mount Vernon he took an active interest in the appearance of the Bright Morning Star over the surrounding lands, and also took the trouble to cut out and preserve detailed comments from his local almanac about the astrological effects of the appearance of the planets. It also seems likely that he knew about Sir Christopher Wren's Masonic plan for London before L'Enfant suggested using it as model for the Federal City of Washington, D.C.

Preston's Masonic writing drew attention to the significance of key focal points of London. Wren had planned his solar alignment to mark the date of the beginning of building work on the Temple of Solomon, and George Washington was almost certainly familiar with Preston's famous work. Moreover, Washington also had sufficient practical surveying knowledge and astronomical data to choose an alignment between his key focal points that marked a Masonically significant sunrise.

When I analyzed the alignment that Washington influenced, I found that it pointed to a date when the Zodiac would appear just as it had on the date of the consecration of Solomon's Temple. There was also an alignment with the Bright Morning Star of Venus. The Masonic significance of this was not yet clear, but it might have something to do with Masonic geomancy. So my next task was to look at Masonic astrology, and the role of the Bright Morning Star, to see what it might mean. In the next chapter, I present what I found out.

# Chapter Five

# Achievement and Masonic Astrology

## The Masonic Shekinah

For nearly fourteen years, from his marriage until the time he was called away to serve his country during the War of Independence, George Washington devoted considerable time and effort to observing the appearances of the Bright Morning Star. As we've seen, he cut out and pasted alignment charts and notes on astrological effects into the pages of his diaries from 1760 until 1774. But what did he learn about the morning star from his observations? And why did he think its appearances important enough to warrant fourteen years of detailed study? I decided to begin my search for answers to these questions by looking more widely at the Masonic traditions of the Bright Morning Star to see what else Masonic ritual might have told him about it.

Nowadays, many of the mythical tales of Freemasonry, once told as part of the tradition of the Craft, are hidden in side degrees and obscure orders. One such story tells of the appearance, in a 480-year cycle, of a special Bright Morning Star, known to the ritual as the Shekinah. A lecture taken from workings of the degree of the Holy Royal Arch of Jerusalem says:

*The First or Holy Masonic Lodge was opened after the Exodus of the Israelites from the Egyptian bondage, by Moses, Aholiab, and Bazeleel, on consecrated ground at the foot of Mount Horeb, in the Wilderness of Sinai. Here the host of Israel had assembled and pitched their tents to offer up prayers and thanksgivings for their signal deliverance from the hands of the Egyptians. In this place the Almighty had thought*

97

*fit to reveal Himself to his faithful servant Moses. Here the Most High delivered the forms of those mysterious prototypes, the Tabernacle, and the Ark of the Covenant; here was delivered the Sacred Law, engraven by the hand of the Most High, with those sublime and comprehensive precepts of civil and religious policy which, by separating His favoured people from all other nations, he consecrated them a chosen vessel to His service. For these reasons this is denominated the First or Holy Lodge.*

It goes on to describe how one Masonic function of the tabernacle was to direct the pre-dawn light of this Shekinah onto the Ark of the Covenant. This idea is then carried forward into the ritual description of the construction of Solomon's Temple:

*Bazeleel was the inspired workman of the Holy Tabernacle which he built to house the Ark of the Covenant and to allow the light of the Divine Shekinah to shine upon it. His design afterwards became the model of King Solomon's Temple, and conforms to a pattern delivered on Mount Horeb by God to Moses, who afterwards became the Grand Master of the Lodge of Israel.*

This ritual lecture goes on to explain that King Solomon's Temple was designed to allow the light of this special Bright Morning Star to enter, and its rays to shine on the Ark of the Covenant. It then gives details that say that the appearance in the dawn sky of the Divine Shekinah represents the favor of God appearing to the Brethren. But the ritual also warns that God can remove this sign of His favor, if He chooses:

*At the consecration of the Holy Tabernacle, and afterwards at the dedication of the Temple of the Lord by King Solomon, the Divine Shekinah descended so its light shone upon the Ark or Mercy seat as it stood in the Holy of Holies, covered by the wings of the Cherubim, where it appeared for several generations, until the Israelites proved unfaithful to the Most High. And so may the light of Masonry be removed from all who prove unfaithful to their God!*

This lecture says that the Bright Morning Star of the Shekinah is the source of the light which Freemasonry is searching for.

A ritual of the Ancient and Accepted Scottish Rite describes a scene outside Solomon's Temple, when the Candidates for Initiation enter the inner chamber of the Temple before the rising of the Sun, and are exposed to this sacred light of the Bright Morning Star:

*In the grey dawn of morning, even before the Sun rising over Mount Olivet flushed with crimson the walls of the Temple, the chosen few, awe-stricken and grave, had assembled. The light from the seven-branch candlestick in the East was reflected back from the golden floor, from the brazen laver of water, with hyssop and napkins, but fell sombrely on the heavy drapings of the sack-cloth on the walls. Amidst the prayers and exhortations, and the solemn chanting of the Levites, the seven entered into a mystic bond, and the duty of secrecy and silence was laid upon them. And then the doors of cedar and olivewood heavily carved and gilded were opened, the veils of blue, and purple, and scarlet, and richly embroidered white linen were drawn aside, and the mysteries of the Holy of Holies revealed to them.*

*None but the Priests and Levites had entered the Sanctum Sanctorum since the Sacred Ark had been brought thither, and now, as the Seven Secret Sentinels put off their shoes and washed their feet, and stepped over the golden threshold, they stood in silence blinded with the light that burst upon them.*

This is a vivid description of how the light of the Bright Morning Star burst into the pre-dawn darkness of the inner sanctum of Solomon's Temple, the Sanctum Sanctorum, and overawed the Initiates who saw it.

The first lecture of the Craft degrees says that Moses' tent was orientated in an East-West direction and became the model for the Temple of Solomon, complete with its dormer opening to allow the light of the Bright Morning Star to enter:

*And for the better solemnization of Divine worship, as well as a receptacle for the Books and Tables of the Law, Moses caused a Tent or Tabernacle to be erected in the wilderness, which by God's especial command was situated due East and West, for Moses did everything according to a pattern shown him by the Lord on Mount Sinai. This Tent or Tabernacle proved afterwards to be the ground-plan, in respect to situation, of that most magnificent Temple built at Jerusalem by that wise and mighty Prince, King Solomon, whose regal splendor and unparalleled luster far transcend our ideas. This is the third, last, and grand reason. I as a Freemason give, why all places of Divine worship, as well as Masons' regular, well-formed, constituted Lodges are or ought to be so situated.*

In the degree of Secret Master, the ritual says:

*The morning star has driven away the shades of night, and the great light begins to gladden our Lodge. As the morning star is the forerunner of the great light which begins to shine on our Lodge, and we are all Secret Masters, it is time to commence our labors.*

There is a Masonic Order of Chivalry, known as the Royal Order of Scotland, which dates back to the seventeenth century. Its ritual says this Order was set up "on the holy Mount Moriah in the Kingdom of Judea" and re-established, first "at Icolmkill, and afterwards at Kilwinning, where the King of Scots first sat as Grand Master." The ritual reason given for setting up this order is "to correct the errors and reform the abuses which had crept in among the three degrees of St. John's Masonry" (a reference to Craft Masonry, which celebrates the two feasts of St. John at the Summer and Winter Solstice).

The Royal Order ritual has a lot to say about the importance of the Bright Morning Star, and links it to highly successful Masons in history, such as Moses. The ritual poses two questions that have to be answered in a set way:

*Q: What does the Blazing Star represent?*
*A: The Glory of God appearing on Mount Sinai at the deliverance of the Law.*
*Q: Why do the Star and circling G appear?*
*A: The Star and circling G declare, The Shekinah, wherever it appear. Whether on Sinai, Salem or the place where the Eastern Magi saw the blessed face.*

The star is mentioned again when the ritual says:

*Q: Whom did you meet in the Middle Chamber?*
*A: Three wise men.*

*Q: How did they dispose of you?*
*A: They led me to the Cabinet of Wisdom.*
*Q: How were you conducted?*
*A: By a Blazing Star appearing in the East.*

The significance of the appearance of this Bright Morning Star is described in the following piece of ritual:

*Q: I desire to know what was the first and highest honor ever conferred*
*on Freemasons.*
*A: The descent of the Divine Shekinah, first at the consecration of the Holy*
*Tabernacle, and afterwards at the dedication of the Temple of the Lord by*
*King Solomon, placing itself on the Ark or Mercy-seat of the Holy of Holies,*
*covered by the wings of the Cherubim, where it continued to deliver its*
*oracular responses for several generations.*
*Q: How many?*
*A: Fourteen*
*Q: Was the Shekinah ever removed?*
*A: It was.*
*Q: Why so?*
*A: Because the Israelites proved unfaithful to their God. And so may the light*
*of Masonry be removed from all who prove unfaithful to their God.*

After a little astronomical detective work, I had found that there was a bright conjunction of Mercury and Venus that appeared with a frequency of 480 years, as described in the ritual. The full story of this research is told in *The Book of Hiram.*[87] But when I looked at the correlations between high-achieving societies and the appearance of this Masonic Bright Morning Star, I began to suspect that there might be some observational science hiding behind the ritual. Did George Washington feel this motivational effect during the fourteen years he spent at Mount Vernon watching the Bright Morning Star arise from the general direction of Jenkins Heights? I decided to look again at the work of Harvard's David McClelland.

## Reaching for the Stars: A Need to Achieve

Over the years, behavioral scientists have noticed that some people have an intense need to achieve. Others, perhaps the majority, do not seem to be as concerned about achievement. Professor David McClelland of Harvard University studied the life cycles of six high-achieving societies in history. These were the Pre-Inca civilizations of Peru (circa 960 BCE); ancient Athens; Spain between 1200 and 1700 CE; Florence during the fourteenth century; England during the Industrial Revolution (in the seventeenth century); and the USA from 1800 to 1950 CE. I had noticed that there was a correlation between some of his high-achieving societies and the appearance of the Masonic Shekinah.

Mercury and Venus can both be bright objects, and when they appear in the same part of the sky they can look like a single very bright star. Sometimes when this happens they form a Bright Morning Star which rises just before the Sun. I had found that this conjunction fitted the times of the appearance of the Shekinah in Masonic legend.

Five of the six societies McClelland looked at thrived when Venus and Mercury were rising close together just before dawn. I ran a statistical check to see what the odds were of these conjunctions occurring at exactly the same time as high-achieving societies arose. There was less than one chance in a thousand of the two sequences of events happening at the same time by accident. This suggested that some real mechanism might be causing the linkage. My first thought had been that perhaps the people living in these societies saw the Bright Morning Star and thought God was about to help them, and helped themselves as a result. Perhaps McClelland had noticed a motivational effect on those societies which were growing at the time these brilliant astronomical events were happening in the dawn sky. Or was there something more?

This link between the Masonic myth of the appearance of a Bright Morning Star and the rise of high-achieving societies had not been examined before. But as I was speculating about George Washington's motives, it was beginning to seem that Masonic geomancy might utilize this motivational effect of the Bright Morning Star.

For over twenty years, McClelland and his team at Harvard University had studied the urge to achieve. McClelland calls successful people "high-achievement motivated individuals" and says it is their need to achieve that makes them a success. Had George Washington become aware of some source of motivation and harnessed it to favor the new United States? Perhaps he did, because one of the examples that first caught McClelland's interest was the high-achieving USA from 1800 onwards.

McClelland recognized that the need for achievement is a distinct human drive. He showed that it can be isolated and assessed. In 1961 he named this factor, which makes us want to do well, "*n*-achievement," shorthand for "*need to achieve*." He went far beyond the current bounds of psychology to explain why we strive to do well. He invented ways of looking at the success levels of a whole range of societies spread across time from Ancient Greece to the U.S. Republic, and in geography from western Europe to South America. His methods have become standard tools used by business analysts to measure levels of economic performance.

McClelland thought that people's level of *n*-achievement drive could be improved, and he developed a range of training sessions to spur it on. But he never managed to account for the natural levels of *n*-achievement that he found in societies at different times. His work showed that societies went through cycles of economic growth followed by decline, and that the *n*-achievement level in those societies was closely related to the stage of the cycle.

This is how he described the problem.

*Suppose we accept, for the sake of the argument, that a part of the "push" for economic development comes from a psychological characteristic which is roughly reflected in our measures of* n*-achievement. What then? Why do some people have more* n*-achievement at some times than other people? Is it a question of racial heredity, challenge from the environment, or perhaps certain economic, political or social disadvantages?*[88]

By investigating George Washington's Masonic inspiration, had I stumbled on the answer to McClelland's problem? Does Masonic astrology, with its belief in the benevolent and motivating power of the Bright Morning Star, explain why people born at some times have more *n*-achievement drive than people born before or after? And, if it does, do the people involved have to know about the myth to be motivated by it? (How else can the positions of the planets be affecting human motivation?) Freemasonry does not put forward any sensible reasons to explain its myths, and McClelland was not at all interested in Masonic astrology; he had looked only at factors which caused success. But five of the six peaks of success he looked at occurred at times when the Bright Morning Star of Masonic myth rose close before the Sun. At these times, more successful people were born. I felt that perhaps looking more closely at McClelland's ideas on the causes of success would help me understand Bro. Washington's Masonic astrology.

McClelland said this about the way his high $n$-achievers behave:

1. They often use a wide range of expressive gestures and try not to repeat things. This love of novelty helped McClelland spot such people in non-literate societies. He even learned to recognize their style of decoration on the things they made.
2. They always do better when offered achievement incentives.
3. When using colors, they prefer blues and greens to reds and yellows.
4. They move around both in terms of where they live and the social groups they mix with far more than people with low $n$-achievement.
5. They enjoy competitive games more than lower $n$-achievers do.
6. They feel that time is passing more quickly than do individuals with lower levels of $n$-achievement.

McClelland ends his summary by saying.

*People with high* n-*achievement behave in certain characteristic ways, but if asked, they do not consistently respond with the attitudes and beliefs that their behavior seems to imply.*[89]

He describes an experiment in which a group of children, whom he had previously tested for levels of $n$-achievement, were asked to throw a ring over a peg. They were allowed to stand as close to, or as far from, the peg as they wished during the experiment. The children with high $n$-achievement scores chose to stand a moderate distance from the peg. Children with low $n$-achievement scores stood either very close to or very far from it. McClelland explained this result by saying that high *n*-achievers prefer to take "moderate" risks, and so they stand where their skill is most likely to pay off in subjective feelings of success. If they stand too close to the peg, the task is too easy and gives them no personal satisfaction. However, if they stand too far from it, they are less likely to hit it and less likely to obtain success. They are more likely to regard any "hits" as caused by luck, rather than skill.[90] High *n*-achievers set moderately difficult but potentially achievable goals.

But do people with a high need for achievement behave like this all the time? McClelland concluded that they only behave in this way if they can influence the outcome. In tests of pure chance, and in gambling situations, they behave no differently from anybody else. Achievement-motivated people are not gamblers; they prefer to work on a problem rather than leave the outcome to luck. Low *n*-achievers might veer towards gambling and take a big risk, because the outcome is beyond their power. They can easily rationalize away their personal responsibility if they lose. However, if they are conservative, they will take tiny risks. Their gain is small, but secure, and there is little danger of anything going wrong for which they might be blamed.

High *n*-achievers will go for the middle ground. They will take a moderate degree of risk because they feel their efforts and abilities can influence the outcome. In the business world, this aggressive realism is the mark of the successful entrepreneur.

McClelland also studied how high *n*-achievers liked to be rewarded. He found that they were not motivated by what economists call the "profit motive." He looked at the histories of groups such as the Quakers and Dissenters of England, and found that, although they were often successful in business, they did not seem to be interested in the money they made. Often they would plough their large profits back into business expansion. He pointed out that the Quakers were forbidden by their religion from showing off or enjoying wealth. Unless they were total hypocrites, money could not have been the force that drove them to achieve. Their behavior did not show evidence of being driven by greed, so the amassing of money must have had a different purpose. He believed that personal wealth played a key role because it is a symbol of achievement: "A man with a large income is likely to gain respect, not because of the income itself but because of the presumption that it is an index of his competence."

To test this idea, McClelland went back to his ring and peg experiment. This time he asked his subjects to say how much cash a child should get for making a successful throw, at successively increasing distances from the peg. He found that children with high *n*-achievement believed that the rate of pay for success at more difficult tasks should increase more rapidly than the low *n*-achievers did. He explained that success meant more to the high *n*-achievers, so they wanted real recognition. This result confirmed that high *n*-achievers were motivated to earn lots of cash but, paradoxically, had little interest in the money for its own sake. They wanted it only as a means of showing the world they were successful. He also pointed out that offering high *n*-achievers more money to do a boring and repetitive job would not increase their motivation at all.

McClelland concluded that high *n*-achievers do not reject rewards, but they matter less to them than the exploit itself. They get more satisfaction out of winning or solving a difficult problem than they do from any money or praise they receive.

High *n*-achievers seek money as a means of comparing their progress and success to those of other people. They also like to get concrete feedback on how well they are doing. McClelland suspected that this need is related to a concern for personal triumph. But they don't respond favorably to comments of a personal nature, such as how cooperative or helpful they are. They are only interested in facts about their work.

He also showed that high *n*-achievers spend a lot of time thinking about how to do things better. He gave as an example that college students with a high need for achievement get better grades than equally bright students with weaker needs for success. He noted that companies that employ many achievement-motivated people grow faster and are more profitable. And he extended this idea to countries. He pointed out that countries with large groups of achievement-motivated citizens had higher rates of national economic growth.

To sum up, here is a list of characteristics that McClelland found to be common among people with a high need to succeed:

1. The capacity to set high ("stretching") but obtainable personal goals.
2. A concern for personal achievement rather than the rewards of success.
3. A desire for job-relevant feedback (how well am I doing?) rather than for attitudinal feedback (how much do you like me?).

I have already mentioned that five of the six historical societies that McClelland studied overlap with pre-dawn coinciding risings of Venus and Mercury. These two planets together would have looked like a very bright star rising just before the Sun. This bright astral display might have caused religious fervor and, as a result, created economic activity in connection with the service of a god. This was an explanation that McClelland suggested when discussing the Israelites in the context of a study of American Jews.[91] But was there anything else happening in the morning skies when these economic peaks crop up?

McClelland had found a peak of achievement centered around 967 BCE. At that time, in addition to Venus and Mercury, Jupiter and Saturn were rising close to the Sun. The year 487 BCE was in the middle of the next cycle that McClelland identified as one of peak achievement. Saturn, Jupiter, and Venus were close to the Sun, and would have been rising as morning stars when a high proportion of that year's births occurred. He also found that 474 CE was another year when a high-achieving society arose—and, at this time too, Saturn, Jupiter, and Venus were rising before the Sun. His next high-achieving society occurred in 1434 CE, when Saturn, Jupiter, Mars, and Venus were all rising together close to the Sun. McClelland says that many children born at this time were high achievers and successful.

McClelland found another high-achieving society in the late seventeenth century. This one did not fit with the patterns of pre-dawn rising of the Venus/Mercury conjunctions that had started me looking into astrology. There was no conjunction of Mercury and Venus then, but, once again, Venus, Jupiter, and Saturn were individually rising close to the Sun. They would appear as a series of Bright Morning Stars, and Masonic astrology implies that this phenomenon should result in the birth of a large number of successful and well-balanced people. And McClelland's work confirmed that it did. This line of reasoning was pushing me towards an investigation of the claims of astrology.

## A Cozy Superstition

For belief in astrology to thrive, it must offer some value to its followers. Even Masonic astrology should offer some proof of its claims if it is to be accepted as a science, rather than a ritual myth. What might this be? Why did a sensible politician such as George Washington choose to align the city that was to bear his name using the ideas of Masonic astrology?

I decided to ask archeoastronomer Robin Heath about astrology. As well as being an academic archeoastronomer, Robin once edited a periodical called the *Astrological Journal* and is the author of a number of books on astrology. (Incidentally, he is not a Freemason and has little interest in Masonry.)

When Richard Dawkins, the Charles Simonyi Professor of the Public Understanding of Science at Oxford University, wrote a critical article about astrology,[92] Robin put forward answers to the points Dawkins made. Here is what he said:

*This article tackles the recent media attacks against the axioms and practice of astrology. At the head of this wave of criticism came Professor Richard Dawkins's article in* The Independent on Sunday, *published on New Year's Eve . . . Dawkins's words need to be picked over carefully by astrologers who wish to understand better the mind that refutes astrological lore . . .*

*The main topic is the value of Sun sign work within the media. Within the context of Dawkins's tirade, it is this aspect of astrology which is most under attack, but we might also recognise that the professor knows nothing, nor apparently wishes to know, of that which lies beneath the surface of this shallow gloss.*

*There are several issues mixed together here. The first concerns the morality of media Sun sign work. Have professional astrologers sold out when they agree to undertake such work? Some are open about their involvement whilst others adopt pseudonyms and can be unbelievably coy about this lucrative off-spin of their work. The APA (Association of Professional Astrologers) currently accepts several such astrologers into its fold. One of these, whom I shall refrain from naming here, provided the perfect justification for Dawkins's attack within the self-same newspaper edition. His ill-conceived words further influenced serious public opinion against astrology and it would be hard to imagine a better assistant to Dawkins in his task of running astrology down.*[93]

Two factors were making me think there might be some real effect behind the beliefs of Masonic astrology. The first was the statistical correlation between Masonic lore and high achievers. The second was curiosity about why Wren and Washington, two Masons whom I respect, should want to use ideas of Masonic geomancy to lay out cities. The whole idea seemed to be getting too close to astrology for my scientist's world-view to accept. But I decided if I was ever to understand Bro. George's motives in positioning the Capitol and the White House, I would have to look at the claims of astrology.

In my general view of astrology, I found myself siding with Richard Dawkins, who said:

*A statistical tendency, however slight, for people's personalities to be predictable from their birthdays, over and above the expected difference between winter and summer babies, would be a promising start.*[94]

The only evidence I had found so far to make me think Masonic astrology might be worth looking at was statistical. On his Web site, Dawkins talked about statistical studies of astrology which had been made by a Dr. Michel Gauquelin. Dawkins said:

*It is, of course, Sun sign astrology's well-heeled practitioners in newspapers and on television that I am attacking as exploitative charlatans. If there is good evidence (i.e. better than the often quoted but non-robust Gauquelin attempt) that some other kinds of astrology work, well and good. I have to say that I'd be extremely surprised.*[95]

Dawkins felt Gauquelin's statistics might support astrology, but he did not say why he thought the work was non-robust. I e-mailed Robin Heath and asked him about astrology in general and Gauquelin's work in particular. He replied:

*It is my view, formed over 25 years of being very interested in both the history and practice of astrology, that "doing a chart" is quite similar to the act of prayer. The cosmos (sky, God, gods, the "above," heaven) is being contacted, knows that this is happening, and responds accordingly to the circumstances prevailing at the time and the consciousness of the astrologer.*

*Such an interpretation of the process fits modern physics quite well and is holistic. It's just that physicists don't like God anymore. Predestination is another of those chestnuts that the Church has washed its hands of, whilst astrologers grapple with it every time they perform astrological acts.*

*Personally, I have a feeling that the life plan is laid down quite tightly—a spine of fate if you like—whilst the details are fleshed out by the conscious will of the individual. It is impossible to not form such a view when you've worked with over 3,000 clients over a quarter of a century. When transiting Neptune falls on Sun or Moon, then there are always losses, scandals, deceptions and a need to accept one's mortality. None of which is fixed of course, yet it sure feels like fate to the individual undergoing the transits.*

*I loath most astro research and many of the researchers. I found Gauquelin a strange and remote personality [Robin speaks fluent French], whilst his wife was both arrogant and awkward. He committed suicide and there were strange things going on with his data collection just before, as I remember.*

*So, what was he measuring? A single factor within a cosmos of potential. The pigeonholing of science followed by the Gaussian analysis of the statistician. He was looking for a recognizable quantum of "meaning" within his data. I doubt whether he found anything, for such is the nature of this kind of research.*[96]

Many years ago, I worked with Robin Heath at Ferranti Electronics in Oldham, and I knew him to be an able and creative engineer. Yet his account of doing astrology as "something rather like praying" did not sound at all logical. It may be his opinion, but it's not proof that astrology works. It is, however, an opinion from someone whose ability in other fields I respect. Robin's belief that there might be a reality underlying astrology encouraged me to look more closely at it.

This was not the first time an assertion of belief in astrology had been made to me by people whose work I respect. A previous instance involved writer and researcher Colin Wilson. This is how it happened.

## A Suitable Subject for Study?

In the *Daily Mail* of Thursday, March 22, 2001, Colin Wilson wrote an article entitled "Why I now believe Astrology is a science." It was about a new Chair in Astrology to be founded at Bath Spa University in the south of England.

Astrology has not been studied at universities since the seventeenth century. At that time, its students used a textbook on fortune-telling called *Christian Astrology* written by William Lilly. (This book had been indexed by Freemason Elias Ashmole, who was also a founder member of the Royal Society.) William Lilly wrote almanacs similar to the one George Washington pasted into the opening pages of his diaries. They were a mixture of astronomical and astrological forecasts, which Lilly wrote under the pen name "the English Merlin."[97]

Astrology was popular during the English Civil War and in Restoration London at the time Sir Christopher Wren was drawing up his plans for a new city of London. In those days it was not a separate discipline from astronomy, and astrologers enjoyed high status and royal support, as this comment from historian Peter Whitfield shows:

*The years 1640-1670 seem to have witnessed a last frantic outburst of astrological activity in England. Turbulence in the political and social world may partly explain this, nor was there as yet any clearly-defined gulf between science and occultism. Daniel Defoe asserted that in the years around the Plague and the Great Fire, "people were more addicted to prophecies and astrological conjurations than ever they were before or since." As late as 1673 King Charles II consulted Elias Ashmole to seek astrological advice about his relations with Parliament.*[98]

Soon after this, Sir Isaac Newton discovered the law of gravity. The new scientists gave up occultism, and astrology was no longer thought academic or respectable. Colin Wilson had said that this trend might be reversing, and there was serious interest in reviving fortune-telling as an academic subject. Colin ended his article with these words about the person who had endowed the new Chair at the university:

*The woman behind the £500,000 donation has no reason to feel ashamed of wanting to reintroduce astrology as a university subject, even though it has been dismissed by the universities for more than three centuries. I can assure her that while we still do not know quite why it works, it undoubtedly does.*[99]

In his article, Colin wrote of his own experience of astrology:

*I decided then that I ought to study astrology more closely, but never seemed to find the time. Then a Sunday newspaper asked me if I would write an astrology column and I decided this was the opportunity I had been waiting for . . . and rather dubiously launched myself on a career as an astrological journalist.*

*It proved harder work than I had expected. There can be no guesswork involved. The position of all the planets had to be worked out, together with their aspects (oppositions, conjunctions, etc.) and this took days.*

*But gradually I began to get a feeling for horoscopes. And this was confirmed when I received a letter from a woman whose son had committed suicide, enclosing the exact time and place of his birth. I spent a day casting his horoscope, and as I did so, the hairs on the back of my neck began to rise.*

*What was emerging was a personality—his enthusiasms, his hopes and his doubts about his future. It was these doubts that had led to his suicide. I sent the horoscope to his mother and she replied that the description of her son had shocked her with its accuracy.*[100]

After reading this, I phoned Colin and asked him if he thought there was any sort of scientific basis for astrology. He was helpful and not at all self-conscious about his belief. He explained that he had been skeptical about the claims of astrology before he studied it, but while writing a regular astrology column for *The Observer*, and reading the letters he got from readers, he became convinced there is a reality at the root of the subject. When I pressed him what that "reality" might be, he admitted that he just did not know. His belief was based on his observation that the insights he gained from astrological methods were accurate far more often than he would expect by chance. About one thing, however, he was quite clear: "What influences human beings is not the stars but the positions of the planets." The Bright Morning Star of Freemasonry is the planet Venus, so Colin's views fitted in with Masonic astrology.

Colin was convinced that there is a link between the personalities and actions of people and the positions of the planets. He said:

*My advice is not to dismiss astrology out of hand. I know it works, but I can only offer you anecdotal evidence and you want more than that. So why not look for your own evidence?*[101]

Colin Wilson was sincere in his belief. He thought there was a yet-unknown scientific principle that made astrology work. But his faith was not evidence of a scientific cause, and I couldn't accept a "yet-unknown scientific principle" as proof that astrology works.

I had a problem with the idea that two people whom I respect held what was to me an irrational belief in astrology. Neither of them was able to justify his position with scientific reasoning; on the other hand, neither could I sway either of them to denounce astrology as superstition.

While reflecting on the outcome of my brief survey of astrologers, I chanced to read Professor Stephen Hawking's thoughts on the matter. I felt he summed up my view on astrology when he said:

*The real reason most scientists don't believe in astrology is not scientific evidence or the lack of it but because it is not consistent with other theories which have been tested by experiment.*

*Why should the positions of other planets against the background sky as seen from earth have any correlations with the macromolecules on a minor planet that call themselves intelligent life?*[102]

Why indeed?

## Facing up to Astrology

Astrology is an embarrassment in a rational scientific world, but it just won't go away. It should have withered and died under the harsh glare of scientific understanding. Instead, it lingers on. Magazines and newspapers encourage its adepts to parade their lack of logic and air their superstitious "truths." Scientists denounce it, yet top astrologers are more widely trusted by the public than top scientists. They also earn more. It wasn't supposed to be this way.

In 1885 the philosopher Friedrich Nietzsche made a famous statement that God was dead. He was dramatizing a popular claim among intellectuals that the

113

idea of God was a vestige of an unscientific past that mankind would soon out-grow. At God's funeral pyre a whole range of superstitious beliefs, including astrology, were supposed to throw themselves into the flames, never to rise again. But astrology not only survived, it prospered. Rationalist thinkers hoped that as educational levels rose and science provided more realistic explanations for the mysteries of existence, the appeal of astrology would fade away. But they were wrong.

To survive, astrology must meet some human need, or we would let it go, along with the idea that the earth is a flat disc supported on the backs of four turtles swimming in a sea of milk. If George Washington thought it worth-while to use ideas from Masonic astrology to design his Federal City, then I needed to understand why he thought so. But, unfortunately, I couldn't phone him up and ask him. I would have to copy the example of his diaries and study the appearances of the Bright Morning Star, then use my own knowledge of Masonic ritual to see if I could deduce what he had discovered and applied.

The Father of the United States of America had drawn on two tenets of Masonic belief that seem to be firmly rooted in astrology. First, he had arranged the line between the President's House and the Capitol to align with the sunrise on a day of high Masonic significance. In this he was drawing from the tradition of Sun sign astrology. Second, he had arranged his align-ment to match the rising of the Bright Morning Star on a Masonically significant day. The Masonic significance of this was that the sunrise align-ment was linked to the day that the Temple of Solomon was consecrated. Masonic myth says that on this day, the Shekinah shone into the newly built Temple. The alignment that Washington had chosen also coincided with the rising of the Bright Morning Star of Venus above the Capitol. But was this Masonic idea tied into the classic astrology of the planets?

Like the dry old bones stored on the shelves of museums, astrology is fos-silized. Nothing has changed since the ancient Greeks laid down its basic principles. It has just become more commercial and now wears a pseudo-mathematical fig leaf to cover the lack of logic behind its claims. Nothing astrologers say, not even Masonic astrologers, explains why the positions of distant stars should make things happen to humans. Astrologers don't try to explain themselves in terms of physics. I wonder if this is because people who know physics aren't encouraged to investigate astrology, and the people who spend most time thinking about the physics of the stars are astronomers, who don't have any interest in astrology?

In the modern cities, where today's astrologers find their clients, there is so much light pollution that people have largely forgotten just how awesome the naked sky can be. Few city-dwellers see the vast number of stars that are visible peppering the heavens in areas where the comforting glow of street lights is absent. A few of these stars stand out, much brighter than others, and are known as first-magnitude stars. These bright stars do not appear to move about the sky but remain, sitting in well-defined positions, forming patterns that we call constellations.

The two most obvious bright objects in the sky are the Sun and the Moon. They are so bright they cast a shadow, and can been seen by day and night. But there are other bright objects, the visible planets, of which the most brilliant are Venus, Mars, Mercury, Jupiter, and Saturn. They vary in brightness and move about the sky. The ancient Greek inventors of astrology called them "wanderers," a name we preserve today in the Anglicized word "planet."

How potent these heavenly objects must have seemed to ancient people! The Sun, when its rays were beating down, affected their daily lives. They got hot, they sweated, their skin burned. They couldn't doubt its power. Then, when the Sun withdrew behind the clouds, they become cold and their world was beset by storms.

They might have noticed how the Moon seemed to affect the fertility of their womenfolk. When it shone full in the night sky, many of the women of the tribe would trickle menstrual blood at the same time. When the Moon was new, the sea came farther up the seashore and drew out farther, giving them access to beds of shellfish they could not usually reach. Surely the Moon-god was showing an interest in their affairs and favoring their welfare!

At certain times, Venus is so bright it also casts a shadow. If our imaginary ancient people went out under dark, clear, moonless night skies when Venus was a bright evening star, they could not have avoided seeing their "Venus shadow." In the dark winter days just before the winter solstice of 2005, Venus was an extremely bright object in the evening sky. For a few days just before the new Moon, it was by far the brightest object in sky. I live in the Pennine Hills of Yorkshire, and on one of those clear frosty evenings, I walked up a local hill as the Sun set. As the sky darkened, I saw I was casting a distinct Venus shadow. Any one of the three bright sky lights of the Sun, the Moon, and Venus can cast a shadow. How magical is that?

When you move, your shadow moves with you. If you dance, it will follow every movement, no matter how quick. If you try to run away, it will run as fast as you can. Such displays of power, and interaction with people, could have planted the idea that these animated bright lights in the sky were either gods or signs given by gods.

But why in this modern world do so many people want to believe that an astral dictatorship can rule the most private details of their lives? If any government tried to impose such a regime on them, there would be instant rebellion. I can see that it might offer a reassuring feeling to know that something is looking out for you. Is this why people want to believe in astrology? Does it offer an order and structure for complex adult lives that reminds them of the cozy certainties of childhood? Or do these awe-inspiring bright planets really change people's lives?

Professor McClelland asked just this question about the USA:

*What happened between 1800-1920? A number of countries experienced the "take-off" into rapid economic growth: e.g. Germany, France, the United States, Japan. In all of them, our theory would have to predict, a wave of achievement motivation should have preceded the economic "take-off." For one of them—the United States—there is very good evidence that such a thing was indeed the case. . . . A characteristic wave of achievement motivation appears very clearly in the data: it rises from 1800 to a peak in 1890.*[103]

George Washington set up a key alignment, based on Masonic geomancy, in the Federal City of Washington, D.C., in 1791, and the government of the United States moved there in 1800. Is it just coincidence that a wave of achievement motivation followed this move? McClelland says that "the psychological and technological basis for American prosperity in the early twentieth century appears in the record of the nineteenth century."[104] Did Bro. George Washington know something modern Masons have forgotten?

## Conclusions

The legends of Freemasonry attributed a tremendous force that motivated individuals towards useful actions to the appearance of a special Bright Morning Star, called the Shekinah. My research had linked this Shekinah to a long-term cycle of conjunctions between Venus and Mercury, which appeared as a bright object rising just before the Sun.

The work of Professor David McClelland of Harvard had found that there had been waves of achievement in societies throughout history. Many of these high-achieving societies thrived when the Shekinah appeared in the morning sky, and when I looked more closely at the data, I found that all these high-achieving societies surged forward when bright planets rose just before the Sun. (And all the conjunctions bar one—which involved Jupiter and Saturn—concerned Venus and Mercury.) I was disturbed to notice that this is exactly what the legends of Masonic astrology say should happen. I was disturbed because the whole thing had no scientific basis, and when I spoke to astrologers with scientific backgrounds, they were unable to offer me any explanation beyond the anecdotal evidence that they knew astrology sometimes worked.

Looking at the thoughts of the scientists Richard Dawkins and Stephen Hawking on astrology, I instinctively sided with them in feeling it must be nonsense. But I couldn't deny that George Washington had taken a keen interest in the rising of the Bright Morning Star, and it appeared to have been a key factor that had motivated him to lay out the focal points of the Federal City of Washington, D.C., in the way he did. McClelland had confirmed that the USA was highly achievement-motivated from a period which began when the Government moved to the new Federal City. Why?

To move on from this impasse, I decided to investigate the claims of Masonic astrology more closely to see if it offered clues to any scientific link between the rising of morning stars and the improvement of human abilities.

# Chapter Six

# Following in
# Newton's Footsteps

## Measuring the Unknown

Where was I to start my analysis of Masonic astrology? As I sat and pondered the problem, two sources of inspiration came to mind. The first was Sir Isaac Newton himself, whose work shows that it is not always necessary to understand the physical causes of a system to analyze it. The other is Richard Dawkins, Charles Simonyi Professor of the Public Understanding of Science at Oxford University, who wrote an article attacking astrology, and in it suggests how its claims might be tested.

There is a superficial case that Masonic geomancy might work, but it relies on unknown forces. I have no idea what those forces might be and have not found a modern astrologer who can explain them to me. They talk only of "planetary influences." To satisfy Richard Dawkins, I must base my explanation on accepted physical theories.

Sir Isaac Newton had access to records of how and when planets moved. These had been noted down by the German astronomer Johannes Kepler over many years. The facts showed that something was happening, and, by analyzing past events, Newton deduced the existence of the law of gravity.

I needed to find a similar set of recorded facts about what happens to humans as the stars move above them. Harvard professor David McClelland had used statistical studies of high-achieving societies to help him understand how high-achieving people behaved. Masonic ritual says that when a Master Mason is raised beneath the benign rays of the Bright Morning Star:

*A vital and immortal principle inspires a holy confidence that the Lord of Life will enable him to trample the King of Terrors beneath his feet, and lift his eyes to that Bright Morning Star whose rising brings peace and tranquility to the faithful and obedient of the human race.*

There are not many clues as to what makes this happen. But it looks as it if the concept worked when Bro. Washington applied this Masonic principle to his Federal City of Washington, D.C. History shows that he succeeded in promoting a surge of what McClelland calls *n*-achievement. But was this surge caused by Washington's own inspirational actions, rather than an application of Masonic geomancy? I needed more than anecdotal evidence.

### The Science of Celestial Interactions

For an effect to result from a cause, there must be a route from the actions of the cause to the effect on the subject. But my scientific background suggests nothing to connect my personality and actions to the movements of distant celestial objects. I decided to start my analysis by listing the possible ways in which celestial objects might interact with people on the earth, according to science rather than astrology. And I could think of only three ways.

**1. By gravitational attraction.** Gravity pulls every particle of mass towards every other particle of mass in the universe. The force of attraction is proportional to the amount of mass involved and inversely proportional to the square of the distance between the two masses. The effects of gravity work at any distance, but changes in gravitational fields take time to travel across space. The "speed of gravity" was first measured by Dr. Ed Fomalont of the National Radio Astronomy Observatory in Charlottesville, Virginia, and found to be the same as the speed of electromagnetic radiation such as light and radio waves. Gravity works over very long distances, but its effects travel no faster than light (168,000 miles or 3,000,000 meters per second).

**2. By sympathetic excitation of electromagnetic fields.** If a star or planet has a natural magnetic field, then as it rotates it will generate electromagnetic (EM) waves (these are like radio waves but have a much wider frequency range). EM waves from distant objects can interact with the local EM field of a planet or star and cause interference effects. You may have seen this sort of interference when "ghosting" appears on an analogue TV signal at certain times of the year, caused when conditions allow interference from foreign TV stations. Light is a special case of this sort of radiation. The speed of light is the same as that of every other EM radiation, and of gravity (again, 168,000 miles or 3,000,000 meters per second). This means that there is a delay between what is happening and when we get to see it. By the time we see the light from the Moon, it shows what was happening there five minutes ago. The light from the Sun is about twenty minutes old when we see it. Light from the zodiacal stars is even older. The rays from the nearest star takes about four years to reach us, and the light we see from the nearest star in the constellation of Gemini (Pollux) has traveled for 35 years to reach us. The light from one of the more distant stars in that constellation (Mebsuta) is 192 years old.

**3. By particle emission.** The nuclear processes that cause stars to give off heat also fire off small chunks of "stardust," often at very high speeds. There are two major types, cosmic rays and ionized particles. Here's a bit of background on them:

*Cosmic rays.* During the first *Apollo 11* moon missions, the astronauts reported that they kept seeing bright flashes of light out of the corners of their eyes. *Apollo 16* astronaut Charles Duke was asked to observe and report on this phenomenon. He recorded many instances, especially while he was outside the ship. After his safe return, Duke's helmet was examined under an electron microscope, and minute punctures were found in it. These had been caused by cosmic rays passing right through his helmet and his head. If they happened to pass through his eyes, he saw them as a bright burst of light. These cosmic rays are made up of the nuclei of hydrogen atoms that are ejected from nearby stars, often during the great explosions of nova stars. These particles travel much more slowly than light and take much longer to travel between stars than EM radiation or gravity.

*Ionized particles.* The other sorts of particles that can be emitted from a star consist of elements (other than hydrogen) that have had their outer electrons stripped off. Helium, for example, has two outer electrons. It is denser than hydrogen and, if ionized, carries twice the electric charge of a typical cosmic ray (which, I have already mentioned, is a highly energetic hydrogen ion). Our Sun has an active EM field and it also has weather. Just as we have thunderstorms on Earth, when it rains and the sky lights up with electrical discharges, the Sun also has storms. These are much bigger and better than the puny ones that make us hide under our bedclothes. When they erupt, great plumes of ionized particles are flung up from the Sun's surface so fast that they stream out into space. During big storms, these particles can cause damage on Earth. They destroy the electronics of communications satellites and cause the lights in the northern sky that we call the aurora. In 1989, a wave of particles from a massive solar storm swamped the electrical power distribution grid of Canada and took out the whole system with a series of overloads. These particles take days to travel from the Sun, and we have set up an early warning system to let us know when they are coming. (A satellite called SOHO has been stationed halfway to the Sun, and when it detects an increase in ionized particle emission, it sends a radio alert ahead to Earth, warning satellite controllers to close down vulnerable systems and minimize damage.)

This list shows the only ways, according to my knowledge of science, that the stars and planets might affect my personality and actions. The stars have a better chance of changing me than the planets, as they have more ways to do it. They can use gravity, electromagnetic radiation, or streams of energetic particles to make me change. Planets can use only gravity or, occasionally, EM radiation.

Electromagnetic radiation from the Moon takes a few minutes to get to Earth. (The *Apollo 11* mission set up a laser reflector on the Moon's surface to bounce laser pulses back to Earth. We use the time of travel of the light rays to measure the distance between the Moon and the Earth.) If you listen to recordings of the *Apollo* Moon missions, you will hear the delay as the radio messages travel backwards and forwards between Houston and the spacecraft.

Pulses from the Sun take longer to reach Earth, and from the stars in Aquarius, the Water Carrier, the radiation takes many years to get here. All the stars in this constellation are at different distances, so the time light takes to reach Earth from each of them differs: working from west to east, the figures are 325 years, 85 years, 191 years, 70 years, 540 years, 156 years. The reason astrologers describe the constellation as looking like a water carrier (a flight of romantic fancy in itself) is because of the positions its component stars occupy when viewed from the Earth. But when I last saw the light from the farthest star in Aquarius, it had been on its way for 540 years—since long before I was born.

I find it impossible to believe that there is some immense plan which makes this light, or any other type of radiation from these stars, affect my personality here on Earth. Just as an example, Skat (one of the brightest stars in Aquarius) could have blown up eighty-four years ago, and we wouldn't know a thing about it yet. As for the particle emissions now emerging from Skat, I will be long dead before they get anywhere near our solar system.

But am I being unkind to the astrologer's arcane and mysterious art? Does the gravity of Skat, and the other assorted stars of Aquarius, cause the subtle effects they claim to detect in me? Gravity works across vast distances, which is why the galaxy has stars in it. Without its long-range pull, no stars would ever have condensed out of the thin gas that makes up most of the universe. But gravity gets steadily weaker over longer distances. If you double the distance between two objects, the pull of gravity between them is reduced four times. This means that small things that are close to you have a stronger pull than big things that are a long way off. The gravitational attraction between me and the printer on the corner of my desk is many orders of magnitude bigger than between me and Skat (and I don't have a massive printer).

The effects of gravity coming from Aquarius, or any other group of stars, are tiny. Their effect on me is millions of times smaller than the pull of my printer. If an astrologer wants me to believe that the gravity of the stars affects me, then he must also show how my future romantic prospects will be improved by the gravitational pull of my printer tugging at my heartstrings.

## Science versus Astrology

Richard Dawkins, the Oxford professor who studies the public's understanding of science, has strong views about astrology. Robin Heath suggested I read the article Dawkins wrote for *The Independent on Sunday* of December 31, 1995:

*For us to take a hypothesis seriously, it should ideally be supported by at least a little bit of evidence. If this is too much to ask, there should be some suggestion of a reason why it might be worth bothering to look for evidence.*

Dawkins went on:

*Scientific truth is too beautiful to be sacrificed for the sake of light entertainment or money. If the methods of Astrologers were really shown to be valid it would be a fact of signal importance for science. Under such circumstances astrology should be taken seriously indeed. But if—as all indications agree—there is not a smidgen of validity in any of the things that astrologers so profitably do, this, too, should be taken seriously and not indulgently trivialised. We should learn to see the debauching of science for profit as a crime.*[105]

When scientists take something seriously, they look for ways to describe links between what they see happening and what they think is causing it. But they need a plausible link before they can start to look for evidence. It is the lack of any link between the stars and personality which makes a scientist distrust astrologers' claims. Dawkins says there are just two influences which can act over stellar distances. These are gravitational attraction and tidal forces. (I would suggest that he is being over-generous, and that these are really just symptoms of the same force, gravity.)

Dawkins goes on to make a strong point about the lack of cause to prompt a serious inquiry into astrology:

*The brain is the seat of the personality and the brain controls handwriting, so it is not in principle unlikely that style of handwriting might betray personality. It seems almost a pity that no good evidence has been forthcoming. But astrology has nothing going for it at all, neither evidence nor any inkling of a rationale which might prompt us to look for evidence. Astrology not only demeans astronomy, shrivelling and cheapening the universe with its pre-Copernican dabblings. It is also an insult to the science of psychology and the richness of human personality.*[106]

What does Dawkins mean when he talks about personality? The term comes from the Greek word *persona*, which is the name for the mask that actors in Greek drama wore to show which character they were playing. So its roots lie in understanding character.

Some researchers say that a person's personality grows out of his or her temperament. This is a distinct way of doing things and reacting to others that is part of the individual's makeup from an early age. Temperament is measured by the way a person relates to the outside world. Those who interact strongly with other people are called extroverts, while those who keep to themselves are known as introverts. These patterns of temperament are thought to be genetic in origin and a result of the way the brain grows.[107]

This implies that personality traits have a bodily basis and are a manifestation of the structure of the brain. But personality is hard to measure, and the way it develops is not fully understood. However, it's an aspect of humanity that astrology claims to be able to predict. So how can the way a personality grows fit into a theory of astrology? Dawkins does not think that astrology can predict human behavior or tell fortunes. He says that to do so, it should be able to explain how personality, and the structure of the brain, is affected by the movements of the stars. This is something astrologers never attempt to spell out.

As we saw, Dawkins considers gravity (in its dual aspects of gravitational attraction and tidal forces) to be the only force that works over vast distances. I think there are two other forces to consider. These are light or radio waves and cosmic rays, and they travel at different speeds. The speed of gravity is the same as that of light, but that is something which was only recently discovered. (When astrophysicists work out the orbits of spacecraft and satellites, they assume gravity to have an instantaneous effect within the solar system.[108] This seems to be a good enough approximation to work in most cases.) Light, however, takes over a quarter of an hour to travel from the Sun to the Earth, while active particles take many days, so any causal mechanism has to account for these facts. Any hypothesis of Masonic astrology must explain how these factors affect the behavior of the brain in ways that can be measured by psychology.

In the eighteenth century, when Sir Isaac Newton began to study tides, the everyday view was that they were caused by the Moon. The scientists of the time thought this idea was astrological tomfoolery. Galileo, who proved that the Earth moved around the Sun, dismissed the Moon's effect on tides as nonsense. Newton knew of no force that would pull the sea towards the Moon. Rather than try to find a force, Newton adopted a simpler way: He *assumed* there was a force, and then worked out how it would work. He called the unknown force (which gives all objects on the Earth their feeling of weight) "gravity." By assuming that gravity was real, Newton found he could predict the tides and the orbits of comets. The return of Halley's comet proved the accuracy of his calculations, and now we no longer think of gravity as astrological nonsense.

Astrology's claim to explain how human fortune is caused by the stars has the same low status with scientists that tidal theory once enjoyed. But there are parallels to Newton's dilemma. Popular opinion is convinced there is a real effect. As I will discuss later, a number of studies show conflicting statistical evidence that such an effect might exist. The popular folklore of tides was confused and wrong, but by assuming that a force existed, Newton discovered the reality of gravity. He worked backwards from the facts to figure out the force involved. I wondered if I could understand Masonic astrology by taking a similar line of reasoning.

I had a limited set of observations from Harvard professor David McClelland that suggests there is a phenomenon to investigate. But I had no model of science to guide my investigations or to suggest experiments. In similar circumstances, Sir Isaac Newton came up with a method that served him well. Could I adapt his methods to my own purpose?

Newton based all his explanations on forces known to the physics of his day. He would not have accepted the unknowable "cosmic influences" invoked by writers about astrology. If I want to use a force to explain Masonic astrology, it must be one that is known to science—Newton didn't use any special argument to fit the circumstances, so neither can I. For example, I can not assume that "thought waves" travel faster than light unless I can show that this is part of documented and accepted scientific theory. If facts clashed with his theories, then Newton accepted the verdict of reality. So must I. If a simple and a complex theory can both explain his evidence, then Newton took the simpler option.[109] So must I.

Having decided on a course of action, I was now ready to look at Richard Dawkins's ideas on how to test astrology.

### Rules for Testing Astrology

In his article in *The Independent*, Richard Dawkins explains why he does not take the claims of astrology seriously. He also makes positive suggestions for any investigator of astrological claims. He outlines minimum tests that astrology should pass to be worthy of study. They can be summed up as follows:

Test 1: *If astrology claims to predict personality, it must put forward a means by which the positions of the stars at the moment of birth affect the growth of personality.* Dawkins extended this idea, saying:

*Personality is a real phenomenon and psychologists (real, scientific psychologists, not Freudians or Jungians) have had some success in developing mathematical models to handle the many dimensions of personality variation. The initially large number of dimensions can be mathematically collapsed into fewer dimensions with measurable, and for some purposes conscionable, loss in predictive power. These fewer derived dimensions sometimes correspond to the dimensions that we intuitively think we recognise—aggressiveness, obstinacy, affectionateness and so on. Summarising an individual's personality as a point in multidimensional space is a serviceable approximation whose limitations can be measured and are known. It is a far cry from any mutually exclusive categorisation, certainly far from the preposterous fiction of astrology's 12 dumpbins. It is based upon genuinely relevant data about people themselves, not their birthdays. The psychologist's multidimensional scaling can be useful in deciding whether a person is suited to a particular career, or a couple to each other. The astrologer's 12 pigeonholes are, if nothing worse, a costly and irrelevant distraction.*

Test 2: *Any astrological prediction should be independently verifiable and unambiguous.* Dawkins said:

*All astrology works on the "Barnum principle" of saying things so vague and general that all readers think it applies to them.*

A brief textual analysis of the "Sun sign" forecasts in a reputable Sunday newspaper convinced me that Dawkins is right. The predictions were so vague they were little more than invitations for the readers to fill in the blanks with what they want to hear. Most of the so-called predictions seemed to be saying "Make up your mind and then do what you think is best for you."

To show you what I mean, this is a typical example of a horoscope that I pulled at random out of a popular Sunday paper:

*There are certain much-cherished hopes that you've barely allowed yourself to consider, much less discuss. But today's aspect of the planet of growth and opportunity, Jupiter—which is in the portion of your chart that accents love and life's joys— triggers a cycle of change.*

Who could disagree with that? It's not saying anything to disagree with. In fact, it's not saying anything. Is it change for the better or the worse? Why should the orbital position of Jupiter matter? What's any of this got to do with growth and opportunity?

I decided to use Dawkins's two tests. Only if I could discover satisfactory responses to the first test would I proceed to the second. But I must admit, I couldn't see how the position of the stars and planets in the sky could have the least effect on what's happening to me down here on Earth.

If I were ever to understand Masonic astrology, I needed to be able to explain how stellar movements can control brain activity. And this case would have to be strong enough to let me make accurate and testable predictions. It looked like a formidable task.

**Conclusions**

To help me understand the Masonic astrology which had inspired George Washington, I reviewed the way Sir Isaac Newton discovered the law of gravity, and decided to apply his experimental methods to my own quest. I also looked at the criticism of astrological explanations put forward by Professor Richard Dawkins, and his two proposed criteria for testing astrology:

1. If astrology claims to predict personality, it must put forward a means by which the positions of the stars at the moment of birth affect the growth of personality.
2. Any astrological prediction should be independently verifiable and unambiguous.

At this point, I was armed with a method of analysis and a means to test any evidence I found. I had a set of working tools to address the problem of understanding the Masonic astrology that seemed to have served George Washington so well.

Now I was ready to look at the published facts. Would they contain useful patterns or clues? Was it really possible for the rising of a Bright Morning Star to form a new personality? I would need to begin with a look at the statistics that Richard Dawkins had suggested might support astrology if they could be trusted. So I set off to read the work of Michel Gauquelin.

# Chapter Seven

# Lies, Damned Lies, and Astrology

## Statistical Proof of Astrology?

Dr. Michel Gauquelin was the pioneer of the statistical investigation of astrology. He was born in Paris in 1928 and took a first degree in psychology and statistics at the Sorbonne before obtaining a PhD in psychology. He was interested in astrology as a child, and later, as a trained statistician and psychologist, made it his lifelong study. When he married, his wife Françoise became his full-time assistant and co-researcher.

At first, Gauquelin looked only at astrological claims such as "professional soldiers are often born under the sign of Aries or Scorpio and rarely under Cancer" but failed to find any evidence. He went on to look at the relationship between planetary positions at the time of birth and death, and he rejected the astrological claim that "death occurs more frequently under the influence of Saturn." Then he looked at the times and dates of birth of famous individuals in various professions. He found that certain planets tended to be in similar positions at the time they were born. He spent much of his life searching for evidence of how such a pattern of planetary positions at the time of birth could arise by accident, but as professor of psychiatry Hans Eysenck said:

*For all his work he has not been able to disprove his basic finding: the planets really do seem to bear some inexplicable relationship with how a famous person develops.*[110]

Gauquelin first noticed this when he and his wife looked at 576 members of the French Academy of Medicine. From medical directories they selected doctors who were successful researchers. These eminent men tended to be born when Mars or Saturn had just risen, or had just passed their zenith.[111] This puzzled Gauquelin:

*What made the phenomenon singular was that it did not occur with all persons. We compared it with a sample set of normal individuals selected at random from official census records. The normal subjects were not born more frequently as Mars and Saturn rose or culminated; that is, the planetary clocks did not work the same way with the famous physicians as they did with the average person. The inexplicable phenomenon was embarrassing to us; we decided not to question its meaning too closely, but rather to repeat the investigation and see whether the bizarre relationship would repeat itself. We thus assembled a second sample of 508 eminent physicians. The work involved was not simple; we had to find not only the names of these doctors but also the date and locality of the births; then we had to write to the mayors of their home towns to obtain the exact time of birth . . . At the end of our second study, the evidence reproduced itself with a stubborn resistance: as in the first group, the birth dates of the famous physicians clustered after the rise or culmination of Mars or Saturn. An undeniable statistical correlation appeared between the rise and culmination of these planets at the child's birth and his future success as a doctor.[112]*

When I read this, I got just a little excited. Gauquelin seemed to be suggesting that successful individuals are born when a bright star is rising. This is exactly what Masonic astrology claims. But Gauquelin was not a Mason and had no interest or knowledge of Masonic myths. I obviously needed to find out more.

Gauquelin repeated this test over and over, with larger and larger samples, until finally he had data on a total of 46,485 successful individuals. He found a statistically significant tendency for them all to be born with when any of the moon, Venus, Mars, Jupiter, or Saturn was rising or at culmination.[113]

In an attempt to explain this, Gauquelin speculated that children who were predisposed to become famous choose to be born as a particular planet rose. This is how he explained this extraordinary idea:

*Perhaps, at the time of birth, each child manifests an inherited sensitivity to planetary clocks . . . This would mean that the birth of a child when Mars appears over the horizon is not mere chance. The birth occurs at that moment rather than another because his organism is ready to react to the perturbations caused by this particular planet at its passage over the horizon. In other words, the position of a planet at a child's birth might be linked to his heredity. This idea is the exact opposite of astrological predestination, because it would mean that the action of the celestial body would not be fixed for ever into the organism of the new-born; it would only have temporary effect during childbirth.*[114]

To test this hypothesis, he assembled birth data for over 30,000 parents and their children. He reported a probability that a person born under either a rising or culminating Mars would have children who also showed a likelihood of being born as Mars was rising or culminating.[115] He offered this explanation:

*The child inherits from his parents a tendency to be born when Mars rises, in the same way he inherits the colour of his hair.*[116]

Such particular properties of genetic inheritance are a radical and unsupported concept, with no recognized mechanism to explain how they might work. When Gauquelin invented this "planet clock" he said it controlled a tendency to be born under the same planet as one of your parents. He really struggled to explain it:

*What is already clear is that the infinitely varied reactions to the cosmos seem to fall into five general categories. These categories are apparently related to the five "planet clocks": the Moon, Venus, Mars, Jupiter and Saturn.*[117]

Because Gauquelin's planet clock has no basis in accepted scientific theories, I reject his explanation. But the events he described are real, as I soon found out.

Astronomer Dr. Percy Seymour, of Plymouth University, reports that Gauquelin's findings on the planetary position at the birth of famous individuals were tested independently in Belgium by the Committee for the Scientific Investigation of Alleged Paranormal Phenomena.[118] They tested a different group of 535 sports champions from France and Belgium but found the same pattern.

In 1989 Suitbert Ertel, Professor of Psychology at the University of Göttingen in Germany, published an extended study of famous and successful individuals. He confirmed Gauquelin's findings, but expressed reservations about Gauquelin's explanation. The abstract to his research paper says:

*The author's previous research with M. and F. Gauquelin's data confirmed the existence of the planetary effects for eminent professionals. However, the present research casts doubts on Gauquelin's physical explanation.[119]*

Gauquelin thought that the child triggered a hormonal release into its mother's bloodstream that precipitated its birth when the fetus was "somehow influenced by the rising of the planet which affected it." He replied in the journal *Correlation*, saying:

*In my theory, the planets would only trigger the birth according to the genetic structure of the child. Cosmic influences at birth neither modify the heredity of the child nor add something to it: rather they would be linked to it.[120]*

I join with Ertel in not accepting this explanation. Hans Eysenck also rejects it, saying:

*This solution is by no means as straightforward as it might appear. If the planet sends some kind of signal that initiates the birth process, there will obviously be a lag between the signal and the resulting birth that is equal to the duration of labour. That duration varies considerably from a single hour to many hours . . . In other words, even if the births of all future sports champions began the moment that Mars was in one of certain specified positions, the resulting spread in the durations of labour should be enough to degrade the effect virtually beyond detection. This objection would be lessened if the planetary signal came after the onset of labour and closer to birth, but in that case the signal would be unnecessary![121]*

Towards the end of his life, Gauquelin expressed doubts about planetary heredity. In his last work in English, *Planetary Heredity*,[122] he confirmed the tendency for successful people to be born with rising or culminating bright planets, but admitted that his later surveys failed to link children to their parent's birth planet. His only repeatable finding is that successful people are more likely to be born with the any one of the Moon, Venus, Mars, Jupiter, or Saturn either rising or culminating. But there are so many objects involved that the chances of at least one rising or culminating as somebody is born has to be quite high.

Is this all that Gauquelin noticed: That a higher proportion of successful people were born with any one of five planets rising at the their birth? The lack of any scientific explanation for this effect remains a problem. The only person to attempt to set it in a scientific context is the astronomer Dr. Percy Seymour. He put forward this theory:

> *It is as if the nervous system can act as an antenna through which we can detect some of the vibrations of the Earth's field. This field has fluctuations which are linked to the Sun and the Moon, and to the spinning of the Earth on its own axis. There are further subtle variations on these basic changes which are linked to the Sunspot cycle. My theory proposes that this cycle is in itself linked to the positions and movements of the planets, including Earth, around the Sun. This means that the whole Solar System is playing a "symphony" on the magnetic field of the Earth . . .*
>
> *According to the theory I have proposed, we are all genetically "tuned" to receive a different set of "melodies" from this symphony. Whilst in the womb, the organs of our familiar five senses are still developing, so they are less effective in receiving information than they are once we are born. However, the womb is no hiding place from the all-pervading constantly fluctuating magnetic field of the Earth: so the symphonic tunes which we pick up can become part of our earliest memories. It is in the womb that some of the "magnetic" music of the spheres becomes etched into our brains. The first role of our particular response to this music is to provide the cue for entry onto the stage of the world.*[123]

This is an interesting thought, but still suggests that the fetus somehow manages to time its own birth (see bold text, above). It fails to answer any of Eysenck's objections. So Seymour's theory of astrology ascribes to genetic inheritance a role in creating the human nervous system that is not supported by evidence.

Turning the Solomon Key

**Gauquelin's Disturbing Findings**

Hans Eysenck was disturbed by the vast array of statistical evidence that Gauquelin amassed. He said, "there is something here that requires explanation." But he did not know what it was.[124]

This sums up the response of most scientists, and also expresses the unease I felt reading Gauquelin's work. His statistical methodology is impeccable, and he was prepared to change his stance in the light of his findings, as he showed by dropping the idea of planetary inheritance just before his death. But I found his attempts to explain his results, first in terms of astrology and later in terms undefined planetary influences, unsatisfactory. Seymour's attempt to substitute subtle variations in the Earth's magnetic field instead of vague "planetary influences" is no better, since it assumes responses from the genetic structure of humans via unknown mechanisms.

Gauquelin's findings lack any plausible reasons why they should work. By the end of his life Gauquelin had studied the planetary birth charts of a large number of professionals. He looked at the horoscopes of actors, scientists, sports champions, soldiers, and writers. He summarized his findings by noting statistically significant evidence that great actors tended to be born when Jupiter was rising or culminating; sports champions and soldiers when Mars is rising or culminating; great scientists when Saturn is rising or culminating; and great writers when there is a rising or culminating moon. He died before completing a vast survey of what he called planetary factors in personality.[125] He was trying to identify unique qualities in each planet to account for these "planetary factors." Astrology predicted Mars factors, Jupiter factors, Moon factors, Saturn factors, and Venus factors, so Gauquelin looked for them; he had no theory to guide him except astrology's supernatural "planetary factors."

Gauquelin went to great lengths to try to identify the personality traits associated with each occupation. He called his list of actors' personality traits Jupiter factors; those of scientists and writers he dubbed Saturn and Moon factors respectively; and the personality traits of sports champions and soldiers he called Mars factors. He devoted a whole chapter to discussing the effect of personality on success and character formation.

Part of his difficulty stemmed from the fact that his data fitted only what he described as "successful" individuals, but he was not able to define any measure

136

of success. He tried categorizing his sports champions as "weak-willed" and "strong-willed" champions. The strong-willed individuals had Mars rising or culminating; the weak-willed didn't. I thought this approach looked like a desperate attempt to explain data that did not fit his expectations.

Gauquelin set out to prove or disprove astrology. As a result, he used astrological rules and techniques to explain his data. He looked for Mars in the horoscope of soldiers and sports champions, because astrology predicted it would be there. He used the same logic for Saturn, Jupiter, and the moon, and applied it to other professions. He found these planets in the right place for his "successful" individuals, but they were in totally the wrong place, when he analyzed less "successful" people in the same occupation.

Then, in a final stroke of desperation, he suggested that the fetus must be controlling the exact moment of its birth. He needed a mechanism to explain why it was born when the right planet was in the correct quarter of the sky. But he struggled with the implications of this idea. He said:

*The mysterious physical knowledge the foetus has of cosmic conditions when it comes to the time of his birth is only a reaction phenomenon . . . The child reacts to the passing of the planet which is simply evidence of his temperament. It in no way modifies the child's future personality at birth and does not give him anything not already in his genetic constitution.[126]*

He never proposed an explanation of this "mysterious physical knowledge" that requires an unknown force to make it work. On these grounds I reject his explanation, although I do not reject his observations.

Eysenck, reviewing Gauquelin's work says:

*Potentially the most serious objection concerns the tendency for significant results to apply only to the elite of a given profession. Gauquelin has shown that the connection is really with personality and not with occupation, so the planetary effect should apply to the whole of a profession that is characterised by a particular personality, not just to its elite.[127]*

This comment encouraged me to keep looking, as this is exactly what Masonic astrology attributes to the rising of the Bright Morning Star.

Masonic myth says that the rising star is supposed to provide motivation to achieve for the *individual*, not his whole profession. Eysenck pointed out that Gauquelin encountered failures in his research that were as inexplicable as his successes. He found no link between astrological Sun signs and personal destiny; and, in a study of 6,000 diagnosed psychotic mental patients, he found no correlation between mental illness and planetary positions at birth. Eysenck added the comment:

*Thus, even with such a clearly marked-out group as functional psychotics, there is no connection with planetary influences. The fact that the method can result in failure is a reassuring indication that the successes are not merely statistical artefacts.*[128]

The astronomer George Abell also studied Gauquelin's results:

*Gauquelin's findings represent an anomalous result that remains unconfirmed to the degree necessary to be accepted as scientific fact. If the results were in accord with some already established theory, then there would be no problem. The case is already stronger than that for almost any area of research in psychology. It is only because of the nature of the findings, which seem to invoke planetary influences unrecognised by science, that a higher level of proof is called for.*[129]

The only theory that these results fit lies in the inexplicable assertions of Masonic ritual. But I have no scientific basis for Masonic astrology. Masonic ritual is not scientific evidence, but it does represent a summation of human observation and understanding that has been refined over hundreds of years. Perhaps Bro. Washington knew something that modern science does not.

Gauquelin's unfortunate fixation with astrology had made him stay within its rules, and this tunnel vision blinded him to any other behavior patterns that might be present in his data. Toward the end of one of his last books—in the last appendix, almost as an afterthought—he prints a table showing that when he combines the birth data for 46,485 "successful" individuals drawn from all professions, there are highly significant peaks when either Mars, Jupiter, Saturn, or the moon are in the pre-dawn sky or have just passed their zenith, when they would not be visible.[130] Elsewhere in the same book, he shows statistical evidence that the pre-dawn risings of the moon, Venus, Mars, Jupiter, and Saturn all figure significantly in the birth charts of "successful" people, but that Mercury, Uranus, Neptune, and Pluto do not. Looking at this list, I realized there was a pattern, and it was a pattern that reflected one of the few ways that celestial objects can affect individuals on earth: the pull of gravity.

The planets that show no significance in the composite charts of Gauquelin's successful individuals are Mercury, Uranus, Neptune, and Pluto; these are the planets with the least gravitational influence on the earth. Of the five celestial objects Gauquelin does list as significant, Mars, even when it is closest to the earth, has the weakest gravitational pull. However, Mars at its farthest is an order of magnitude stronger than Uranus at its closest, and that is a further order of magnitude stronger than Neptune at its best. The feeble gravitational pull of little Pluto is four orders of magnitude less than Neptune's, and, perhaps more significantly, Pluto has a moon of its own that is almost as big as the planet itself, but this moon is not even mentioned by astrologers, although it must have almost as much effect on Earthly gravitational attraction as Pluto itself. The gravitational force of Mercury is an order of magnitude less than that of Mars.

Here are the planets, sun, and moon in order of gravitational attraction at the earth's surface. (For full details of how I worked this out, see Appendix 1.)

### Celestial Body

Sun

Moon

Jupiter

Venus

Saturn

Mars

Mercury

Uranus

Neptune

Pluto

It does not surprise me that scientist and statistician Eysenck is unhappy with Gauquelin's results. Gauquelin's evidence, at best, suggests that only a subset of celestial objects has statistically significant effects on individuals' birth charts. (I do, however, find it interesting that the statistically significant objects are those with the highest gravitational influences on the earth, a fact Gauquelin overlooks.) His findings show that any of these objects can figure on the eastern horizon, or just past the zenith, at the birth of a "successful" individual. Clearly, these planets do not have the particular characteristics astrology ascribes to them. But I was beginning to wonder if their gravitational effect was important.

This posed a new problem. The actual gravitational force on a newborn baby caused by the pull of the rising Mars is almost three orders of magnitude less than the gravitational attraction of the doctor delivering it. I must point out that most doctors are considerably less massive than Mars, but to compensate for their lack of bulk they stand much, much closer to the event. Based on this reasoning, it seemed unlikely that the direct gravitational pull of Mars on the newborn infant could be the cause of the differences Gauquelin discovered.

Gauquelin's evidence did not show what he wanted to find. It did not prove a link between chosen profession and a planet of birth. However, it did show a correlation between high levels of success in many professions and a planet with a strong gravitational field rising just before the sun. No way is this conventional astrology. But it might be statistical evidence to support the Masonic belief that the rising of a Bright Morning Star motivates people. I needed independent facts to test out this idea—and fortunately, there were some.

### Sachs and His Stats

In 1994 the German film-maker and photographer Gunter Sachs undertook a statistical and mathematical investigation into the claims of astrology. He is not an astrologer, and none of his collaborators are either. Their study was motivated purely by curiosity, and when they began, none of them knew much about astrology. But they drew up a series of guidelines, which they then followed very carefully. I have reproduced their guidelines here, as I consider the results of their work to be important.

Their main aims were:

1. To examine, by means of a broadly structured scientific study, the possible effect of star signs on human behavior;

2. Not to try to prove that there *is* such a thing as astrology above and beyond mythology, but to investigate *whether* it exists, allowing for an open result;

3. To publish their study even if it failed to prove the existence of non-mythological astrology, as that would also be of interest;

4. To base their research exclusively on empirical data and not to interview any astrologers;

5. To examine and explain scientifically any factors that might distort their statistical results;

6. To indicate as significant any noticeable deviations from expected results that could not be explained as pure chance;

7. To have their calculations and their results checked by a suitable neutral authority such as a university.[131]

They worked with the Foundation for Public Opinion Research, at Allensbach in southwest Germany, which acted as their independent adjudicator, and used a statistician from the Institute of Statistics at Munich University, Dr. Rita Kunstler, to advise on statistical methodology. Their results are both fascinating and unexpected.

They took their raw data from public authorities, insurance companies, and market research surveys, collecting a vast database about the birth dates of criminals, traffic offenders, sick people, suicides, and much more, including marriages and divorces. The data protection rules prevented them from identifying individuals, but they were able to obtain dates of birth linked to outcomes. Once they had the raw data, Sachs's team set about analyzing it and publishing the results.

The study used very large samples, and significance tests were carried out and verified by the Institute of Statistics. One thing is clear: The tests were unbiased, and Sachs's team went to great trouble to eliminate systematic sampling errors.

The team started by looking at sales of astrological star-sign books and compared the figures with the proportion of individuals born under those signs. He found statistically significant differences in ten out the twelve star signs, a result which would occur by chance only once in every ten million trials. This level of significance is way beyond the one chance in ninety-nine used for most workaday statistical tests, such as engineering quality control. Here is Sachs's own summary of his findings about this test:

> *The subject of the investigation was sales of the paperback series "Zodiac Signs." The survey was based on data relating to the sale of 313,368 books in the period 1991-1994, divided into star signs. We observed ten highly significant deviations. The influence of chance elements on the observed deviations can be excluded with odds of 1:10,000,000.*[132]

Sachs found that people born under the sign of Scorpio bought the most astrological books. Intrigued by this initial result, he went on to look at ten different areas of life where he could obtain data.

The technique used to test these examples is firmly based in the statistical idea that it is not possible to prove anything; we can only be really sure if an idea fails to work. In practice this means setting up two possible explanations for a set of circumstances, called the null and the alternative hypotheses. For example, we could say that if I am lying in bed, then I cannot have gone out for a walk: The null hypothesis is that I am lying in bed, and a possible alternative hypothesis is that I have gone out for a walk. You could test the null hypothesis by looking to see if I am lying in bed. If my bed is empty, then the null hypothesis is *dis*proved, but this does not prove the alternative hypothesis, that I have gone for a walk. I could, for example, be sitting watching TV.

However, as Sachs set up mutually exclusive null and alternative hypotheses, he makes the case for accepting the alternative much stronger. This is why in most of the following examples, he sets up his null hypothesis to be that all the effects he has measured are random. His mutually exclusive alternative is that the observations are non-random. This, however, says nothing about the cause of the non-random results, and does not prove the existence of astrological influences.

Here is a summary of his main findings:

1. *Who marries whom?* Sachs took a sample of 717,226 married people and looked at their star sign matches to see if they fulfilled astrological expectations. His null hypothesis (the result to be tested) assumed the matches would be randomly distributed between star signs. They were not. He identified 144 possible star sign combinations, and in these he found 25 pairings that deviated significantly from the expectations of chance. When he checked the probability of this result occurring by coincidence, the odds were 1 to 50,000 against it. This means that it is 49,999 times more likely to be due to some unknown factor than to mere chance.

I have summarized the detail below.[133]

*Pairings with a statistical significance higher than expected*

| Man | Woman |
| --- | --- |
| Aries | Aries |
| Taurus | Taurus |
| Taurus | Libra |
| Gemini | Gemini |
| Leo | Aries |
| Virgo | Virgo |
| Libra | Libra |
| Scorpio | Pisces |
| Sagittarius | Sagittarius |
| Sagittarius | Aries |
| Capricorn | Capricorn |
| Aquarius | Aquarius |
| Pisces | Scorpio |

Sachs comments that he finds it extraordinary that this group of thirteen combinations includes no less than eight pairings in which both parties were born under the same sign.

*Pairings with a statistical significance lower than expected*

| Man | Woman |
|---|---|
| Aries | Scorpio |
| Taurus | Gemini |
| Taurus | Leo |
| Cancer | Aries |
| Leo | Aquarius |
| Scorpio | Gemini |
| Sagittarius | Pisces |
| Sagittarius | Capricorn |
| Aquarius | Scorpio |
| Aquarius | Taurus |
| Pisces | Virgo |
| Pisces | Libra |

2. *Who divorces whom?* The sample size for this test was 109,030 couples. The method used was the same as that used to test marriages. Once more, of the 144 possible combinations, Sachs found 25 significant deviations, but this time, there was a much lower level of significance. Once in every 26 tests, the result could be expected to occur by pure chance. This was not at a level that made it statistically meaningful.

3. *Who is single?* This test was based on census data from 1990 covering the entire population of Switzerland: 4,045,170 people. For this test, Sachs looked only at people of marriageable age, which he defined as between 18 and 40, which gave him a sample size of 2,731,766 people. He found that people born under certain star signs are more prepared to commit to marriage than those born under others. The 7 significant deviations from random behavior were statistically significant at a level of one in ten thousand. This shows that there is a definite behavior pattern within this sample.

4. *Who studies what?* For this test the data came from the Universities Clearing House in the U.K. and covered 231,026 applicants for 10

restricted-entry courses. The null hypothesis was that the star signs would be randomly distributed across the range of disciplines. There were 120 possible star sign/degree course combinations, and Sachs found 27 significant deviations from chance. The odds of obtaining this result by coincidence were 1 in 10,000. This result is nothing less than monumental. People have been condemned to death on the basis of DNA evidence with a lower probability of being correct than this.

5. *Who does what job?* Here the sample was taken from the 1990 Swiss census of 4,045,170 entries and 47 categories of occupation. This gave 564 possible combinations of job and star sign. Sachs found 77 significant variations, at odds of one in ten thousand against their being coincidence. Again, only a fool would deny he had a correlation here.

6. *Who dies of what?* This test was conducted on all registered deaths in Switzerland between 1969 and 1994, a sample size of 1,195,174. To make the test meaningful, only deaths from natural causes were tested, with violent and accidental deaths excluded from the study. This reduced the sample to 657,492 individuals. (I couldn't help thinking the Swiss must be extremely violent, accident-prone, or both, if almost half the deaths in their country are caused by non-natural means.) The 240 possible death/star sign combinations revealed five significant deviations from chance, at a significance level of 1 in 270. This result seems modest compared to some of Sachs's results, but it is still of statistical interest.

7. *Who commits suicide?* From the same death register, Sachs was able to extract a sample of 30,358 people who committed suicide. He found five significant deviations from chance expectations of star sign distributions, with a likelihood of the result being coincidence of only 1 in 1,000.

8. *Who drives how?* The sample was taken from the British Car Insurers VELO database and covered 25,000 claims made during 1996. Once more, Sachs found significant deviations for 4 star signs, at

a significance level of 1 in 10,000. He also took a sample of 85,598 Swiss traffic offenders from the Swiss Central Crime Register, and again found the same 4 star signs showing statistically significant deviation from chance, at odds of 1 in 5,000 that the result was not random.

9. *Who commits what crimes?* The sample was 325,866 convictions for 25 different types of offense. The data came from the Swiss Central Criminal Records Office. Of 300 possible crime/star sign combinations, 6 were found to vary from the expected level, and they were statistically significant, with odds of 1 in 10 million against coincidence.

10. *Who plays football?* From a sample of 4,162 professional footballers in Germany, Sachs found nine star signs deviating significantly from the expected chance value. The odds of this being coincidence are 1 in 10,000.

Having completed these statistical tests, Sachs asked his statistician advisers to carry out an extremely logical data check. The previous data sets were scrambled, and the dates were arranged into twelve artificial star signs before repeating the tests. Basically, he used a random number generator to group the 356 days of the year into twelve completely arbitrary blocks. Here is his own description of the process:

*The statisticians were able to mix the data at random and create artificial star signs in the same order within the year but provided these with artificial (i.e. false) birth dates. In this way an artificial year resulted beginning with 6 April, for example, followed by 11 Nov etc.*

*If the astrologer's statements about the effects of star signs were invalid there would be significant findings here too. However, there were no significant correlations between the artificial signs.*[134]

This demonstrated that the patterns he had found were related to the days of the year on which the events happened, not to any other factor that might be causing a bias.

Sachs also carried an analysis of a market research databank called, in English, the Allensbach Media Market Analysis Survey, which is known by its German initials of AWA. He introduced this test by saying:

*Over the past fifty years, representative surveys have become so widespread throughout the world that we now have a wealth of data which can employed for secondary statistical analysis. In other words, the data can be used to look for answers to questions which were not on the agenda of the original surveys.*[135]

The AWA has been conducted annually since 1959 to provide advertisers and advertising agents with information about various advertising media. It aims to link individuals who are observers of particular media with their demographic and psychological characters and with their consumption patterns. The objective is to combine these data to arrive at the best possible strategies for advertising campaigns.

The standard questionnaire includes three demographic questions that are useful for astrological assessment. These are:

1. What is your date of birth?
2. Were you born during the day or the night?
3. What was your exact time of birth?

To apply the laws of probability to astrological questions requires a very large database, and the AWA survey met this criterion, with 10,758 individuals sampled in the year that Sachs carried out his analysis. And the advantage of this particular approach is that the questions asked contain no direct references to astrology, so there is nothing to direct the respondents' thoughts towards astrological preconceptions.

The results are startling. There is a wide range of significant differences in behavior between people born under different star signs. (Some are bizarre. For example, Sachs found people born under Aries are more likely to use aerosol deodorants and watch sports on TV than people born under other star signs. Not the sort of prediction one finds in the astrology columns of any popular newspaper!) The most important outcome of this test is that there are a large number of small, but significant, differences in the behavior of people born under different star signs. These findings, however, did not predict success in love, good fortune or propitious times to take decisions—the sort of predictions astrologers usually claim for their arcane art. Instead they found small differences in behavior in large groups of people, which correlated with the dates they were born.

Sachs summed up of his work as follows:

> *The main purpose of our study was not to produce interesting individual results—these were, in fact, no more than entertaining by-products of our project. Rather, the declared aim of our research was to establish whether there was a correlation between star signs and human behaviour and predispositions.*
>
> *We have proved it—there is a correlation.*[136]

I can appreciate the magnitude of what Sachs has detected here, although this study shows only that a mapping between astrological birth signs and variations in behavior cannot reasonably be rejected. Sachs proved the significance of this correlation, but he did not produce any mechanism to explain how astrology "works."

Is this why the study is largely ignored by both the scientific and astrological communities? The scientists see it conflicting with their other theories, while the astrologers doubt it because its findings do not confirm what they want to believe. It seems few people are prepared to look at the facts in a neutral manner.

My skepticism was shaken by Sachs' findings that there are patterns in human behavior that can be detected using an astrological sorting filter. Why should this be? His work gives no clues. He simply observes, and shows a consistency in his results that is way above random chance.

When researching *The Book of Hiram*[137] I had been struck by the way the growth of a number of high-achieving societies coincided with appearances of conjunctions of Venus and Mercury in helical rising, that is rising in the dawn sky just before the sun as a Bright Morning Star. I had calculated that the correlation between the pre-dawn rising of Venus/Mercury and the societies with a greater proportion of higher-achieving individuals was statistically significant.[138] Now I realized that I would have to revisit this data. Gauquelin's significant planets appear as Bright Morning Stars as they work their statistical magic. And this is just what Masonic astrology says they should.

### Success, Achievement, and Your Stars

As we've seen, Professor David McClelland and his team at Harvard University spent over twenty years studying the urge to achieve. Gauquelin's work also looked at "successful" people: those with an urge to achieve. He had showed that they were significantly more likely to be born when one of the closer or larger planets was either on the western horizon or had just passed the zenith. This finding is summarized in figure 11 below, which shows the time of day as a clock face. Three o'clock is sunrise, twelve o'clock is midday (zenith), six o'clock is midnight (nadir) and nine o'clock is sunset—so the west is shown to the left of the diagram and the east to the right.

Is there is a link between Gauquelin's successful people and McClelland's high-achievement-motivated individuals? Successful people have a high need to achieve, after all; it's what makes them a success. I decided to test this idea.

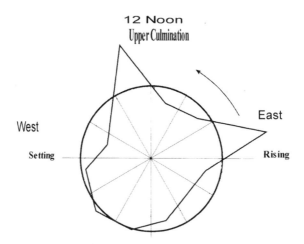

*Figure 11: The distribution of the times of birth of successful individuals. The circle shows the line of equal probability of birth at any time of day: how births would be distributed throughout the day if they occurred randomly. The irregular shape shows how the births of Gauquelin's 46,485 successful individuals were grouped, relative to the position of the sun in the sky.*

Gauquelin included a large number of biographies of the individuals who made up his sample. In that of medical scientist Louis Brocq he uses phrases that fit the characteristics of a McClelland high *n*-achiever (as outlined on p. 104):

*In the course of his career he never sought honours. He did not apply for University teaching positions and never sought membership of the Academy . . . His scientific work as a dermatologist was extensive . . . he worked without affectation or pedantry.*[139]

And similar sentiments are ascribed to the famous botanist René Maire:

*In scientific matters, he was animated by a [single-mindedness] . . . that left people amazed. Maire related everything to his work . . . He was always ready to help his colleagues, who were always welcome to use his abundant library, of which he was extremely proud.*[140]

I decided to check just where the planets were when these scientists were born. At Brocq's birth Saturn was culminating above him, and at Maire's Jupiter was in a similar position.

Of the great comedian Charlie Chaplin, who was born as Jupiter rose just before the sun, Gauquelin says:

*He has an extremely sensitive professional conscience . . . he repeated the same gag nine times running before the cameras and because he was still not satisfied, he made another nine takes the following day.*[141]

And he adds that Chaplin could not be motivated by money alone. He turned down $877,000 for a series of 25-minute radio broadcasts and, when asked why, responded, "I can't come that close to the public, I have to remain remote and mysterious."

Gauquelin also summed up his strong-willed sports champions thus:

*Those who manage to do this [succeed as sports champions] can boast of having mental capabilities similar to those of great war leaders or the major captains of industry.*[142]

Harvard's McClelland says that young men behave more vigorously as entrepreneurs if they have higher *n*-achievement levels, and that high *n*-achievers tend to be successful leaders of industry.[143] He says that major captains of industry have high levels of *n*-achievement, while Gauquelin says his strong-willed champions have attitudes like "captains of industry." They seem to be talking about the same types of people.

Gauquelin's sketches of successful individuals have a great deal in common with the high *n*-achievers that McClelland looked at. McClelland also noticed that the level of achievement motivation in a society changed over time. Gauquelin has shown that the time of year a person was born could affect their level of success in adult life. Sachs has shown that academic success varies according to the star sign of the individual (i.e. the time of year they were born), but also that star signs change over time. Were they all taking slightly different views of the same unknown phenomena?

McClelland plotted changes in levels of achievement motivation and degree of economic activity over time for many different societies, as this typical graph, reproduced on page 152, shows. It shows that surges in the achievement activity of a society are followed by increases in its economic activity.

Could I use McClelland's analysis of particular societies to make sense of Gauquelin's and Sachs's results? All three researchers seem to be talking about the same type of people. But there is a difference in their approaches. Gauquelin found that "successful" individuals were born when certain planets were rising, or directly overhead. McClelland, while interested in economic development, had isolated personality factors that drove individuals to make their societies achieve. And Sachs just noted that the star sign a person was born under was linked to achievement. Yet Gauquelin's detailed biographies used the same descriptive phrases that McClelland linked to high levels of achievement motivation. Was there a connection? And, if there was, where did Sachs's findings fit into this strange statistical view of the world?

Is there a pattern of human behavior that is tied into the positions of the planets? Could I test this idea? If I could reconcile these three different views of the world, they might give me an insight into how Masonic astrology works . . . if it does.

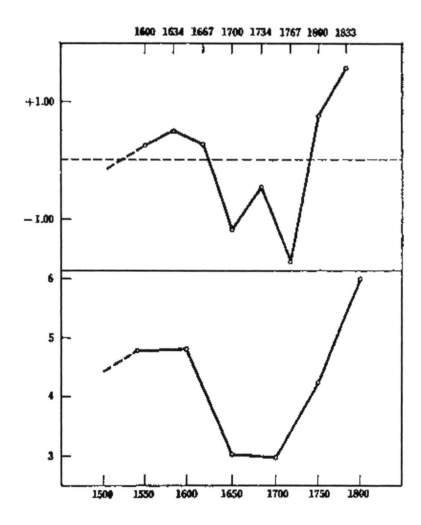

*Figure 12: The upper graph shows economic activity; the lower shows McClelland's Measure of the Society's Achievement Level, derived from published sources, fifty years earlier [after McClelland (1961)].*

152

## Harmless, Harmful, or Statistical?

There are a lot of odd facts—and some even odder guesswork—about success-ful people in Gauquelin's work. In Sachs's study of university entrants there are hard facts about the star signs under which people achieve academic success, without guesswork or context. And finally, there is a detailed scrutiny of how the success-related behavior of groups of people vary over long periods of time in the work of McClelland. All three sources say that the proportion of suc-cessful people born at any time into a society varies over time. McClelland and Sachs don't know why this is, and Gauquelin thinks it's caused by certain planets triggering the birth of a successful person.

None of this is the sort of data that usually appears in astrologers' horo-scopes. But do these three separate approaches offer a chance of a new insight into why George Washington took Masonic astrology seriously enough to use it to lay out the Federal City of Washington, D.C.?

Hans Eysenck, whom I've already mentioned, was an authority on statis-tics at the London University Institute of Psychiatry. He does not dismiss Gauquelin's work:

*If there is any value in the scientific method as usually employed in studies of this kind, and if the laws of statistics apply here as they do elsewhere, then these dis-coveries must stand as clear indications that our conceptions of the universe we live in are not as final and complete as we might like to think.[144]*

This offered me clear encouragement to try to fit these odd facts into a better theory. Eysenck and co-author Nias went on to say:

*A few years ago our own position would have been that of the "hard scientists" who reject astrology and all its works without question . . . The remarkable demonstrations provided by the Gauquelins encouraged us to make a systematic search of the literature to discover just what was the empirical evidence for and against astrology.[145]*

Eysenck showed that much of the astrological literature is flawed. He said this was because astrologers usually lack any grasp of statistics, so they devise unsound tests to try to confirm their beliefs. He gave this advice to any astrologers wishing to use statistics to try to prove their case:

*Those who genuinely believe that they are practising and teaching a valid set of principles must get down to the hard job of finding proper proofs for their hypotheses and theories, using the well-developed methods of the social sciences, particularly psychology. There is no real problem in mounting a series of decisive experiments in this field; the need is to make them sophisticated enough to take into account the many traps we have pointed out in the course of our discussion of previous experiments. We hope, therefore, that astrologers will take seriously the task of building up a science, and provide doubters with the proof that has so far escaped them of the validity of astrological assertions.[146]*

However, no astrologers took him up on this. The cycle of claims and counterclaims continues, with neither side offering factual support for their positions. Followers of astrology talk of a basic paradox that protects them from scientific proof. But this paradox looks just like an attempt to avoid being held to blame for the lack of predictive certainty that Dawkins pointed out to be an essential part of astrology.

Eysenck thinks that Gauquelin became aware of an effect that is not astrological. He calls this strange thing "cosmobiology," and says it might be a scientific effect that is so far little known.

*If, in judging classical or traditional astrology, we have had to side with those scientists who find little good to say about it, the position is rather different when we turn to cosmobiology. Here we find that those astronomers and physicists who have shown any interest in the matter have overdone the cautious, critical attitude which quite properly characterises "hard" scientists, and have treated the Gauquelins and other prominent exponents rather badly, often criticising them in terms of what they might have done rather than judging them on what they actually did. If astrologers of the traditional school are often non-factual in their claims and arguments, so have many scientists been in dealing with the claims of cosmobiology . . . there are certain facts urgently in need of a good hypothesis to explain them.[147]*

As it happens, I seem to have an hypothesis, based on Masonic astrology, that appears to fit the observations. The only real problem is that I know it only as a ritual experience, not as a scientific explanation.

Eysenck says the experimental design of Gauquelin's work stands up to the most careful scrutiny, and the methodology is of as high a standard as the best studies in psychology, psychiatry, sociology, or any of the social sciences. So perhaps I should keep looking to see if Masonic astrology is the best place to find the "good hypothesis" he calls for.

## Where to Start?

But where do I begin to look for a science of Masonic astrology? Perhaps I should revisit "cosmobiology" for a clue. Eysenck and Nias give this definition of it:

*Cosmobiology is not a logically consistent body of knowledge. It is rather a string of "one off" phenomena, equally mysterious, equally lacking in proper physical explanation, and only linked together because of the (probably correct) belief that they are all caused or affected by planetary or other cosmic influences. This is a can of worms which is particularly designed to frighten off cautious scientists, and when to the claims of cosmobiologists is added the taint of astrology the scientific reaction of disdainful withdrawal becomes intelligible.*[148]

The topic is as disconnected as the three statistical studies of success I already discussed. But if I could combine the work of Gauquelin and McClelland to study the claims of Masonic astrology, I might gain an understanding of George Washington's application of Masonic geomancy.

Five of the six societies of the past that McClelland studied occurred when there were risings of the Masonic Shekinah in the pre-dawn sky. I had deduced that a periodic conjunction of Venus and Mercury, which looked like a bright star rising just before the sun, occurred on each of these occasions and formed the basis of the myth of the Shekinah. But what other planets were rising in the morning skies when these economic peaks cropped up?

McClelland had found a peak of achievement in 967 BCE. In addition to Venus and Mercury, Jupiter and Saturn were also rising close to the sun at that time. Gauquelin's charts showed that his successful subjects were born on days when one of the higher-gravity-field planets was rising. In the spring of 967 BCE, many of the children born would have had Jupiter, Saturn, or Venus—all high-gravity-field planets—rising on their birthday. Gauquelin's findings say this means that many of them should have been successful high-achievers. That is exactly what McClelland reported.[149]

The next period McClelland identified as a time of peak achievement was 487 BCE. Saturn, Jupiter, and Venus/Mercury were close to sun then, and so would have been rising for a high proportion of the births; and Gauquelin suggests that a high proportion of the children born at this time should have been successful. Another time when McClelland found a high-achieving society arising was 474 CE, at which time Saturn, Jupiter, and Venus/Mercury were rising before the sun. His next such society occurred in 1434 CE, when Saturn, Jupiter, Mars, and Venus/Mercury were all rising together close to the sun. So, once again, McClelland and Gauquelin seem to agree that many children born at this time should be high-achievers and successful.

McClelland found another high-achieving society in the late seventeenth century. This one did not fit with the patterns of pre-dawn rising of the Venus/Mercury conjunctions I had identified as the Masonic Shekinah. There was no conjunction of Mercury and Venus at that time, but Venus, Jupiter, and Saturn were all rising close to the sun. This was also a condition that Gauquelin's work said should result in the birth of a large number of successful people. McClelland's work confirmed that it did.

To check out this pattern, I looked at the state of the sky when Gauquelin's "iron-willed" champions were born. Were any heavy planets rising close to the sun? This more detailed look at the state of the sky at times when McClelland found high-achieving societies showed that there was an increase in individuals' achievement motivation when any high-gravity planet rose near the sun. What else had been happening in the sky when Gauquelin's high-achieving test subjects were born?

I decided to randomly sample ten of these individuals for whom Gauquelin had included biographies. I found that all of them had heavy planets rising close to the sun at the time of their births. Gauquelin did not mention this in his descriptions. Here is a table of the ten and my results:

| Name | Date of Birth | Heavy Celestial Bodies Close to the Sun |
|---|---|---|
| Sacha Guitry | Feb. 21, 1885 | Venus, Mars |
| Lucien Guitry | Dec. 13, 1860 | Venus, Moon |
| Tristan Bernard | Sept. 7, 1866 | Mars, Moon |
| Hubert Latham | Jan. 10, 1883 | Venus, Mars |
| Heinrich Himmler | Oct. 7, 1900 | Venus, Mars |
| Reinhard Heydrich | March 7, 1904 | Venus, Saturn |
| Hélène Boucher | May 23, 1908 | Saturn |
| Martin Bormann | April 20,1889 | Mars, Venus |
| Alfred Jarry | Sept. 8, 1873 | Venus, Jupiter |
| Henri Lebesgue | June 28, 1875 | Jupiter |

Gauquelin wanted to explain the traits of these people in terms of astrology. So he looked only for astrological outcomes. Because of this tunnel vision, he ignored the fact that, at every birth, heavy planets were rising close before the sun. And they would appear in the pre-dawn sky as Bright Morning Stars. Could it be that the closeness of a heavy planet to the sun is more important than astrological prediction? Might generations of Freemasons have noticed this fact and incorporated it into their ritual teachings, and could that be what George Washington noticed?

## Weighty Considerations

Gauquelin believed that his findings could be explained if the unborn child played a role during labor and delivery. However, this idea is impossible to reconcile with the uncertain timing of a woman giving birth.

But do you remember our discussion of Sir Isaac Newton's discovery of gravity back in chapter 6? When he was trying to understand gravity, Newton assumed that there was a force between the sun, the moon, and earth, which he could not specify. He called this gravity (the attractive force that gives all objects on the earth their feeling of weight). He then used observations of tide heights at Bristol and Plymouth, juxtaposed with the positions of the moon and sun, and the tide height records for many different latitudes throughout the world, to relate the movement of the sea to the positions of the sun and moon.

From these calculations, he was able to deduce the relative masses of the earth and the moon.[150] Newton went on to show that other quite separate events, such as the appearance of comets, could be predicted using this force of gravity. His reasoning was confirmed when Halley used the method to forecast the return of the comet that bears his name.

I wondered if I could use Gauquelin's observations in a manner similar to Newton's use of the different heights of the spring and neap tides. Gauquelin's data imply that when a heavy planet rises close to the sun, or is directly overhead, at dawn, a greater number of successful children are born. By assuming this to be true, I can predict the proportion of high-achievers who will be born into a society from the positions of heavy planets in the sky. If this assumption is fair, then the forecasts should compare with the findings of McClelland. If it is wrong, then it will not be consistent with McClelland's observations. The computation involves many steps but is simple and repetitive, so it lends itself to a computer simulation. I decided to try it.

### Simulating Star Achievement

The simulation I was designing had to cover the astronomical year as viewed from the earth. By looking at the rising time of each of heavy planet each day, I could work out where that planet fitted in a description of the solar system. Einstein's theory of relativity says that no particular viewpoint of the universe is special in any way, so I decided to work with the earth as my center and calculate how the sun and the planets revolve around it, thus making it easy to compare my results to astrological data. (I did this simply to keep the sums easy, not because I think the earth is the sole immoveable center of creation.) To see how this works, if you think of the sun as moving around the full circle of the sky once in every 24 hours, then each hour represents 15° of this orbit. This way I could map areas of the sky as hours of the day, and work out where the heavy planets were. Gauquelin had defined two critical areas, one where a heavy planet is on the eastern horizon and the other where it is almost directly overhead. These zones are easy to check to see if higher proportions of high-achievers are born when those planets are in these parts of the sky.

The simulation also had to take account of seasonal changes in the birth rate throughout the year. As all the figures I was using related to the northern hemisphere, I decided to base the model on the seasonal birth rate pattern for Britain. To make it easier to compare with Gunter Sachs's work, I transposed calendar days into "star signs."

Birth rates are recorded and published for each day of the year. I built a table showing the percentage of births, averaged over the period 1950-1980, for each of the "star signs" used by astrology. If the birth rate is constant throughout each season of the year, then each star sign will show 8.3 percent of the total, and indeed the graph shows little variation in the proportion of children born under each sign (indicating that it is unlikely that any of the effects Sachs had found were a result of seasonal variations in the number of births).

Next, I worked out where the moon, Venus, Mars, Jupiter, and Saturn were in the sky for each day of the year. Then I adjusted for the slight annual variation in the birth rate caused by the seasons. This told me how many births to expect each day. Next I used my program to simulate what proportion of the births would take place with one of the heavy planets in a critical position. (I called these Morning-Star zones, as Gauquelin had found that a heavy planet, which would appear as a Bright Morning Star, in this zone resulted in the birth of a successful individual.) Finally, I totaled the predicted proportion of successful individuals to be born and grouped their totals by star signs.

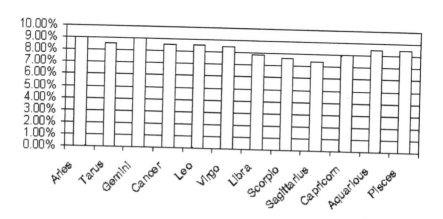

*Figure 13: Distribution of all births by star sign.*

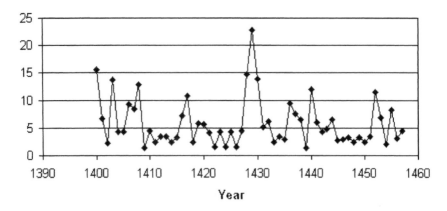

*Figure 14: The percentage of births occurring in morning-star zones, when heavy planets are close to the Sun.*

McClelland said he found a peak of achievement in 1440 CE. My program worked out the fraction of likely "successful" babies that Gauquelin's rules forecast to be born around this period (1400-1460 CE). The resulting chart (figure 14 above) shows a high proportion of babies predicted to be high-achievers would have been born around 1430. This was caused by Mars and Jupiter being near to the sun for long periods.

Newborn children cannot have an instant effect on the level of achievement of a society. So to make the results more meaningful, I averaged the effect of the proportion of high-achievers over their working lifetimes. I assumed that by the age of 18, people would start to have an effect, and that they would continue to contribute for a further 18 years, until their mid-thirties. After this I assumed, at this period of history, they would start to die off. The result of this calculation is shown in figure 15.

The peak of achievement that McClelland found shows in this forecast of active high-achievers.[151] It begins around 1428 and continues until 1445 before falling again, just as McClelland had seen. I was using Gauquelin's findings to predict the levels of achievement in a historic society, and the results were fitting the real data.

In effect, I was using the prediction of Masonic astrology that highly motivated individuals are created when the Bright Morning Star appears in the east.

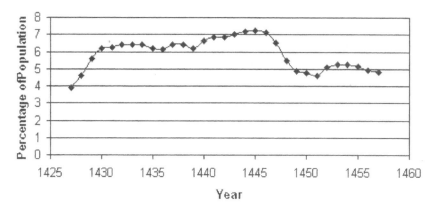

*Figure 15: Morning-star-zone births averaged over their working life.*

But, even after these calculations, I was no closer to knowing *why* heavy planets in key parts of the sky should turn babies into "successful" adults. I found this result so disturbing that I quickly decided to search for another way of testing the Masonic-star predictor against real data.

There was another piece of evidence I could check out. Sachs had found differences in behavior for people born at various times of the year. How did this fit in with using morning-star zones to predict numbers of high-achievers? Did the fraction of people born when high-gravitational-field planets are in key positions in relation to the sun vary over the time period Sachs considered?

He had looked at university freshmen in the year 1994. Most young people go to college at the age of eighteen, so the majority of this group would have been born in 1976. This time, I used the computer model to simulate the births in 1976. I wanted to see what groups of individuals had been born in morning-star zones, with one of Gauquelin's critical planets in a key part of the sky. These babies would be eighteen years old at the time of Sachs's test. The resulting chart (figure 16) shows the fraction of the expected births for each star sign when the Masonic rules of the Bright Morning Star predict the babies should grow up to be successful. The total number of births for each star sign is about 8.3 percent of the total, but this chart shows big differences in the number of Masonically predicted high-achievers born to each sign.

161

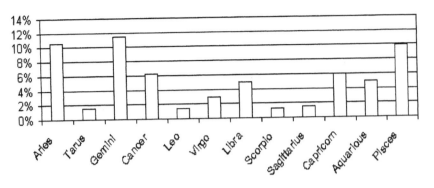

*Figure 16: Proportion of predicted high-achievers born in 1976 by star sign.*

But how likely was it that this pattern would arise by pure chance? There is a statistical test, the chi-square test, that can work out the probability of the result just being coincidence.[152] To use it, I have to compare the pattern I have with a pattern I want to disprove. I did a chi-square test to see if I could accept that the predicted high-achievers were randomly distributed over the star signs. (If I could, then it would mean that the morning star effect was not significant.) But I could reject this hypothesis at odds of a thousand to one; this means that the Morning Star effect is causing a significant impact on the number of high-achievers born under each star sign.

But would this effect remain the same every year? That seemed unlikely, as the pattern of appearance of heavy planets in the key zones changes over cycles much longer than a year. It was unlikely that the pattern in figure 16 would repeat each year, so I also tested the other year Sachs had looked at, 1977. The next chart, figure17, shows a different distribution but is just as irregular as the first one, although this time different star signs are favored. When I applied the chi-square test to these new results, it too showed that, at odds of one in a thousand, I could reject the hypothesis that high-achievers are randomly spread across star signs. This means that there is a real pattern to the number of individuals born with a heavy planet in the critical parts of their birth sky, which I was now calling their "morning-star zones." But this pattern changes from year to year.

This does not agree with Sun-sign astrology, which says that the sign you are born under always fixes your fortune in the same way; if you are born an Aquarius, it doesn't matter what year you were born in, your forecast is the

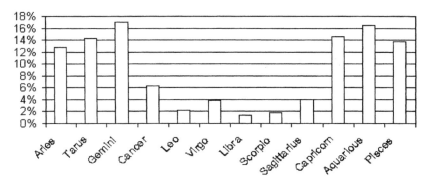

*Figure 17: Proportion of predicted high-achievers born in 1977 by star sign.*

same. But comparing the proportion of Gauquelin's high-achievers born under Aquarius in 1976 with those of 1977 shows a dramatic difference. This is not a result that fits comfortably into astrological belief systems or their spin-off trade of newspaper horoscopes. But it does agree with what Sachs found, and it also agrees with the myth of Masonic astrology that it is better to be born, or Masonically reborn, when the Bright Morning Star is rising in the dawn sky.

This test has wide-ranging implications. If Gauquelin's rule that successful people are born with any high-gravity object such as the moon, Venus, Mars, Jupiter, or Saturn rising or culminating is correct, then the spread of the time of birth successful babies born under each star sign is not random. My initial idea that Venus/Mercury conjunctions might be significant was not explaining the data, but the idea of the morning-star zone was. The morning-star-zone idea predicts that the proportion of high-achievers born to each sign will change from year to year. Western astrology does not incorporate this idea, so Gauquelin had found something else. And these morning-star-zone results fit in well with the observations of both McClelland and Sachs. So what is going on?

I carried out a series of simulations to test further predictions. The forecasts are based on an assumption that when heavy planets appear in morning-star zones, they have an effect on the level of motivation-to-achieve of children born under their "rays." I have found significant variation in the expected personalities of children born in different years and star signs. These differences fit in with the findings of McClelland and Sachs. But I have no idea what mysterious "rays" might be causing this effect.

Using morning-star zone has given me a method of predicting real events, even though this result is not a logical outcome. But it explains why Sachs found significant differences in behavior for people born under different star signs. That is just what the morning-star-zone model predicts if the newborn babies have the differing levels of achievement motivation that McClelland's data says they do. But there was one further test I needed in order to confirm that I could reproduce all of Sachs' findings.

Sachs had shuffled the membership of the star signs in his sample. When he did so, he found that the significant behavior disappeared. I needed to take the predictions from my simulations for the proportions of high-achievers born each day of the year and create a similar random sequence of days. These could then be placed into a set of non-sequential, artificial star signs. I followed Sachs's technique, as described on page 146, to see if my findings would duplicate his. The significance of the star sign groups then vanished, and my results confirmed what Sachs found. I could repeat all of his findings by using the predictions of Masonic astrology. His results are explained by assuming that the occupation of Morning-Star zones by heavy planets can predict the fraction of high-achievers born into any society.

This was a disturbing outcome. Gauquelin tried to make forecasts; he tried only to explain astrology. But I have gone down a different road. By using the Morning-Star-zone rule, which I deduced from Gauquelin's work, I forecast the results found by McClelland and Sachs for personality behavior linked to achievement motivation. Like it or not, I had predicted a pattern that seemed to be driven by the "mysterious astral rays" of a series of Bright Morning Stars.

Now I had a statistical explanation for the results of Gauquelin, Sachs, and McClelland. Just assume that, if the moon, Venus, Mars, Jupiter, or Saturn is rising or culminating as the sun rises at the moment of a baby's birth, then that baby will have a higher level of achievement motivation than average. It will then go on to develop personality traits that will help it be successful in later life. What an uncomfortable finding! There is no accepted way in which a heavy planet passing close to the sun in the sky, as viewed from Earth, should cause major differences in a baby's nature. I am reduced to saying that this is caused by some sort of vague astral force, which, for want of a better name, I am calling "mysterious astral rays." That is not acceptable to me as a scientist.

Is it a real physical effect on the babies' brains, or is it just a statistical artifice which I have failed to detect?

Nonetheless, my quest to understand the Masonic geomancy of George Washington was moved forward. These results meet one of Richard Dawkins's tests of astrology. The cross-matching of the separate work of Sachs, McClelland, and Gauquelin satisfy his second test, that any astrological prediction should be independently verifiable and unambiguous. Gauquelin's morning-star-zone rules, when used to make forecasts, are confirmed by the independent observations of Sachs and McClelland.

I was uncomfortable and suspicious of my findings. If, to explain the actions of George Washington, I have to show that Masonic astrology is able to predict personality, I must put forward a mechanism by which the positions of the stars at the moment of birth affect the development of a child's personality.

I needed to avoid the trap that seduced Gauquelin. When he found an unusual result, he slipped up by trying to prove that "there is something of value in astrology for the world today."[153] This led him to make wilder and stranger claims. I must now look at the human brain and its role in creating personality. The only clue I can take forward from Gauquelin's work is the significance of the strength of gravitational attraction of certain planets when they rise near the sun. But how can gravity affect the development of personality?

## Conclusions

Dr. Michel Gauquelin's statistical studies of astrology did not reveal any proofs of the validity of traditional astrology, but they did show a strong tendency for successful people to be born when a planet with heavy gravity rose close to, or at right-angles, to the sun. This outcome was unexpected, and has never been satisfactorily explained by Gauquelin or any other scientist or astrologer.

The patterns in his data indicated that more successful people were born when a bright planet rose before the sun. I compared some of the biographies of his successful subjects with the characteristics of Dr. David McClelland's high-achievers and found a good match. Using the Morning-Star zones, implied by Gauquelin, I predicted the proportion of high-achieving people that McClelland had measured in historical societies, and found that I could match the data that McClelland had observed.

Gunter Sachs had carried out a large-scale survey of Sun-sign astrological effects using public databases, and found that the Sun sign a person was born under correlated with different personality-based behavior patterns. Using my morning-star-zone method of predicting the proportion of high-achievers born in any month of a year, I was able to replicate the observations Sachs made on college freshmen.

By applying this morning-star-zone method, I was able to make predictions which could be independently checked against previously collected data, and my predictions fitted. This meant I had a method of satisfying Dr. Richard Dawkins's second test of astrology, which required that any astrological prediction should be independently verifiable and unambiguous.

But I was as far as ever from satisfying his first test, which said that a theory of astrology must put forward a means by which the positions of the stars at the moment of birth affect the growth of the brain (the brain being the seat of personality). The only explanation I have is that Masonic ritual seems to have encapsulated ancient wisdom and encoded it in a series of legends. That is a long way from scientific proof. If I was ever to understand how Bro. George Washington used Masonic astrology to bring about a surge of achievement motivation in his Federal City of Washington, D.C., then I needed to know more about how a newborn brain grows a personality. Only then could I begin to consider the mechanisms that might be behind the "mysterious astral rays" of the Bright Morning Star. In the next chapter, I'll begin at the beginning—from the moment of conception.

# Chapter Eight

# The Journey from Single Cell to Complex Genius

## Where It All Begins

Once upon a time we were all infants, or so we are told. But how much of our early experience do we actually remember? Certainly nobody remembers being born, and, for most of us, our earliest memories date from about the age of two or three, by which time we have a personality, although we cannot remember growing it. We remember only after we have developed what the psychologists call "a sense of self" or a "higher consciousness." Perhaps our memories begin then because we are starting to learn the basics of language.

There is no evidence inside our minds that we existed before our memories began. The only proof we have is the collection of embarrassing photographs our mothers produce of bare-bottomed babies smiling up from sheepskin rugs. Much as we may protest that these images look nothing like us, we are assured they are our proto-selves. But we cannot recall being photographed in that state of innocent unawareness. To ourselves, we appear to have lived only within the range of our own memories.

At the other end of life, older people who suffer from dementia also have no memories. They forget who they are and what they have done. In the disease process, their personalities disappear along with their memories. A much-loved, caring parent can be become an inconsiderate and unaware monster. Common sense suggests that our sense of self is formed from the sum of our memories. This view is also held by neuroscientist Professor Steven Rose, director of The Brain and Behaviour Research Group at the

Open University in the U.K. Commenting on one particular form of dementia, he said:

*People suffering from Alzheimer's disease experience a frightening loss of their own identify and access to their store of personal memories—those memories which for all of us form such a central buttress to that very personal identity.*[154]

As I started to read about the subject of personality formation, it became clear that there were a number of key issues, but one area of certainty stood out. The relationship between our innate sense of "self" and the memories that remind us who we are is important. But exactly how our past actions form the basis of our present personality remained a puzzle.

Then I was lucky enough to be invited to lecture at the Orkney Science Festival when Karl H. Pribram was also speaking. Pribram, a sprightly man in his early eighties, is Distinguished Professor of Cognitive Sciences at Georgetown University in Washington, D.C., and Distinguished Professor of Information Sciences at George Mason University in Virginia. He is also an Emeritus Professor of Stanford University and has been Director of the Center for Brain Research and Informational Sciences at Radford University. His energy and enthusiasm would not have been out of place in a man a third of his age.

Dr. Pribram was at the Festival with his wife, the writer Katherine Neville, who also was speaking. After the day's lectures, I went to dinner at the Kirkwall Hotel with Professor Pribram, his wife Katherine, and the Slovenian physicist Dr. Andrej Detela of the Josef Stefan Institute in Ljubljana. It was a fascinating evening. Karl has spent most of his life exploring the properties of the brain and its structure. The talk after dinner ranged from quantum physics to brain science, with Karl telling us about thought transfer experiments Ed Mitchell conducted with the crew of *Apollo* 8 while working for NASA. He also outlined his ideas on the nature of consciousness. As he was talking about the transition from sleeping to waking, I took the opportunity to ask him about something that was puzzling me about self-awareness.

I knew that sometimes when I was awakened by early morning sunlight, I could be aware of my body, but not of who I was, or where. I'd noticed that over a brief space of time—objectively, it could be no more that a few seconds—I would find myself becoming aware of my surroundings: I would then remember my past and finally recall who I was. I asked Karl if it was possible that, as I awoke, I was living through a stage of consciousness in which I existed without any awareness of self. This was quite likely, he said, before launching into an impromptu lecture to explain the difference between "primary" and "higher-level" consciousness.

He explained that, before I could have any sense of self, I had to have primary consciousness. This he defined as an ability to generate a mental scene in which I could integrate a large amount of diverse data to relate my immediate behavior to the demands of my environment. He went on to explain how this level of consciousness is similar to the sort of awareness that an animal such as a dog experiences, or that a young baby may have before it acquires language. Awareness of self grows as you react to the inputs of your senses, and is only possible when your brain has developed an ability to construct and connect past and future events.

In other words, you have no sense of self until you can remember your past and imagine your future. This acquired memory, Karl went on to explain, is a physical property of the brain. It is formed by neurons firing together and forming links.

On those occasions when I awoke without a concept of who I was, I was experiencing the state of consciousness that a young child lives in before it acquires language. Only as my memory of what I could do, and the skills I had learned, interacted with and influenced the area of my brain that was the focus of my waking thoughts, did I remember my personality and become fully conscious. Only then did I know who I was. Karl explained that this process often happens as you wake up, but you accept that you're disorientated by sleep, so it's not a problem.

Karl said that our personalities change and develop as the structure of our brain alters to accommodate new concepts as we learn them. The implication of this is that a child develops a personality as physical changes take place in the structure of his or her brain. But what sort of changes occur in a growing human brain? What roles do brain activity and memory play in forming our personality? I asked Karl for his opinion.

He answered that a baby, in the early days of its life, experiences only primary consciousness. Yet, at this time, it has three times as many separate brain cells as there are people alive in the whole world.

"If I set out to count each individual neuron and am fast enough to check each object off at the rate of one a second, it will take me around thirty million years to complete the full numeration," he told us.

"Should we order pudding first?" asked the practical Andrej.

Karl grinned, obviously pleased that he had encouraged us to visualize the awesome complexity of a baby's brain.

But one thing still puzzled me. When does the undifferentiated, lightly structured brain of a newborn baby change into the complex personality of an adult?

As I read more of Karl's work on memory and how it contributes to consciousness, I began to understand that human memory functions in a different way to the digitally based computer memory I am used to working with. Human memory is non-representational, which means that memories are not simply stored in a single location, but appear in our conscious mind when there is a match between the electrical activity of the brain and trigger signals from the environment.

Karl had written how we all experience this phenomenon:

*Events dimly remembered become vivid when we return to the scene of the experience. Meeting old friends, hearing familiar music, re-reading a long-neglected topic, all call forth re-constructive power of thought long gone. We are little aware of the amount of our memory that is carried "out there"—not in our brains but in our homes, jobs, and libraries. Given these highly structured inputs, the machinery of our brains can restructure—reconstruct—a remembrance from the bits and dabs actually stored in the head . . . For education, the moral is clear. Instruction (shared discovery of structure) should supplement teaching (showing).[155]*

Professor Steven Rose of the Open University, who has spent over twenty years studying how memories develop, says remembering is a process of making connections:

*Early brain development in the foetus and new-born is itself associated first with a massive proliferation of cells, and then by a steady drop in number, but the space once occupied by lost cells is taken up by an increase in the branching and synaptic connections made by those that remain. Is this a "good thing" or a "bad thing" so far as brain function is concerned? We don't know; it seems to be part of the normal development sequence, but one should not be seduced into a simple assumption that more means better.*[156]

How did this process, where a baby is born with a whole bundle of disconnected brain cells that are then stimulated by the outside world to link together to grow a personality, fit in with the claims of traditional astrology?

## Cutting the Cord

Traditional astrology claims that an individual's personality is fixed by the influence of the stars at the moment the umbilical cord is cut. But from what I now knew about the development of brain and personality, this just did not make sense. Could any mechanism fix for life a baby's unformed personality at the exact moment of birth?

The idea that such a complex structure should arise in an instant, "midwived" by the "cosmic influences" of distant stars, seems to have no basis in reality. The human brain begins to grow soon after conception, but it does not appear fully formed at birth. Your brain grew from a fertilized egg, but at what point in its development did it become conscious? I somehow doubt it was at the moment of "cutting the cord," which is when astrology would have you believe your personality was fixed for the rest of your life.

The moment the outer tissue layer of a human egg is penetrated by a sperm, a single-cell being (called a zygote) is created. The zygote contains all the genetic code needed to grow itself into a complete human being, with a conscious brain and a distinct, highly individual personality. But this amoeba-like zygote does not have a self-conscious brain. Let's follow its progress and see when it starts to grow brain tissue.

Within some thirty hours of conception, the zygote starts to split and divide into a tiny multi-celled creature, now called a morula. The main problem this growing morula has is how to feed itself. So far, the developing zygote has been living off the fat of its mother's egg. Dad contributed only genetic plans with his sperm; he didn't send any food parcels to help his young zygote on its way. Fortunately, there is a source of food fairly close by, but it belongs to the little zygote's mom. Her blood is full of all the nutrients and chemicals the morula needs to keep on growing, so the obvious solution is to swim to the wall of the womb and start suckling. About six days after conception, the fast-developing morula, now called a blastocyst, attaches itself onto the wall of its mother's womb and starts to draw oxygen and food from her blood.

As the blastocyst taps into mom's food supply and starts to feed, it becomes an embryo. Admittedly it is a young and simple embryo, but it has another thirty-nine weeks of cheap board and lodging in front of it, before its mom's body gets fed up with the freeloader and throws it out to fend for itself. So how does the fast-developing embryo use this carefree period?

This is when it starts growing a brain, a nervous system, and all the other parts of a working body. Within twelve days its brain is growing quite quickly. The central part of the embryonic disc, known as the neural plate, now starts to specialize in growing brain cells. By the end of the first month the embryo has a primitive, but complete, brain. At that point, it's just a lump on top of the embryo's developing backbone, but it will grow up to be that part of the brain known as the cerebellum.

Now that the little embryo has a basic brain, it starts to plan ahead. Perhaps it realizes that the free lunches its mom provides will end one day. It starts to get itself organized to cope with the outside world. Does it know that, unless it grows more than a cerebellum, it may not be able to get the best-paid stock-broking jobs in the city? Maybe it's so afraid of not being bright enough to pass its SAT tests, and of being excluded from Harvard or Oxford, that it really focuses its efforts on growing a much more complex brain. This ambition can be seen clearly by the rate at which it grows neurons, the basic brain cells. About five weeks into its life, the embryo is growing neurons at a rate of a million every four minutes! As every thought the embryo will ever think involves the triggering of interconnected neurons, this is a serious investment in future intelligence. However, it's not enough to build enormous stockpiles of neurons and hope for the best. Those billions of neurons have got to link together, so that they can contribute to the thinking processes of the new brain.

When does that process start? The best way to start to understand how the neuron-rich embryo uses its enormous stock of unconnected brain cells is to look at one of these cells and what it can do.

A single neuron looks like a very tiny daffodil plant, with a stem, a bulb, and lots of little roots, called dendrites. The bulb is the cell body, the long stem is called the axon, and finally the flowering of terminal endings are called the synapses. Neurons receive signals from other neurons via their dendrites. If enough dendrites become excited, the electrical potential within the cell body rises to a level called the trigger potential, and the neuron "fires." As it fires, it sends a pulse of electrical power along the axon towards the synapse area, where the pulse is passed on to the dendrites of other neurons. The process is quite simple. Tickle enough of the neuron's roots and it sends a compulsive sneeze up its stem, so its flower tickles the roots of the next neuron in line.

All right, perhaps there is a little more to the theory than that. But my point is that neurons are essentially digital in operation—all or nothing. They either work completely or they don't work at all; there are no half-measures in neuron-triggering. They either reach a threshold voltage (between -50 and -70 mV) and trigger, or they just sit there doing nothing. Only triggering neurons cause thoughts, and without thoughts you don't have memories, reflexes, or consciousness. And you need memory, reflexes, and consciousness if you are going to develop a personality. But one neuron on its own cannot sustain a complete thought and become self-aware. If the embryo wants to become conscious, it needs lots and lots of neurons, all connected together, all triggering one another and interacting in a way that makes the brain aware of itself.

The embryo won't be able to become consciousness until it develops a large enough interconnecting tangle of neurons. And when might this be? Brain expert Professor Susan Greenfield of Oxford University points out that, although the newborn baby has grown lots of neurons, they are packed in pretty tight by the time the baby pops out of its mother.

*By nine months' gestation, we have most of the neurons in our brains that we are ever likely to have. So now we are born! Birth allows the brain to go on growing, since otherwise the head would soon become too big for the birth canal of the mother. At birth, the human head is roughly the same size as a chimpanzee's, some 350 cubic centimetres. By six months, it will be half its eventual size, and by two years it will be three quarters the size of an adult head. At four years old the human brain is four times the size it was at birth, some 1,400 cubic centimetres.[157]*

But when does this rapidly growing brain become conscious? Greenfield explains:

*We are born equipped to adapt to stress and with a certain number of reflexes. But are we conscious? This perplexing question has never been satisfactorily answered. All the possibilities seem bizarre. One scenario is that we are conscious in the womb, but then the problem arises of identifying exactly when this momentous event occurs. Clearly, the single fertilised egg is not conscious, so when would consciousness suddenly intervene? And of what could a foetus be conscious? Another idea might be that the baby becomes conscious precisely as it is born. Again, this is a strange idea, as many babies are born prematurely. So is it the act of birth itself that evokes consciousness? It seems hard to accept this line of thought, as the brain itself is completely unaffected by the birth process.[158]*

A newborn baby has lots of neurons, but few connections between them. It takes two years for the density of neural connections to get anywhere near the levels found in an adult brain.[159] And it is the connections between neurons that make the brain conscious. This does not agree with the astrological idea that an individual's personality is switched on at the moment the umbilical cord is cut, and from that moment is fixed forever.

Dr. Gerald Edelman, President of the Neurosciences Research Foundation in La Jolla, CA, and Dr. Guilio Tononi of the Neuroscience Institute have a theory about the start of consciousness:

*Conscious experience appears to be associated with neural activity that is distributed simultaneously across neuronal groups in many different regions of the brain. Consciousness is therefore not the prerogative of any one brain area, instead, its neural substrates are widely dispersed throughout the so-called thalamocortical system and associated regions . . .*

> *To support conscious experience, a large number of groups of neurons must interact rapidly and reciprocally though the process called re-entry. If these re-entrant interactions are blocked, entire sections of consciousness disappear, and consciousness itself may shrink or split . . .*
>
> *Finally, we show that the activity patterns of the groups of neurons that support conscious experience must be constantly changing and sufficiently differentiated from one another. If a large number of neurons in the brain start firing in the same way, reducing the diversity of the brain's neuronal repertoires, as is the case in deep sleep or epilepsy, consciousness disappears.*[160]

In other words, if the baby's brain doesn't create a vast range of distinct and separate neural interconnections, then it will never achieve higher consciousness, let alone enable its owner to become a high-achieving individual. A wide range and variety of neuron connections are essential.

But what role does memory play in this process? Edelman and Tononi explain:

> *In a complex brain, memory results from the selective matching that occurs between ongoing, distributed neural activity and various signals coming from the world, the body and the brain itself. The synaptic alterations that ensue affect the future responses of the individual brain to similar and different signals.*[161]

The network of neural connections within the brain is changed as that person lives in, and responds to, the environment. The changes in the brain cause new memories and new responses. This fits perfectly with Karl Pribram's comment that external events such as revisiting a place can trigger memories that you did not know you had. When you repeat the environmental stimulus, you trigger the neurons that hold the memory.

Steven Rose goes even further when he talks about the vivid picture memories that most children experience:

> *Scientific knowledge about the world comes from two types of study: the search for underlying regularities in seemingly dissimilar phenomena; and the analysis of the causes of variation—small differences in seemingly similar phenomena. Eidetic memory [vivid picture memory] is interesting for both reasons. First, because it is*

*so different from the ways in which most adults seem to remember things; by its very difference it opens up questions about what is for most of us normal memory that we would otherwise not think of asking . . . Although eidetic memory is rare in adults, it seems to be much more frequent in young children. Think back to your own early memories, and it is probable that you will recollect them as a series of snapshots, fixed or frozen in time.*[162]

My own earliest memories go back to about the age of three. At that age, on Saturdays I was looked after by my aunt. I decided to test my memories by calling her and discussing things I could remember, such as the kitchen of the house she moved out of two months after my third birthday. I could accurately describe features that I had never seen as an adult and had not been told about. This simple test confirmed the accuracy of my early memories, which, although vivid, were disjointed and unconnected. As I grew older, my memories were of more than isolated incidents; they became a continuous picture.

So my personal experience fits in with Susan Greenfield's comments that a child develops consciousness gradually over the first two or three years of independent life, not at the moment of birth. It also agrees with Karl Pribram's view that a baby has only primary consciousness, without any awareness of self, and it fits with the technical descriptions of Edelman and Tononi and of Rose. But none of this background knowledge supports astrology's view that this complex path of development is preordained. So does this mean there is nothing more than visual inspiration in the Masonic astrology that Brother George Washington adopted?

Bro. Washington was too astute a politician to have done anything without good reason. So I decided to set myself another question. As we are born with most of the neurons we will need for the rest of our lives, how does a newborn infant change its brain from a great disconnected bundle of neurons into a well-ordered network? How do all those neurons know where to link? If I understood how this happened, I could then ask if the rising of the Bright Morning Star could possibly have any influence on the process.

I returned to Susan Greenfield's writings. She says that the primary linking of neurons is driven by genetics, but fine-tuning is caused by local factors. She says that the growing neurons of this network are not "irrefutably fixed in their course." They are guided in particular directions by chemical traces. The substance that does this job is a hormone called nerve growth factor, and it is given off by neurons that want to attract links. The particular links that form are fixed by two factors: the emission of chemical growth stimulants and shared electrical activity. Electrically active neuron links grow together.[163]

There are critical development stages in this process. If a child is deprived from birth of the opportunity to hear speech, it will reach a stage where it can never acquire it, despite the inbuilt tendency to learn language that Steven Pinker has shown to be a fundamental part of human makeup.[164]

I found a good example if this in a case reported by psycholinguist Roger Brown.[165] Kamala and Amala were two children abandoned in the forests of India. They were adopted and raised by wolves. Kamala was eight when he was found, and he never learned to speak, even though he was taught to walk erect and to wear clothes. His sister died soon after being found. There are numerous cases in the literature that all agree: If children do not learn language at an early age, they never learn it.[166] There are certain stages in the development of the interconnections of your brain when you can learn particular skills. If you wait too long, you never develop the neural pathways to carry out these functions.

Linguist Eric Lenneberg said that there are critical periods of your life when you can learn certain basic things, such as how to speak, and, if you miss the chance, it never comes again.[167] And Susan Greenfield cites the case of a boy who was blind in one eye, even though the eye had nothing physically wrong with it. The eye itself worked perfectly and had all the correct reflexes to light, the optic nerve triggered when the retina was exposed to pulses of light, yet the boy was totally blind in that eye. During the first few weeks of his life he had suffered an eye infection, and his blind eye had been bandaged. During this critical period, the neurons in his brain were trying to make contact with the light-sensing cells in his eye by growing an optic nerve. As one eye was deprived of light, it was not stimulated, and his brain linked all the neurons for seeing into the eye that was not covered. He never saw anything from the eye which had been masked out at this critical period.[168]

This boy was born with both eyes capable of linking to the brain. If he had been treated for the infection without having a light-proof bandage put over his eye, then he would have developed quite differently. This outcome is confirmed by Professor Steven Rose, who says:

*The optic nerves terminate in a region deep in the brain called the lateral geniculate; there they make synapses with a set of many million neurons from which runs a set of further connections to a region of the cerebral cortex, the visual cortex . . . If the brain is to interpret images arriving at the retina of the eye, these pathways have to be organised in an orderly manner . . . The "wiring" that connects eye to brain must therefore be remarkably stable . . . How is such stability achieved, despite the tremendous changes that occur in size, cell number and experience during development? There is a lot of evidence that during early phases of brain development there is a huge overproduction, a veritable efflorescence, of synaptic connections, which are later steadily pruned back in number; redundant or irrelevant synapses are discarded, and the remainder in some way stabilised. This pruning and stabilisation process seems to be an important way in which experience modifies brain structure during development.[169]*

This is a case of natural selection of important neurons from a whole bunch of "wannabes." This process is explained by Edelman and Tononi, who noted that one of the most striking features of brains is their individuality and variability. This variability occurs at all levels of brain organization and is so diverse that it cannot be ignored. Given the evidence that similar genetic material and a common pattern of brain development produces a vast range of individual brain structures, each having a separate and distinct personality, they showed how this arises by a process of natural selection:

*[Darwin's principle of natural selection] has deep ramifications. It not only provides the basis for the origin of species, but it governs processes of somatic selection occurring in individual lifetimes. When we say somatic selection, we mean what occurs in a single body in time frames ranging from fractions of seconds to years and, obviously, ending with an animal's death. Thus, selection and variation can also occur in the cellular systems of animals.[170]*

Susan Greenfield sums up the process of brain development:

*It is the connections that are important, and the degree of stimulation from the environment will determine how the connections between neurons are formed, and thus determine your individual memories and so make you into the person you are.*[171]

It's a combination of your neural network and your personal memories that form your personality. We are what we remember. Without our memory, we cease to have a personality. The next question I wanted to research, therefore, was how does our brain make our memories?

## The Pulse of Memory

The neurons of your brain store all your memories. As I described on page 173, a neuron is a single cell split up into three separate sections: the dendrites, the cell body, and the axon. The dendrites are like the roots of a plant, and they grow out of the cell body, which contains the nucleus of the cell. Out of this tiny globular body of the cell extends a long thin cord-like structure which is frayed at the end. This is the axon, and the many frayed branches of the long stem are synapses. These synapses connect to the dendrites of other neurons. When you remember something new, your brain makes some new connections between your neurons.

The brain and the rest of the nervous system are made up of many millions of neurons, so any single neuron is quite small. Its size is measured in microns (a micron is a thousandth part of a millimeter), and a fine human hair is about 100 microns thick. Dendrites are typically a few hundred microns long, and the diameter of a cell body is between 5 and 100 microns. An axon, though, can be a meter or so long, extending from the head to the base of the spine without a break. This basic cell can therefore be rather unbalanced; some motor neurons—for example, those that make up your spinal cord—can have axons far longer then their dendrites. If you imagine the dendrites to be as long as a walking stick, then a motor neuron axon can be the equivalent of up to fourteen miles long.

The basic job of a neuron is to receive electrical signals at its dendrites and pass them on along its axon to the synapses, which link to the dendrites of other neurons. A typical neuron gives out and receives signals from between 1,000 and 10,000 other neurons.[172] A neuron transmits and receives signals using a mixture of chemical and electrical signals. The electrical potential between the inside and the outside of the cell membrane of a neuron, when it is not communicating, is about 70 thousandths of a volt (the inside of the cell is at a lower voltage than the outside, so it's called a negative voltage). A thousandth of a volt is a millivolt and is written mV. So the "rest potential" of a typical neuron is -70mV.[173] But what happens when it sends a signal?

An electrical engineer would say that a resting neuron is polarized, but when its dendrites are excited, either electrically or chemically, then a strange thing happens. As the voltage across the cell membrane drops to about -55mV (this is known as the threshold voltage), the whole system collapses, and the inside of the axon shoots up to a positive voltage. This causes an electrical pulse, which can be as high as +40 mV, that travels to the far end of the axon. There it excites the dendrites of the next neuron at the part of the cell called the synapse. (Firing off a pulse takes quite a bit of effort on the part of the neuron, and, like a male hoping to repeat the sex act, it needs to rest after this electrical ejaculation before it can do it again. )

A pulsating axon obeys what is called the "all or none" law. If the dendrites go higher than the threshold voltage, then a full-strength pulse (+40 mV) travels down the axon. If the dendrites don't get excited enough, then nothing happens.[177] The maximum pulse size of a healthy neuron stays at around +40 mV. But if it gets highly excited, then the voltage stays the same but it fires again and repeats the cycle more quickly. Neurons are quicker to recover from their ejaculations than a typical human male, and they can be ready to fire again after about a thousandth of a second. So a strong stimulus will cause the neuron to give off a train of pulses with a maximum speed of about 1,000 per second.[175] A less intense stimulus causes a slower rate of pulsing.

Memories are formed inside your brain as a repeating series of electrical pulses. But how do you store these pulses, which are finished in a thousandth of a second? Tim Bliss and Terje Lomo, of Department of Neurophysiology in the University of Oslo explained how it happens. They were studying the brain of a rabbit, which they had first anaesthetized before inserting electrodes into a part of its brain associated with memory function. They stimulated the rabbit's brain with a string of electrical pulses at the rate of between ten and one hundred per second for about ten seconds, and were surprised to find that the group of neurons kept on firing again and again for over ten hours.[176] Once a new memory link formed, that memory was literally burned into the linkage by the newly connected neurons firing over and over. A single short burst from external trigger pulses was enough to start this burn-in process running in the brain. They called the phenomenon LTP, standing for long-term potentiation. Professor Stephen Rose summarizes its properties:

> *First . . . it [LPT] occurs only in the cells to which the conditioning train is delivered, rather than spreading across to others—it is thus the result of the functioning of a network of specific connections rather than a wave of diffuse activity.*
>
> *Second . . . it requires a repetitive train of reasonably high-frequency pulses; the same number of pulses delivered more slowly is ineffective, so there is a threshold below which LTP cannot be induced . . .*
>
> *Third, and perhaps most interesting from the point of view of cellular analogies to memory, it has been shown that a form of associative LTP is possible. In this a weak input which cannot sustain LTP in its own right may be encouraged to do so if combined with a strong stimulus arriving from a second pathway.*[177]

In another experiment, rats were trained to cross a barrier on command, using a mixture of rewards and inputs of LTP-inducing pulse trains. Food was placed beyond the barrier, and when a rat crossed it to reach the food, its brain was bombarded with a train of pulses, using electro-magnetic induction. The rat could be made to repeat the learned task simply by beaming impulses at it, without offering any reward. LTP was used to create radio-controlled rats, or perhaps it could be said the rats' personalities were changed by beaming electromagnetic pulses at their brains.[178]

This phenomenon of long-term potentiation is important. A brief period of electrical exposure causes permanent changes in the connections within the brain, and by doing so creates memories.

Rose carried out a further experiment to test this idea. He taught young chicks to avoid pecking at bitter-tasting pellets. As he explains:

> *It requires only a single peck for the bird to learn . . . avoidance because the result of learning is for the bird to stop doing something it otherwise would; and it is passive*

*because the bird is not required actively to avoid, as it would if it had to escape from some unpleasant condition, but merely to refrain from pecking.[179]*

Rose let the chick create its own memory of an unpleasant taste when it pecked at a pellet. He could tell which chicks had this memory and which had not just by offering them neutral-tasting pellets to see if they pecked.

He created sample batches of chicks with and without these memories, then he looked for changes in the chicks' brains. He took batches of trained and untrained chicks, anaesthetized them, and inserted electrodes into their brains to record the electrical activity. The chicks with the memories had different patterns of electrical activity from the chicks who had not been trained.[180] The chicks that were assimilating the new memories had bursts of high-frequency pulses firing off inside their brains. This is how Rose described his results:

*This bursting activity was massively up—fourfold higher—in the trained animals than in the controls . . . The increase in bursting seemed to continue for up to twelve hours after training. It was an LTP effect, generated not by the artificial injection of current but by a behavioural experience.[181]*

As a chick creates a new memory, there is an increase in electrical activity that grows new synaptic connections and an increase in the number of active dendrites in the chick's brain. Creating memories causes a physical rewiring in the animal's brain as bursts of electrical activity form new connections. But does this mechanism also work in humans? Rose thinks it does:

*At the cellular and biochemical level neurons from the human brain are virtually indistinguishable from those of other vertebrates; there are no obviously unique human brain cell types or even brain proteins, and the physiological and organisational properties of non-human mammalian brains seem very similar . . . I thus see no good reason to oppose the proposition that when engrams [a name for how memory traces are stored as physical or biochemical changes in the brain in response to external stimuli] are formed in the human brain, their formation employs broadly the same types of biochemical mechanisms as in other vertebrates.[182]*

So science says our personality develops from a genetic predisposition modified by Darwinian somatic selection of neural pathways in early life. These connections are formed by bursts of electrical pulses called long-term potentiation. This explanation does not leave much scope to explain the morning-star patterns Gauquelin had found. I still did not know how the appearance of the Bright Morning Star in the dawn sky could affect the neural pathways of a baby's brain as it grows a personality, and I was still a long way from understanding how Masonic astrology could correlate with such a dramatic increase in the achievement motivation when the U.S. government moved to the Federal City of Washington, D.C.

## Conclusions

Babies are born with an enormous number of loosely connected neurons in their brains. As the neurons form linkages, under the influence of exposure to signals from the baby's senses and by the creation of memories, the baby develops its own personality. The process is one of strengthening links that are useful and pruning those that are not. If a neuron link does not fire regularly, it soon dies off. Experiments with animals show that memories are created by rapid chains of electrical pulses, which are usually created by the senses reacting to outside events and result in new physical links in the brain. But this process of creating new links in the brain can also be caused by beaming bursts of electromagnetic pulses at the animal's brain.

I have not yet found a mechanism which can shape a child's brain for life as it is being born. Yet all the statistical evidence I have found says that being born when the Bright Morning Star is on the dawn horizon gives that child a better chance of being successful and being more achievement-motivated. Traditional astrology is obviously wrong when it says that a child's personality is formed for life at the moment the umbilical cord is cut. But what mechanism *does* explain the accurate predictions that I have made by applying the rules of Masonic astrology? Perhaps a closer look at the electrical processes that create memories, consciousness of self, and personality would give me a better handle on this puzzle.

This investigation was leading me a long way from the rituals of Freemasonry and into unexpected areas of scientific research. But if I wanted to understand the Masonic astrology which so inspired George Washington, the electrical processes of the brain were the next thing I would have to look at.

# Chapter Nine

# Powering the Enchanted Loom

### Sparks in the Bell Jar

Your brain is vulnerable to the power of electricity. The use of electric force will change your personality forever, as the unsettling story of electroconvulsive therapy (ECT) clearly shows.

ECT is a medical process in which patients with severe depression have their brains zapped with a powerful flux of electric current. It overwhelms normal brain activity, causing an epileptic-type fit. Researchers at Dundee University found that about three-quarters of patients treated in this way report that their condition gets better.[183] This is indisputable evidence that electric current can change your state of mind, and, if that change can be made permanent, it can change your personality.

ECT began in 1930 with the work of Italian psychiatrist Ugo Cerletti. He believed that epileptic fits would help the brains of confused and disoriented patients become more ordered. Electricity was known to induce seizures, so he tried to produce epileptic fits under medically controlled conditions. First, he went to his local slaughterhouse and watched pigs being stunned and killed by an electric current through the brain before they were butchered. Next, he tried different current strengths on dogs, learning how to induce a fit without actually killing his subject. Finally, in 1938, he was ready to test his technique on a human.

His luck was in when he found a man wandering round the local railway station, mumbling incoherently. Cerletti took him back to his laboratory, strapped him down, applied electrodes to his temples, and put a rubber tube in his mouth to keep him from biting his tongue. Then he pulled the switch. The patient's muscles spasmed, but he stayed conscious long enough to spit out the rubber tube and yell, "Not again, it's murderous."

The next jolt rendered him unconscious and induced the desired fit. The man was given eight further shocks before he was released and reported to be "in good condition and well orientated." (After all, to mumble anything else might have provoked further "treatment"!)

The poet Sylvia Plath, who suffered from severe depression, described her own ECT treatment.

*"Don't worry," the nurse grinned down at me. "Their first time everybody's scared to death."*

*I tried to smile, but my skin had gone stiff, like parchment. Doctor Gordon was fitting two metal plates on either side of my head. He buckled them into place with a strap that dented my forehead and gave me a wire to bite.*

*I shut my eyes. There was a brief silence, like an in-drawn breath. Then something bent down and took hold of me and shook me like the end of the world. Whee-ee-ee-ee-ee, it shrilled, through an air crackling with blue light, and with each flash a great jolt drubbed me till I thought my bones would break and the sap fly out of me like a split plant.*

*I wondered what terrible thing it was that I had done.*[184]

Electroconvulsive therapy is a treatment of last resort for people whose personality disorders are so severe that they are unable to live with themselves. The electric current, as it pulses through the neurons of the brain, changes their personality, but it can improve their ability to live a normal life. It doesn't always work, however. Sylvia Plath committed suicide. The writer Ernest Hemingway was given a dozen shocks to try to relieve his recurrent depression, but the treatment wiped his memory; he hated his new self so much that he shot it. Evidently the human brain and the personality it houses are changed dramatically by electric current flows. Just before taking his life, Hemingway wrote in his diary:

*What is the sense in ruining my head and erasing my memory, which is my capital, and putting me out of business?* [185]

In an article in the *Sunday Times*, Professor Ronald Duncan of Yale University says that ECT makes new neural connections grow; after ECT, new neurons form, and existing ones sprout new connections. Professor Ian Read of Dundee University added that severe depression damages neurons, and that successful antidepressant treatments cause neurons to regenerate and relink. He said, "some of the treatments that people think of as rather crude, such as ECT, are in fact effective rescuers of the dying neuron."[186]

If you lose too much of your memory to disease, then your personality also goes. The film made about the last days of the novelist Iris Murdoch showed this in touching but horrific detail. What ever else it might do, ECT affects memory. I was now convinced that externally applied electric current changes the way the neurons connect to each other, and this changes both memory and personality.

Electrical activity in the brain of a young child seems far more important in creating a personality than the positions of the stars. But knowing this just makes explaining the statistical effect of the Bright Morning Star harder to explain. I needed to know more about the electrical processes of brain growth.

## The Electric Brain Maze

I decided to study the neuron in greater depth. It is a cell like any other in the body and is completely enveloped by a membrane. Like other cells, the genetic material of its nucleus is lodged in cytoplasm, and its metabolic power is derived from mitochondria. But, as we've seen, neurons have special features. As a neuron grows, it sends out two types of extensions from its membrane that create connecting threads to other neurons: One type is a single filament, which can be very long and is called the axon, while the others look like the branches of a tree and are called dendrites. Neurons pass electric current in one direction only; the current enters through the dendrites and leaves through the axon. It is this tangle of electrically conducting threads that make the cells of our brain different from those of the other organs of our body, such as the heart or the kidneys.

Within the brain, there are two classes of neuron. The first type is called a projection neuron. These have lots of dendrites that connect with adjacent neurons, and an axon that terminates far away in other parts of the brain.

Projection neurons can grow axons over 3.28 feet (a meter) long, and they provide long-distance signaling to more remote parts of the brain, or even to other parts of the body. The second type of neuron is called an interneuron. Both its dendrites and axon are shorter, so they terminate locally. Professor of Brain Science at the University of California, Walter Freeman, describes their function:

*These two types of neurons could be compared to road systems. The interneuron is like the local streets, providing connections within a neighborhood of neurons, whereas the projection neuron, like a system of main roads, provides the long distance connections across the brain and to the spinal cord.*[187]

Each neuron receives inputs from many other neurons, and sends its output to the input-dendrites of many other neurons. When an axon joins with a dendrite, it forms a synapse.

Neurons have two main jobs, to excite or inhibit. Excitatory neurons increase the current flow to their targets, while inhibitory ones reduce the current flowing through their targets. Excitatory neurons turn up the intensity of your thoughts, whereas inhibitory neurons damp them down. Projection neurons are usually excitatory; interneurons can be of either type.

Any single neuron can have thousands of synapses attached to the branches of its dendritic tree. Freeman explains how they work together.

*The growth of dendritic trees continuously adds new surface area for more contacts, not only in childhood but also into adult life, even into healthy old age. Axons and their lateral branches also grow and divide, connecting with other neurons. The competition for synaptic space is intense, and success in finding and maintaining a connection depends on the synapses being active. If they are inactive, owing to damage or disuse, the connections decay and the synapses disappear. Even the neurons may vanish. The health of neural connections in old age, like muscles, requires exercise. The lifelong growth and maintenance of active connections provide the basis for learning, remembering and adapting through modifications of the numbers and strengths of synapses, and they require daily exercise.*[188]

The brain is a congregation of neurons that keep triggering each other. Consciousness and personality arise from the complex conversation of electrical signals this population generates. But how do they arise?

A newborn baby starts life with a large bundle of unconnected neurons, no memories, and little personality. During the first months of life outside the womb, its neurons make connections. As the web of connections gets more and more dense, higher consciousness, self-awareness, memory, and personality appear.

By now I was quite sure that this blooming of personality is not caused by the magical intervention of mysterious astrological "rays." The more I found out about the way personality is formed, the less likely it appeared that it could be the result of the process suggested by Michel Gauquelin:

> *The child who is about to enter the world carries on an obscure dialogue with the planetary gods.*[189]

All the same, despite Gauquelin's failure to explain his results, I am convinced that the beneficial effect of the Bright Morning Star is as real as any statistical hypothesis can be. But what is it that causes the effect? Where do these high-achieving personalities come from?

## A Visit to Brain City

The brain works like a great city. Imagine it as a vast community of specialized individuals (neurons) all living together in this city, each carrying out its own separate and independent occupation. They have local communities, each with connecting streets and pavements, where people meet and shop; they have trunk roads that connect the different neighborhoods of the city together. Butchers, bakers, and electric-light-bulb-makers all toil away at their own jobs, making sure that all the needs of the city are supplied. Some groups, like nurses and sanitation workers, carry out their tasks day and night every day of the year, to make sure that we stay healthy and don't drown in our own waste. Others, such as stockbrokers and merchant bankers, work only during the hours of daylight and sleep at other times.

Rumors waft through this city. When the news spreads that the latest pop sensations are giving a free concert in Central Park, people surge into the park to listen to the music. And when night falls, the people go home to rest, leaving only essential workers to toil on through the night. The structure of the city grows and changes to accommodate the people who want to live in it. Old, worn-out buildings are knocked down; new offices and shops are built to replace them. As traffic density increases, new roads are built to carry the citizens between their homes and places of work. Old, unused networks of local roads, which once served rows of houses now empty and neglected, are erased, and new avenues are built.

When one watches a film of a city in speeded-up time, the city appears as a living being. Yet its macro-activity is nothing more than the sum of the micro-activities of the many individuals who live there. So it is with the brain. Each neuron sits in its place, its dendrites continually receiving trigger pulses, and its axon sending a pulse of its own when it becomes excited enough. Watching a single neuron is like watching the actions of a single person within a city: it tells us very little. We see only the mundane regular routine, and get no impression of the vibrant city life that this individual takes part in and contributes to.

To get a real overview of a living city, we need to watch how the communities within it react with each other. If we look at groups of individuals, we can use mathematical techniques to work out how they relate to each other. It is the same when trying to understand the brain. Walter Freeman of the University of California found that the apparently chaotic behavior of any individual neuron can be analyzed when enough of them form a group. There are billions of neurons interacting in a human brain, and they form what he calls a nonlinear dynamic system. This complexity allows him to use statistical analysis tools to predict how the neurons will behave as a group.

Returning to the city analogy, imagine that you are watching from a helicopter hovering above the city at the time when the schools all finish for the day. You will see the movements of all the school buses and car-driving mothers on the school run briefly causing the roads around schools to become crowded until the children have all been collected and the roads return to normal. Dr. Freeman would call the schools "point attractors," but he is speaking in mathematical language, so to make his idea clear I will try to explain it in non-mathematical terms.

## Of Pots and Woks and Memories

Let's begin by visualizing a physical model of a point attractor. Imagine that you have a conical pot, or a very steep sided wok, and a marble. If you toss the marble into the pot, it will roll around for a while but will always settle at the bottom. If you repeat the experiment, each time the marble will travel over a different path but it will always settle at the lowest point of the container. That low point is the "point attractor," and the various paths that the marble follows as it rolls towards that bottom point are what Freeman called "itinerant trajectories of brain activity."

He discusses a "state transition between attractors," which you can visualize by imagining two conical pots, side by side. If you throw your marble into the first pot very hard, it is possible for it to bounce out of that one and to fly into the second one, where it will run round and finally settle to the bottom. The surplus energy that made the marble fly out of the first pot into the other one causes the "state transition" from the state of being attracted by the lowest point of pot 1 to the state of being attracted to the lowest point of pot 2. A thought in the brain is similar to a marble bouncing across a whole landscape pitted with woks, all of which are trying to capture it so that it rolls towards their particular bottom. Freeman calls this "a landscape of attractors," and these craters in the brainscape are where our memories are stored.

Freeman had one more comment on how a brain becomes conscious:

*Neurons initially grow from embryonic cells that divide and multiply in very large numbers to give densely packed spherical cells. When the axons and dendrites begin to grow, they extend rapidly with prolific branching between the cell bodies. Many neurons die if they fail to make adequate connections. Even so, in the adult cortex, the density of cell bodies is so high that there are typically a million or more other neurons within the radius of the dendritic arbor of a given neuron . . .*

*The initial connections between neurons in the embryonic cortex seem to form blindly, based on chance encounters between cells . . . as the axons and dendrites branch and extend. The strengths of connections are maintained by continuous activity at low levels, while the cortex waits for changes in synaptic strength to be made with learning and habitual use.[190]*

Now, armed with a basic explanation of how the adult brain creates thoughts—by stimulating or inhibiting different communities of neurons within the brain—I could return to the question of how these densely interconnected groups of neurons grow out of the unlinked bundles of newly hatched neurons of the newborn child.

I next consulted a textbook on behavioral neurology. This is what it said:

> *There is strong evidence that environmental influences at certain stages of life can produce permanent changes within the nervous system . . . The immature nervous system is highly susceptible to change.*
>
> *The number of nerve cells does not substantially change after birth, yet the brain increases in size tremendously during the first year of life and does not complete this spurt of growth until adolescence.*[191]

This confirmed that the brain forms its personality in the early years of life, as it becomes conscious. It does not happen at the moment of "cutting the cord," as the astrologers would like me to believe, and there is no scientific support for any mechanism facilitating Gauquelin's "obscure dialogue with the planetary gods."

But my quest to understand Masonic astrology was leading me towards the mystical question of consciousness.

## I Am, Therefore I Think

Everybody reading this book knows what consciousness is. It's more than just being alive. It's what you lose when you fall asleep and what pops back into your mind when you wake up the following morning. But knowing what it is and being able to define it scientifically are very different things.

Consciousness was first studied in 1641 by the French philosopher René Descartes. He published his thoughts in a book called *Meditations on First Philosophy*, and his definition of consciousness was in Latin: *Cogito ergo sum* (I think, therefore I am). He also invented the idea of "the ghost in the machine." This he imagined to be the immortal soul, a sort of *homunculus* that was the thinking essence of a human being. The soul made humans different from other animals. It was responsible for self-awareness and was something mystical, to be found outside the brain. It was supposed to communicate with the body through the pineal gland in the center of the brain.

Believers in a soul find no support for their conviction in modern consciousness research, though. One leading researcher in this area, the philosopher Daniel Dennett, calls Descartes's idea "the hopelessly contradiction-riddled myth of the distinct, separate soul."[192]

But if I have no soul, and there is no "me" inside my head controlling my brain and my body, this raises two questions. How did consciousness arise within the chemically modulated electrical network of my brain? And how do the internal mechanics of my consciousness create my personality?

Somehow, the largely unconnected tangle of neurons that I was born with have changed into the highly ordered, interlinked structure of my adult brain. The process seems as mysterious and elusive as the change from a caterpillar to a butterfly. A newborn baby's brain is like the body of a caterpillar, made up of billions of individually striving neurons, but all of them are eating experience rather than leaves. During the early years of life, this caterpillar brain turns into a self-conscious butterfly, a wonderfully ordered thinking machine that Professor Freeman can describe with his mathematical neurodynamics. It is an organ that can sustain consciousness, and my personality has grown out of its immature incoherent muddle. I can sympathize with Descartes for wanting to avoid asking how this can be. He took the easy way out and blamed God for making the soul in a mysterious and inexplicable way. However, I find his answer no better than Gauquelin's invocation of a conversation with a workforce of planetary gods.

The only scientific candidate for explaining this process is somatic selection. This is how Dr. Edelman of the Neurosciences Research Foundation describes this concept of Neuronal Darwinism:

*Whatever the specialness of the human brain, there is no need to invoke spiritual forces to account for its functions. Darwinian principles of variation in populations and natural selection are sufficient, and the elements invoked by spiritualism are not required for our being conscious. Being human in mind and brain appears clearly to be the result of an evolutionary process . . .*

*Darwinian principles turn out to be important even for a basic understanding of brain functions, especially given the enormous variation in the structure and function of individual vertebrate brains. No two brains are alike, and each individual's brain is continually changing. Variations extend over all levels of brain organisation, from biochemistry to gross morphology, and the strengths of myriad individual synapses are constantly altered by experience. The extent of this enormous variability argues strongly against the notion that the brain is organised like a computer with fixed codes and registers. Moreover, the environment or world from which signals are delivered to the brain is not organised to give an unambiguous message like a piece of computer tape. There is no judge in nature giving out specific pronouncements on the brain's potential or actual patterns, and there is no homunculus inside the head deciding which pattern should be chosen and interpreted.[193]*

I have already described how the light receptors of the eye have to be stimulated to connect to the paths of the brain that process vision. This means that external stimulation is essential for a child's brain to develop. The process involves far more than the axons of the optic nerve simply chasing the scent of the neuron growth hormones towards the relevant parts of the brain. There is a genetic component that causes a basic linking of the nerves connecting the senses to relevant areas of the brain before birth.[194] Yet the creation of vision through these nerves depends entirely on electrical contact being made. Neurons need to fire electrically, before they make a physical linkage. This implies that electrical activity plays a major role in the transition from an uncomprehending baby to a conscious adult personality and is summed it in a phrase I have heard many neuroscientists use. "Neurons which fire together, wire together."

Brain scientist Susan Greenfield explains how a fetus becomes conscious:

*Clearly we cannot expect a fetus, locked away in its black, wet, warm world, and hearing distant and meaningless noises via its mother's abdominal wall, to have the same consciousness as we adults . . .*

*The problem of [understanding] fetal and non-human consciousness is caused, I suggest, by an unnecessary and false assumption that consciousness either is on or off, there or not there. Perhaps a better way to consider consciousness could be to view it as a continuum: not as a sudden blinding light but rather as a dimmer switch.*

*This switch could vary from almost imperceptible light, say, the consciousness of invertebrates, to the floodlit brilliance of adult human consciousness. Quite simply, consciousness could grow in degree as brains do. It seems to make sense, then, that a pivotal property of consciousness is that you can have more or less of it: a continuum. If consciousness is continuously variable as we grow, there is no reason why it should become static once we are mature. If consciousness is variable then it should also be able to expand not just during childhood, from one moment to the next.[195]*

No way is this a description of personality being formed at the moment of "cutting the cord." In Greenfield's view:

*We start simply enough, with neurons getting on with their daily life in a way that is already well understood . . . Such networks of cells, formed after birth and reflecting individual experiences, are the most plausible physical basis for personalizing the brain into an idiosyncratic conglomeration of experiences, generalizations, prejudices, and propensities: a mind.*
*This mind grows slowly as a life story takes shape and persists throughout nightly ruptures in awareness.[196]*

But she stops short of trying to work out an exact moment when consciousness starts and personality appears, simply saying:

*Different brain regions to greater or lesser extents all play a part in what is largely still a mysterious final co-ordination within the holistic brain.[197]*

Brain-wave activity in unborn fetuses has been recorded. Consistent neuron firing activity starts at about eleven weeks. The brain-wave patterns show activity similar to an adult brain experiencing rapid eye movement sleep.[198] Newly forming pre-infants dream their brains towards connections that will form their personality. The neurons, nudged by the genetic release of neural growth hormone, form sensory networks between their growing bodies and their dreaming brains.

How does Darwinian selection drive this process? Darwin's theory assumes differences, followed by the natural selection of any that offer an advantage. At first sight, this process does not seem able to guarantee a smooth transition from unconnected bundle of neurons to smoothly coordinated brain.

The process that takes the dreaming, yet separate, neurons of the unborn child and weaves them into the seamless personality of the adult is complex. Small wonder Gauquelin wanted to invoke "planetary gods" to control the mysterious process his statistics revealed to him. But I have a different problem. I am looking for an "unknown" factor, preferably within the laws of physics, that links the growth of achieving personalities with the Bright Morning Stars—rising high-gravity planets. I am not prepared to accept that it is something that science cannot explain.

Natural selection seems to be the only game in town that can hope to explain the statistical effects found by Sachs, McClelland, and Gauquelin. But how does it work?

As I was puzzling over this problem, I remembered a discussion I had with Professor Archie Roy over a late-night cup of coffee in the Kirkwall Hotel in September 2000. (Earlier in the evening we had shared the stage in the Orkney Arts Theatre to give a joint lecture on "The Megalith Builders" as part of the annual Science Festival.) I knew Archie had spent a lot of time investigating the paranormal, and I was curious why such a distinguished astronomer would get involved in what I rather scathingly called "fringe" activities. His reply surprised me. He said that it wasn't his job as a scientist to prejudge the outcome of any investigation. He just applied all the scientific techniques at his disposal to impartially study unusual phenomena, in case there was a rational explanation.

Remembering Archie's impartial curiosity inspired me to keep searching for a rational explanation. I returned to the problem of how the neurons of a growing brain work out how to wire themselves up, even though the enchanted loom of the brain seemed an extremely tangled puzzle to unravel.

## Inside the Enchanted Loom

It was Oxford physiologist Sir Charles Sherrington who first described the brain as an enchanted loom. I was now fast becoming convinced that the evolutionary success of the human brain is based entirely on its ability to adapt to the environment into which its owner is born. But what was not clear to me was exactly how it manages to weave such a successful pattern.

As we have seen, the process of natural selection that grows a self-aware brain is based on the well-established idea that "neurons that fire together, wire together." The converse of this is that neurons that are not stimulated on a regular basis—at least every few seconds—wither and die. This concept is confirmed by the work of three professors of psychology based at the universities of Berkeley and Washington: Alison Gopnik, Andrew Meltzoff, and Patricia Kuhl. After spending many years studying the way children's thinking processes develop, they determined that when a baby is born, each neuron in its cerebral cortex has around 2,500 synapses (i.e., links to other neurons). By the time the child reaches the age of two to three years, he has grown 15,000 synapses per neuron, which is many more than are found in the average adult brain.[199] At this time, the average number of neurons in his brain is about 100 billion ($1 \times 10^{10}$).

I decided to see how long it would take me to count these individual connections if I did it reasonably quickly, say at the rate of one a second. If each neuron has 15,000 ($1.5 \times 10^4$) connections, this gives the number of possible separate interconnections as 100 billion raised to the power of 15,000, or about ($1 \times 10^{40}$), that is: 10,000,000,000,000,000,000,000,000,000,000,000,000,000.

This number is mind-blowingly big. There are 31,557,600 seconds in a year, so if I count one possible connection every second, without stopping to rest, I can count them all in just three billion, billion, billion years! Unfortunately, that is one million, billion times longer than the age of the Universe. This presents a formidable design task. If some supernatural brain-designer lists the vast number of possible ways of wiring the connections of the child's brain, then tests the behavioral outcomes before finalizing an individual personality connection pattern, this super-engineer must be able to count up and decide very quickly indeed.

The task is well beyond human skill, and even beyond any electronic computing capability in existence. If I could get the research funds to build a Beowulf cluster of a million Cray super-computers, each with a computing power greater than that of Deep Thought, the computer with a brain the size of a small planet in *The Hitchhiker's Guide to the Galaxy*, it still wouldn't have any chance of doing the sums in time. And even attempting the job would bankrupt all the world's research councils.

As I did these rough sums, I was amazed at the complexity and flexibility implied by this fantastic degree of interconnection. Preschool children have brains that are more active, more connected, and more flexible than any adult's. Gopnik, Meltzoff, and Kuhl explain:

*Cells grow in different parts of the brain. In order to influence one another, these cells have to talk one to another . . . Rather than waiting, like the passive computer, for a technician to hook them up, they physically grow their own connections to other cells.*

*New techniques allow neuroscientists to closely examine the brain's cells during their early embryonic development, when the brain begins its primitive wiring. This research shows that the wiring is activity-dependent: brain cells get connected by sending out electrical signals. Even before birth, brain cells are spontaneously firing, sending off bursts of electricity and trying to signal one another . . . Groups of cells send signals in waves trying to reach other cells. Cells that fire at the same time grow connections to one another (a favorite phrase of neuroscientists is "Cells that fire together wire together"). Evidently, cells want to be in touch with others who respond to them . . .*

*This pattern of growing and connecting cells isn't completely random, but it's also far from predetermined. Studies of animals show that some instructions are laid down by the genes, like the basic telephone trunk lines laid between cities. Cells in the retina of the eye do send connections out toward the visual areas in the back of the brain, rather than to the language centers on the sides of the brain. But, beyond that, the wiring depends on activity . . .*

*As cells signal to one another, they lay down these more permanent connections . . . Making these permanent connections is what brain cells live for. As a cell matures, it sends out multiple branches trying to make contact with other cells . . . When two neurons form a synapse chemicals can flow between them and the connection is complete.*[200]

With such a large number of possibilities inherent in a newborn brain, natural selection is the only way to form a working personality. Any possible design and implementation of a neural interconnection diagram would take too long, even for "planetary gods" with awesome powers. Once childhood ends, though, most of the early connections have withered and died, along with our dreams of wanting to be a steam train driver. Gopnik, Meltzoff, and Kuhl describe the process of growing a personality as analogous to pruning a fruit tree. By halting the growth of some branches you encourage growth in others, and so optimize the fruit yield. But it is important not to carry this analogy too far: I don't want to equip Gauquelin's "planetary gods" with pruning shears and let them loose on my children's enchanted looms.

In practice, what happens is far simpler. The neurons that survive in the adult personality are those that fire together most frequently during the first years of life. With this new insight, I returned to Edelman and Tononi and found that they support this concept. They, however, stated it with far more technical precision than I have done. This is what they said:

*All selectional systems share a remarkable property that is as unique as it is essential to their functioning. In such systems, there are typically many different ways, not necessarily structurally identical, by which a particular output occurs. We call this property degeneracy . . .*

*Put briefly, degeneracy is reflected in the capacity of structurally different components to yield similar outputs or results. In a selectional nervous system, with its enormous repertoire of variant neural circuits even within one brain area, degeneracy is inevitable. Without it, a selectional system, no matter how rich its diversity, would rapidly fail—in a species, almost all mutations would be lethal; in an immune system, too few antibody variants would work; and in the brain, if only one network path was available, signal traffic would fail.*[201]

Somatic selection is a sensible mechanism for growing different personalities. Functionally similar clusters of neurons develop all over the brain. These groups contribute different responses to meeting behavioral objectives, such as surviving, mating, feeding, and so on. The responses of these groups are reinforced when the individual reacts appropriately to the environment, and so learns to repeat that response. In such cases, the frequently accessed neuronal connections prosper, while less popular ones die away. But what role can the Masonic Bright Morning Star play in this process?

## Conclusions

The brain is electrically powered, and its memories and personality can be changed by passing electric current through it. If a neuron does not continually communicate with its fellow neurons it dies, so neurons that fire together wire together, and those that fail to communicate wither into nothingness. Our consciousness arises around groups of attractor points, which are communities of neurons that behave rather like holes in a flat plane: Our thoughts can either drop into one or bounce from hole to hole.

Our personality grows as our experiences stimulate some neural pathways and allow others to die. Each personality is a result of the history of stimulations its brain received as it grew. The number of possible links is so high that only a natural selection process can choose among the many genetically possible combinations. In this way, a personality develops. This rules out completely the explanation of traditional astrology that a child's personality is fully determined by the positions of the stars at the moment of birth.

But if I want to understand Brother George Washington, I need to explain the statistics of Masonic astrology. Only if the rising of the Bright Morning Star can influence the formation of these neuron clusters in a child's brain can it have a role in the creation of personality. But, since I have ruled out the influence of "benign rays," the only external mechanism I can find that can change these connections is electricity. So I must investigate how external electromagnetic waves might have an impact on the brain. None of the heavy-gravity objects that appear in the statistics as Bright Morning Stars emit radio waves, so how can the time of their rising relative to the sun matter? External electromagnetic pulses can interact with the electrical system of the brain, but how can rising planets cause electric pulses?

The clue to this puzzle came from an epileptic dog, as we'll see in the next chapter.

# Chapter Ten

# Tides, Telephones, and the Phases of the Moon

### The Periodicity of Pi

For many years, my wife has kept a small pack of dogs. The habit started with a single puppy, then she began to add to her collection. The pack size has stabilized at three dogs and a cat, and is organized by age. It is based around one old grumpy dog, who sits in his basket and growls at the other two; one mature dog (the top dog), who runs around chasing balls and getting wet and muddy and stealing any toys or bones the grumpy old dog manages to smuggle into his basket; and one young puppy, whose function is to be subservient to the other dogs while being as noisy and messy around the house as possible. The chief ambition of the puppy's life is to torment the cat. The occupants of each of these roles change every five or six years or so. When the grumpy old dog dies, the mature one inherits its role in the pack, the puppy matures and moves up to top dog, and my wife goes out and gets another pup to make sure the cat doesn't get complacent.

In the middle of 2000 she had a border collie pup filling the role of general nuisance. About six months earlier, when she brought him home, he seemed to delight in running around in tight circles, so we named him Pi. My wife was pleased with him; she kept telling me that he was shaping up to be a nice dog with a friendly temperament and an easygoing disposition. However, around dawn in the light mornings of early June, he started to disturb us.

The three dogs, Domino, the old grumpy Jack Russell terrier; Gelert, a Welsh Corgi who was top dog; and Pi, the pup, woke up soon after first light and squabbled. Whatever the disputes were about, it soon became clear that young Pi was getting the worst of them. On a couple of occasions when I went down to calm things down, I found Pi lying on his back in the middle of the kitchen floor with the others piled on top of him, growling and snapping. When I called the other dogs off, Pi seemed a little groggy on his feet but otherwise none the worse for the tussle.

We were at a loss to understand what was happening, but assumed that the pup must be starting to mature and chancing his luck with the older dogs. We decided to let them sort out their own pecking order, as we knew from past experience that such disputes don't take too long to settle down. But we were wrong. The dawn scuffles were the beginning of something much more serious, which would soon flare up into a condition that needed urgent treatment and would open a window into the workings of Pi's brain.

On the morning of June 20, 2000, we were awakened by the noise of scuffling dogs coming from the kitchen. Once again, when they were separated, Pi looked a little shaken by the brawl. But this morning was different. Later on, my wife and daughter set off with the three dogs for their morning walk. Pi dashed off in front of the others, rushing to be first down the rough track towards the narrow footbridge across a stream. The others chased after him, but even as an eight-month-old pup he had the longest legs and was first there. As my wife followed the dogs down the track, she heard what sounded like a serious dog fight. Rushing after them, she found the other two dogs attacking Pi, who seemed to be extremely agitated. His eyes were glazed and he was drooling and making a strange howling sound. As my wife went towards the melee, she called off the two older dogs, who obeyed her.

Pi just lay there howling and writhing—he seemed to be having some sort of fit. My wife went over to him and tried to reach his collar to put him on a lead, but as she did so he clamped his jaws onto her finger. Now my wife was howling along with Pi, but my daughter managed to get a lead around the dog's neck and pull him off.

Aggressive conduct was totally out of character for Pi. My wife said afterwards, "He didn't seem to be my dog at all! His eyes were glazed and he was moving in a jerky way and making a strange howling noise, like nothing I've ever heard before."

They all returned home, and we applied first aid to her injured finger. By now, Pi seemed to have recovered from the attack and was back to his normal friendly self. But we were concerned about his odd and dangerous behavior, and decided that we needed expert advice. My old friend Kevan Judge is a senior partner in Shearbridge Veterinary Hospital in Bradford. I called him and told him what had happened. He asked me to bring Pi up to his office.

After Kevan had examined Pi, I asked him what he thought the problem was.

"I think he's suffering from a type of epilepsy which causes psychomotor seizures," he said. "I'll need to do a few more tests to confirm it. Can you leave him with me?"

I left Pi at the veterinary hospital, and Kevan rang a couple of days later to confirm his diagnosis. I asked him if he could cure the problem and, for once, he was a little uncertain.

"I can give you anticonvulsant tablets which will control his fits, but I'm not sure if they can actually be cured," he said. "The tablets are slightly toxic, so I don't like giving too high a dose of them to a healthy dog. I'll start him on a low dosage. What you'll have to do is get him to sleep separately from the other dogs in case he has any more fits."

"Why does he need to sleep separately," I asked. "It not catching is it?"

"No, but the other dogs will go for him if he fits."

"Why's that?" I asked.

"He be bucking the pack hierarchy and won't stop when the older dogs warn him off. So they'll end up attacking him to keep pack discipline, particularly if there's no human there to stop them."

"We'll keep him separate," I promised.

I already knew a bit about epilepsy, as I had once employed a data-entry clerk who suffered occasional epileptic attacks of a type known as *petit mal*, in which sufferers lose awareness of their surroundings for a few minutes. A number of other people worked in the same office, and they all knew about her condition. She had explained to us what to do if she "went blank." The nearest person was to squeeze her hand tightly and speak her name until she answered them. She said that these attacks didn't happen often, but we must be careful to make sure she didn't get hold of the fingers of any person helping her, because once, while having an attack, she tried to braid the fingers of her father's hand and broke one of them.

During attacks, she lost all awareness of who, what, and where she was. "It's as if my mind dissolves into bubbles of fizz," was how she described it.

During the five years she worked for me, she was a conscientious and reliable worker. She had only three *petit mal* attacks during that time, but I happened to be near her when one of them happened. At first I thought she was just pre-occupied with the data on the screen of the computer terminal she was using. She was staring intently at the screen and rocking slowly backwards and for-wards in her seat. As soon as I realized what was happening, I took one of her hands, which were lying limply on the keyboard and causing the computer to bleep in protest.

She did not respond. As I looked into her eyes, it was as if there was nobody "in there." Her normally lively eyes had a vacant and glazed look. There was no intelligence motivating the twitching movements of her face.

I squeezed her hand and spoke her name. As I did so, I saw expression begin to seep back into her eyes, and her normal personality returned to control her facial expression. During the attack, it was as if her personality was switched off and she became a mindless zombie. I had seen a similar vacant look in Pi's eyes on those mornings when I rushed down to separate the scuffling dogs.

Epilepsy can be controlled in humans, and Kevan thought it could be con-trolled in Pi. We began by giving him a daily tablet and keeping a close eye on him. My wife offered to keep a record of any future fits.

This is how I came to look more closely at the phenomenon of epilepsy, and to notice a correlation between the phase of the moon and Pi's condition.

**What Is Epilepsy?**

Epilepsy is a chaotic electrical state of the brain. When Pi's eyes glazed over, as he rolled on the floor, foamed at the mouth, and thrashed helplessly around, an electrical storm was taking place in his brain.

During an epileptic attack, the brain produces epileptic waves that vibrate at three cycles per second; on an electroencephalogram (EEG) these brain waves have a distinctive spiky shape. Parts of Pi's brain acted as centers of attraction for the 3-cycles-per-second epileptic waves and multiplied them throughout his head. The epileptic waves started in some groups of neurons that were easily excited and spread until the whole brain vibrated at the same frequency.[202]

According to epilepsy experts Drs. Jonathan Pincus and Gary Tucker, the symptoms this produces are:

*lip-smacking, chewing, gagging, retching, or swallowing. Some patients may perform a variety of complicated acts that seem to blend with normal behaviour. Usually the behaviour is inappropriate. A few patients may assume bizarre positions. Some patients have fugue states. Fortunately, outbursts of aggressive behaviour are extremely rare, but these outbursts can occur. Often the patient is not responsible for his actions.*[203]

Poor Pi had all these symptoms. But why had he never shown any warning signs as a pup? The medical textbooks say that, in children, symptoms of most kinds of epilepsy do not appear before three months, and if they are going happen they will begin before the age of twelve months. They also added that these effects could be spotted in the irregular EEG patterns of these children before their first fit.[204] The neurons of the brain have to form a large enough number of links before the epilepsy can appear. If the interconnections of your brain are too simple, you won't suffer from it. This explained Pi's behavior. He had shown no symptoms before the series of spasms started in early June 2000 when he was six months old.

Kevan asked us to keep a close watch on Pi's behavior while he was taking a low dosage of anticonvulsants to see if he had any more fits. For a week or so all seemed to be well, then he had another slight fit, which was so mild that, if we hadn't been watching for it, we would have assumed he was dreaming. This didn't seem too serious, so Kevan told us to keep Pi under observation. For the next few weeks he had no problems, and then he had another series of the "dreaming"-type attacks while he was sleeping by the fire. This went on for about four or five months. The pattern was that about every four weeks or so, Pi would have slight fits and then would be fit-free for another few weeks.

While I was checking our kitchen calendar, I noticed a periodic pattern to the days Pi had suffered slight fits. The pattern looked to be just shorter than a calendar month. When I counted the lapsed days between Pi's attacks, I found it was an exact lunar month. After noting the dates and checking the phases of the moon, the pattern stood out. Pi's attacks were occurring when the moon was full.

I had no idea what was causing this periodicity, and when I mentioned it to Kevan he said he'd look at his records and see if anybody else's dog showed a similar pattern. A few days later he rang to say that he'd checked out the other dogs that his practice was treating for epilepsy, and he'd found out when their owners had brought them in for treatment after attacks. There seemed to be a tendency for the attacks to be around the full moon. As there were too few incidents to make the result statistically significant, he has now started to keep more detailed records about epilepsy to try to build up a larger sample of the time pattern of attacks. At the time of writing, the full-moon pattern is strong, but the sample size is not yet large enough to decide if it is significant.

This link between Pi's epileptic attacks and the full moon started me looking to see if there was any scientific evidence of animal behavior linked to the movements of the moon. I soon found that there was.

## Dancing to the Rhythm of the Heavens

The late Giorgio Piccardi, Professor of Chemistry at the University of Florence, specialized in looking at small changes in chemical processes, with a particular interest in water. He found an unexpected link between the effectiveness of a well-known boiler-cleaning technique and the weather on the surface of the sun, which led him to decide that the sun was somehow adding small amounts of energy into a delicate chemical process. At a conference held in Brussels in 1960, he said that some delicately balanced systems "respond to every external stimulus, even a little amount of energy."[205]

Piccardi was interested in the problem of removing boiler scale (a coating of calcium- or lime-scale deposits in the pipes of steam boilers). It is well known that flowing water creates an electrical field; in fact, during the First World War, a device was patented that used a high-powered jet of water to create an electric charge to set off landmines. And it has long been a standard safety procedure, when using a high-pressure water hose to clean out oil tanker bilges, to ground the hose nozzle to avoid the sparks generated by the fast flow of water, which could set fire to oil vapor.

Water molecules are made up of three atoms—two of hydrogen and one of oxygen. Normally water molecules are electrically neutral, as they consist of a balanced number of positive and negative charges. However, in some circumstances the water molecule can lose an electron and show an electric charge to the outside world.

Water is not a perfect substance—it has been poetically described as "a liquid that still remembers the crystalline form of the ice from which it originates"[206]—and Piccardi found this property had a use in removing lime scale from boiler pipes. A container of water can be made to behave as if it is a single molecule, although in this state its balance of hydrogen and oxygen atoms is unstable. Water that has been arranged in this way is known as "activated" water, and activated water can be supercooled, which means that its temperature can be reduced well below the normal freezing point of water without its turning to ice. If the super-cooled liquid is then disturbed by vibrating it, the change to ice is instantaneous.

Activated water is also far better at dissolving lime scale than ordinary water, and for this reason it has been intensively studied. The individual molecules of water are aligned using an electrical field, but the consistency of water's effect on lime scale is affected by the periodic variations in the earth's magnetic field, as Piccardi noticed when trying to improve the descaling process.[207] The chemical properties of activated water are identical to those of unactivated water, but, as long as the ranks of hydrogen atoms in activated water remain aligned, they neutralize the electrical fields bonding the calcareous deposits to the pipes and dissolve them more easily. However, Piccardi found that sometimes his activated water did not work, so he carried out tests to find out why.

He noticed that the chemical reactions took place at different rates according to when and where the tests were carried out. Eventually he discovered that the changes were linked to the degree of electromagnetic shielding, the altitude above sea level, and the latitude. It was changes in the strength of solar radiation that reduced the ability of his activated water samples to dissolve lime scale. So the activated water was responding, and changing, according to the state of the weather on sun's surface.

Dr. Frank Brown, a biologist at Northwestern University in Evanston, Illinois (near Chicago), approached the question of extraterrestrial influence on natural processes form a rather different angle. He did a whole series of tests to see how the phase of the moon affected animals. Oysters are well known for opening and closing their shells according to the state of the tide, and Brown knew from the work of Newton that the state of the tide is dependent on the position of the moon in its orbit. So the oyster was the first creature he looked at.

Brown had a number of oysters taken from the sea at Long Island Sound. They were packed in closed light-proof water containers and shipped out to his laboratory at Northwestern University, which is quite close to Lake Michigan but a thousand miles from the sea. Brown kept the oysters in constant low-level lighting and timed when they opened and closed their shells. There was no tide in their boxes, but for a while they continued to open and close in time with the tidal flows of Long Island Sound. Then, over a period of fifteen days, they shifted until they were opening and closing in time with the movements of the moon over Evanston.

The oysters were not using the flow of water passing over them to time their daily activity, but were sensing the position of the moon directly. They were moving in time with the nonexistent tidal flow that the moon *would* have caused in Evanston, had the town been on the coast.[208] Evanston had no tides, so the oysters were dancing to the movements of the moon.

Thinking that perhaps only simple creatures can sense the position of the moon, Brown carried out studies on more intelligent creatures. He used rats and hamsters. He kept the rats in an area which had constant light, even temperature, and unvarying atmospheric pressure. Then he recorded when the rats were active and when they slept. They had no way of knowing what time of day or night it was outside the laboratory, but the rats settled into a steady pattern of activity that was keyed into the position of the moon in the sky.

Over a period of many months, the rats were at their most active in the six hours between the moon's rising and when it was right overhead.[209] This lunar day is fifty minutes longer than the solar day, so their peak of activity moved backwards fifty minutes each day, just as tides do. The daily change in the time of high water is a visible outcome of the mismatch between the lunar and solar day. The intercrossing of the gravitational fields of the sun and moon can be seen as they move the sea to and fro. But why should rats be tidal? The effect is there, and statistically unchallengeable, but there is no obvious explanation for it.

Brown then tried the same experiment using hamsters.[210] This time, he kept the experiment going for eight months. At first, the hamsters matched their activity with the solar day, then their twenty-four hour rhythm changed into a lunar-day cycle of twenty-four hours and fifty minutes. But the rhythm was not constant. After a spending some time following the moon, the hamsters' daily rhythms would flip back into time with the sun. The rodents never had any clues as to the external conditions, but still managed to synchronize with either the solar or lunar day, switching between them many times during the experiment.

Brown was puzzled by these results. His main research interest was the biological clocks of living creatures, which are called their circadian cycles. He was looking for some internal clock that let the creatures control their regular daily rhythms, but he was disturbed by the way they all seemed to be able to detect the position of the moon and use it to control their daily rhythms. This happened even when they were totally isolated. He was forced to speculate that there may be some external trigger for the circadian rhythms he had previously observed. He thought there must be some unknown factors intruding into the laboratory conditions that the animals used to reset their internal clocks to the lunar or solar day. He wondered if the animals' internal clocks were really free-running, rather than locked by a rigorous internal timing mechanism, and if the rhythm of their circadian cycles was triggered by the environment.[211]

Now, of course sums can be manipulated. There was a famous proof, or perhaps spoof, of this when a Dr. L.C. Cole published the life-cycle properties of the unicorn, which he derived by careful and sequential manipulation of a series of random numbers.[212] Cole took a series of numbers selected by a computer. He solemnly worked out a series of life cycles for the nonexistent unicorn from them. By careful choice of technique, numbers can be pushed towards almost any desired outcome. And I freely confess that during late-night drinking sessions at various Science Festivals, I have been guilty of using algebraic subterfuge to "prove" that 1=2. But when I do this trick, (for those interested in the oddities of arithmetic I divide zero by zero to get an indeterminate function), I know I am abusing mathematical technique for the sake of cheap amusement. I suspect Cole did too, and he never went on to measure any real unicorns or observe any colonies of them under controlled conditions.

Brown was more scrupulous. He based his findings on experiments with real animals. But he was still left with a lame explanation that this effect might just be an accident—unless something was happening that he did not understand. How did the movements of the moon affect the lifecycles of rats, hamsters, and oysters? He speculated that there might be a sensitivity in the creatures that science did not know about, as he had already removed the effects of light, temperature, and atmospheric pressure.[213]

Rats, hamsters, and oysters are interesting in their own way, but does any of this lunar periodicity appear in animals with more complex brains? It turns out that it does: It happens in women. In 1986 a study of the fertility cycles of a large number of women found that a high fraction of menstruations occur around the new moon (28.3 percent).[214]

However, gynecologist Jeff Aronson, writing in the *British Medical Journal*, studied the timing of births and the lunar cycle. He reported no link between the phase of the moon and the likelihood of giving birth:

> *It is disappointing therefore that the purported link between the time to be born and the full moon is not supported by evidence. Of 27 studies published since 1938 (reviewed in* Psychol Rep *1988;63:923-34 and 1994;75:507-11), most have shown no relation between birth rate and the time of the month, and in those that have, the relation was weak and inconsistent.*[215]

This negates a key point in Gauquelin's argument: that the movements of the moon and planets can encourage a baby to be born.

There was a lunar cycle pattern in Pi's fits, but noticing the pattern did not explain what was causing it. Something had to be changing the electrical activity in Pi's brain. However, there was a snag with this idea: The moon does not have an electromagnetic field.

I looked for evidence that humans might also be able to sense the position of the moon, and I found a report of an experiment carried out by the Max Planck Institute. This explored what happens to human circadian rhythms when subjects are shielded from the earth's electromagnetic field. Here is an account of the experiment and what it found:

> *An experiment in body-time artificial distortion that was carried out at the Max-Planck Institute for Physiology in Germany. Scientists fitted out a bunker-apartment*

*in the institute's subterranean laboratory as a Faraday cage, in such a way that the test subjects living there for the experiment were unaware that the walls and ceiling of their temporary home were lined with hidden metal shielding. Thus they were isolated from almost all known forms of electric and magnetic field effects. A control group spent the same time underground, but without the shielded conditions.*

*Both groups began to develop longer circadian periods than normal, the unshielded subjects averaging 24.84 hours and the shielded group 25.26 hours. The latter also showed more irregularities than their colleagues, notably in periods of urination . . .*

*The scientists then tried the effects of a strong artificial electric field on the group shielded from all other fields. This immediately had the effect of shortening the average "day" to just under twenty-four hours. Some volunteers even seemed to have previously erratic body functions "corrected" by the artificial treatment.*[216]

What was fascinating, even though it was not commented on in the write-up, was that the unshielded control group behaved just like Brown's rats and hamsters, and slipped into a lunar day rhythm of twenty-four hours and fifty minutes. The shielded group moved to a longer cycle. Was this a clue that the moon was creating some sort of electromagnetic effect in the subjects?

I couldn't see any mechanism to explain how the moon might cause this effect. It does not emit radio waves or have a magnetic field. But might it have been reflecting radio waves from another source, such as the sun? I needed to find more about the way radio waves can affect the brain. Fortunately, a government report had reviewed the effect of various types of electrical emission on humans. And this would give me another clue.

## Phones on the Brain

In March 1999 the U.K. Government set up a working group to look at how mobile phones affected humans. Tessa Jowell, the Minister for Public Health, was concerned about any possible health risks from these phones and wanted to know what their radio signals might do to the neurons in the human brain.

The terms of reference of the working group were:

*To consider present concerns about the possible health effects from the use of mobile phones, base stations and transmitters, to conduct a rigorous assessment of existing research and to give advice based on the present state of knowledge. To make recommendations on further work that should be carried out to improve the basis for sound advice.*

These terms of reference gave the group the job of carrying out a full survey of all the ways electrical and magnetic fields can affect humans. I was beginning to suspect that any physical effect caused by the position of the moon had to be some form of electromagnetic effect. This was the only way to explain why the Faraday cage, which blocks all types of electric field, made a difference in the results of the circadian cycle experiments at the Max Planck Institute. Perhaps this report would suggest a mechanism.

If there was new research about the affect of EM fields on the brain and nervous system, then I hoped to find it in the report of this Independent Expert Group on Mobile Phones (IEGMP).[217] The group was set up in 1999, chaired by Sir William Stewart, and its report (known as the Stewart Report) was published in May 2000. Its summary conclusions caught my interest at once:

*The Expert Group has conducted a comprehensive review of the literature and has consulted widely . . .*

*There is now some preliminary scientific evidence that exposures to radio frequency (RF) radiation may cause subtle effects on biological functions, including those of the brain . . .*

*The widespread use of mobile phones by children for non-essential calls should be discouraged . . .*

*[The working group] has concluded that the balance of evidence to date suggests that exposures to RF radiation below guidelines recommended for the UK and those recommended by the International Commission on Non-Ionizing Radiation Protection (ICNIRP) do not cause adverse health effects to the general population. It understands that all mobile phones presently marketed in the UK comply with these guidelines. Exposures from base stations are very much below those from mobile phones.*

*There is now scientific evidence, however, which suggests that there may be biological effects occurring at exposures below these guidelines. This does not necessarily mean that these effects lead to disease or injury but it is not possible to say that exposure to RF radiation, even at levels below national guidelines, is totally without potential adverse health effects. In the light of these findings the Expert Group recommends a precautionary approach to the use of mobile phone technologies until more detailed and scientifically robust information on any health effects becomes available*

I wondered what evidence Stewart had found about "subtle effects on biological functions, including those of the brain," and why this should lead him to advise that children should not make too much use of mobile phones. By now I was interested in any effects on the growing brain by EM fields, and this was the most comprehensive survey I could hope to find. I downloaded a full copy of the report and read it eagerly. Here are the sections I found most interesting.

The report talked about what happens when parts of the nervous system act like tuned radio aerials:

*Radio-frequency radiation could, however, produce other effects . . . . there was a special case in which the biological system were resonantly sensitive at the frequency of the electric field and rather insensitive to fields at other frequencies . . . If the resonance was very sharp . . . **quite small electric fields might produce detectable effects in resonant systems of this type, should they exist in biological tissue** [my emphasis].[218]*

Here was a hint, based on current research, that said a resonant part of the nervous system can respond to very small signals, if they are of the right frequency. This means that human cells could receive radio signals and turn them into neuron trigger pulses. The Stewart Report describes in detail how this works:

*Membranes are known to have strongly non-linear electric properties (Montaigne and Pickard, 1984).[219] When a voltage is applied across the membrane, the current that flows is not always proportional to the voltage . . . The membrane acts*

*as a rectifier . . . . if an oscillating voltage (electric field) is applied across a recti-*
*fier, the total current that flows when the field is in one direction is not balanced*
*by the current when the field is in the other: an AC field produces a net DC cur-*
*rent and hence a net flow of products through the membrane.[220]*

I soon found more evidence to support this idea:

*Another mechanism that has continued to create interest is based on the assumption*
*that biological systems might interact resonantly with microwave fields. This possi-*
*bility was initially discussed by Frohlich (1968,[221] 1980,[222]) . . . [he] also considered*
*whether quite small oscillating electric fields might put energy into this state and*
*hence trigger significant biological changes; that it is to say, whether a living bio-*
*logical system might behave in a manner roughly similar to a radio receiver. A*
*radio can detect and amplify an extremely small signal against a background of*
*very much larger signals. It does this when the operator tunes a resonant circuit to*
*the frequency of the carrier wave. The resonant circuit essentially responds only to*
*electromagnetic waves of frequencies within a narrow bandwidth.[223]*

Was some sort of microwave pulse triggering Pi's epileptic fits? But, if so,
how was the moon causing them? I kept coming back to the basic point that the
moon does not emit radio waves.

Next, I found comments about LTP (long term potentiation), the effect that
Steven Rose says is the way we make memories. There is a section of the Stewart Report dealing with the question "Can RF exposure cause functional
changes in the brain and affect behaviour?"

*In neurons in certain parts of the brain (especially a structure called the hip-*
*pocampus, and in the cerebral cortex, particularly in young animals), changes in*
*the level of intracellular calcium resulting from incoming synaptic activity can*
*lead to long-term alterations in the "strength" of synaptic inputs on to the neu-*
*rons. Such long-term potentiation and long-term depression are thought to be*
*involved in the mechanisms of memory and learning (see Kandel et al., 2000).[224]*

*Repacholi (1998)[225] has recently concluded . . . that RF fields, continuous or*
*pulsed, can affect membrane channels, . . . at levels that do not cause significant*

*heating. There have been reports of decreased rates of channel formation, decreased frequency of channel openings, and increased rates of rapid, burst-like firing [LTP]. However, there is no clear understanding of how low intensity RF fields have such effects.*[226]

In chapter 8 I discussed the memory studies of Professor Steven Rose and the ideas about somatic selection put forward by Drs. Edelman and Tononi. The Stewart Report linked in with what they had said and also extended the possibilities of external influences on the processes. The neuron paths that survive are those that fire most frequently. Stewart says that under some conditions, radio signals can trigger LTP, especially in young, growing brains. Perhaps revisiting the idea of pulsed RF fields causing new neuron connections might help me understand what might be happening in the brains of Gauquelin's "successful" people born under the "rays" of the Bright Morning Star, and so help me understand George Washington's interest in the subject.

The bulk of the Stewart Report deals with issues about the radio signals used in mobile phones. It has, however, answered a number of questions, confirmed some of my own findings, and offered some clues about how the Bright Morning Star effect might work. And, most importantly, it confirms that radio-frequency signals have real effects on young brains.

While investigating Masonic astrology, I've found statistical evidence linking personality effects to the movement of the heavy planets which appear as Bright Morning Stars. I know of only three credible ways by which these distant objects can interact with a person on earth. These are:

1. By affecting the pull of gravity.
2. By changing the electromagnetic field of the earth.
3. By squirting particles towards earth.

None of these mechanisms seems likely to cause the sort of short, sharp pulses of radio energy that the Stewart Report says are most likely to affect the brain. I must continue my search for a mechanism that will allow heavy-gravity planets to influence the growth of a child's brain. The Stewart Report is nudging me to look at radio waves, so that is what I must investigate next.

## Conclusions

Epileptic dogs, oysters, rats, hamsters, and human beings are all affected by the phases of the moon and its position in the sky, even when they seem unaware of it. Research on activated water showed that minute changes in solar radiation will change the behavior of sensitive chemical reactions during the descaling of boilers. I wondered if the moon might be reflecting radio energy from the sun, and by that means causing the responses in animals.

I looked at the Stewart Report on radio absorption by humans to see if it could give any clues. It confirmed many of my own suspicions, including one that the human brain is sensitive to short, low-energy pulses of radio energy and that exposure to quite small pulses of high-frequency radio energy can trigger neurons. The report was particularly concerned that little was known about the effect of these types of radio pulses on the brains of growing children, and it advised that children's use of mobile phones should be restricted as a safeguard.

The more I investigated the way in which personality formed in the growing brain, the clearer it became that electrical energy, and now radio energy, could change the way neurons linked up. But I still had no way of knowing how the rising of a Bright Morning Star could cause pulses of radio energy. If I was ever to understand the secret behind George Washington's application of Masonic astrology, then I would need to find out more about the earth's radio environment. The area of radio research seemed to be the only way left to see if I could find any mechanism to link the formation of personality to the pre-dawn rising of planets.

# Chapter Eleven

# A Mirror in the Sky

## Do-It-Yourself Radio

Even as a young schoolboy, I loved to play with radios. The pockets of my school blazer bulged with bits of wire and "useful" electrical odds and ends. Some of my better-off friends had wireless sets of their own, and, although sometimes I was let loose on my parents' large radiogram, I wanted a radio set of my own.

I couldn't afford to buy one on my pocket money, so the only way to get one was to make my own. It needed to be simple, and it was. I made a crystal set. Toilet-paper rolls, army-surplus wire, and a condenser taken from a broken radio set my grandmother had thrown away, were all pressed into service. All I needed to buy from a radio junk shop was a cats-whisker (the old name for a crystal diode, or rectifier) and a pair of ex-Army headphones.

Finally, I needed an aerial and something to ground the set. I buried two square yards of chicken wire netting in the flower bed under my bedroom window and connected it to the bottom of the coil. This was my ground connection. To the other end of the coil I connected 50 feet of "Army surplus" insulated copper wire, which ran from my bedroom window to the tree at the bottom of the garden. Then there was just one thing left to do: I connected a "bypass" condenser, salvaged from the broken radio set, across the terminals of the headphones. Now I had my own radio set.

It was hardly rocket science, but this simple circuit worked the very first time. As I slowly turned the knob on the tuning condenser, I could hear a whole new world of radio stations. How could a simple collection of bits and pieces of ex-War Department junk be turned into a working radio set? In some ways, radio is simple. If you make your aerial the right length to fit the radio waves of the station you want to hear, you will be able to pick it out from the rest.

At first, I just listened to the comedy shows, but I soon found there were other things to hear on the radio, stations my simple crystal set couldn't tune into. If I twirled the dial of my parents' radiogram down as far as it would go, I heard people who had their own private wireless stations. They were telling each other about the vast distances their "short waves" had gone and bragging about the distant stations they had "worked." Of course, I wanted to know more—and curiosity drove me to get a cheap short-wave radio of my own.

All the theories I have read about the way children's brains develop say that the neurons that fire most often are selected to remain as part of the adult brain. But all the researches assumed that the signals that set off this linking come into the brain via one of the senses, or as a result of thoughts or sense impressions. But the Stewart Report had said that neurons can also resonate like a radio set. So, if a neuron is the length of a quarter of a radio signal's wavelength, it will receive as well as my simple crystal set did. An appropriate frequency of radio signal will make a neuron fire and link.

Could Bright Morning Stars be causing radio pulses that were changing the way children's brains link up? If neurons of a resonant length are fired by radio pulses, and if there are lots of these pulses happening when a child's brain is growing, then they must affect the way its neurons link together.

Child psychologists Gopnik, Meltzoff, and Kuhl, whose work on the development of children's brains I mentioned earlier, had explained how only the neuron links that fire most often survive into the adult brain:

> *By the time babies are born, there is already a great deal of neurological structure in place. But, equally clearly, the brain changes in radical ways over the first few years of life, and it changes in response to experience. In other words, the brain learns. This learning isn't just passive. The brain actively tries to establish the right connections, and it prunes connections that don't get much use.*[227]

This "pruning" is done by flows of electric current. A developing brain makes "the right connections" by triggering them over and over again. Experts on human consciousness, Drs. Edelman and Tononi, confirmed this:

*Neurons strengthen and weaken their connections according to their individual patterns of electrical activity. Neurons that fire together wire together.*[228]

And memory expert Professor Steven Rose had seen this happening in the brains of his young chicks as they learned how to avoid bitter-tasting beads. Their brains changed under the influence of intense bursts of electrical activity.

*The bursting activity, like the biochemical and structural changes, occurs only in the animals which remember the task . . . memory can really be such a simple, mechanical process, a straightforward linking up of neurons into some novel network . . . like rewiring a computer.*[229]

The way the human brain forms first its memories and then its distinct personality all boils down to a repetitive flow of electric currents in key parts of our brain. Personality can be changed by current flow, memories are formed by current flow, and our brain structure favors the circuits that pass current through most often. It's rather like a fast-flowing river eroding a deep canyon into the ground, whereas a meandering stream will silt up and disappear.

But what does this imply for Masonic astrology? The electrical instability of my wife's border collie Pi changed with the phase of the moon. Could there possibly be a radio link between the position of the moon and the electrical effect in his brain? If so, what caused it?

Astrology claims to explain how this happens, but its theory is based on science that is over two thousand years out of date, for the ideas of the Greek mathematician Ptolemy, who died in 185 CE, are still considered valid sources of astrological lore. Claudius Ptolemy, whose major work the *Almagest* claimed that sun and stars moved round the earth, knew nothing of gravity, neurons, or somatic selection. He lived and died almost two millennia before the ideas of Newton, Darwin, or Gauquelin became known. Yet his thinking is still the cutting edge of astrological "science." And he believed in the physical influence of "planetary rays." My investigation has not uncovered any source of such rays.

As I looked at the brain research I've outlined above, I saw how neurons can respond to radio signals, and, once triggered, can form new linkages by the process of long-term potentiation. I began to suspect that there might just be a real scientific process here that could make Masonic astrology work. Radio pulses can affect the neuron interconnections within a developing, or even a mature, brain, and so change the personality, or mood, of its owner. So, if a rising planet gives off radio pulses, it can affect a growing brain. But I still had a problem explaining why Pi had more epileptic fits when the moon was full—because the moon is not a source of radio pulses.

There were two radio mechanisms left for me to investigate: the atmospheric processes that spread radio waves around the globe and cause atmospheric noise. These phenomena are well known to radio and radar engineers, and there are scientific theories that explain how they work. But can they explain Pi's response and give me the key to Bro. Washington's Masonic astrology?

## Listening to the World

Radio waves travel in straight lines. The earth is a ball. Yet I have sent radio signals from Britain to Australia, even though these countries are on opposite sides of the world.

At first sight, these statements seem to be paradoxical. If the radio waves can only travel along a line of sight, then it would appear that, if you cannot see the transmitting mast, you should not be able to hear the station. Trying to send radio waves around the curvature of the earth should be like trying to look around the corner of a building long before you reach it. Radio waves, like light rays, are not supposed to bend. So how is it possible to transmit a radio signal to the other side of the globe?

Well, the trick is done just the same way as you would peer round the corner of a building without actually craning around the side: it's done by mirrors. A radio mirror bends the waves around the curve of the earth. Of course, you need a big mirror, and it needs to be high up in the sky, but fortunately the earth does have a natural "radio mirror" in the sky. It's called the ionosphere.

The earth is surrounded by air, but, as you climb higher and higher, this air becomes less dense; if you climb high enough, all trace of it disappears. The layer of air is about 250 miles (400 kilometers) thick. The electrical properties of the atmosphere change according to how high you are. Close to the earth's surface the air is a good insulator, and it needs a high voltage before it will let any current flow through it; but in the higher layers, where the air is thinner, it conducts electric currents easily. The ionosphere stretches from about 30 to 250 miles (50 to 400 kilometers) above ground level. The area of the atmosphere below 30 miles (50 km) is called the troposphere, and the region above 250 miles (400 km) is called the stratosphere.

When the air gets thin, its molecules don't interact closely, so they easily lose some of their electrons, and the loose electrons buzz around freely. The parent molecules have a positive electric charge, while the free electrons have a negative charge. The sunlight that hits the earth's atmosphere contains a lot of ultraviolet radiation (UV), which is an electromagnetic wave with a very short wavelength, and it is this UV radiation hitting air molecules high above the earth that strips away their outer electrons. The stripped molecules become ions, and the separated electrons are free particles. Ions and electrons don't like being separated, and, given a chance, they will recombine into an electrically neutral molecule, but as long as the sunlight keeps bombarding them, they are kept apart.

Nearer the earth's surface the air is thicker, so there is a great crush of molecules. This means the free electrons quickly recombine. But in the upper atmosphere the air is less dense, and hence there is a much smaller chance of a free electron finding an ionized molecule to rejoin. This means that electrons stay free longer and are slow to recombine. Much of the UV radiation is absorbed in the higher atmosphere, so that by the time it gets close to the ground it is less able to knock electrons off air molecules. (This is a good thing for us humans, because otherwise it would burn our skins and cause cancer to a much greater extent than it already does. )

It is these ions and the matching free electrons in the upper atmosphere that create the radio mirror. A wireless wave will travel quite happily through the non-conducting air at atmospheric pressure, but it can't go through a layer of free electrons without getting bent. Instead of going in a straight line, the radio wave gets pulled sideways by the electric fields of the ions and electrons. Depending on its wavelength, the radio wave will either be slightly bent before it flies off into space, or it will be bent so much that it is reflected back to the earth. (The longer the wavelength, the more strongly it bends. Shorter wavelengths bend less, so they escape into space.)

221

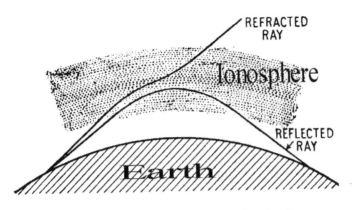

*Figure 18: How the ionosphere reflects radio waves back to Earth.*

This radio mirror was found early in the twentieth century by a scientist named Oliver Heavyside, so it was called the Heavyside layer. Other scientists soon noticed that the Heavyside layer shifted around. During the day it was close to the ground, but at night it moved upward. The effect of this movement is very noticeable in the Medium Wave radio broadcast band—that is, wavelengths from 200 to 3,000 meters (all radio engineers conventionally quote meters for radio wavelengths. During the day you hear only the stations within ten to thirty miles or so, but as soon as night falls, stations from much farther away boom in.

The ionized layer is like a shell surrounding the whole of the earth, but its shape keeps changing. It's made up of clouds of electrons and ionized air molecules. It changes from moment to moment, which means the direction in which it reflects wireless waves also keeps changing. The height of the Heavyside layer (renamed the E-layer after the 1947 Nobel Prize for physics was jointly awarded to Oliver Heavyside and Arthur Kennelly for separately discovering it) is about 60 miles (100 kilometers) at night, but during the day, the force of the sun's rays pushes it lower. Figure 18 shows how the ionized layer reflects radio waves.

The ionosphere is more than a fixed mirror in the sky. It's more like a hall of mirrors at a fair. There are up to four separate ionized layers in the upper atmosphere—now known as the D-, E-, and F-layers—and sometimes the F-layer splits into the F1- and F2-layers. All these layers are at different heights and reflect different wavelengths of radio signals.

The strength of UV radiation in sunlight changes with the time of day and the season of the year. During the day, the ionosphere over the day side of the earth receives the full force of the sun's radiation hits, but at night it is in shadow and receives no direct UV radiation. When the ionosphere is in shadow, the ions quickly recombine with the free elections. But when day returns, there is a rapid rise in the number of free electrons and ions.

By squirting a radio signal straight up at the ionosphere and seeing how much of it is reflected, it's possible to work out the density of electrons in the air. Appendix 3 shows how the thickness of the cloud of free electrons varies over Washington, D.C., during the course of the day. There are few free elections at large during the night, but at dawn there is a rapid increase in numbers. They increase a thousandfold within minutes. By midday, the cloud of free electrons is enormous, but as the earth turns away from the sun, their numbers fall back to the low night-time level.

As I looked at the variations in density of free electrons over the U.S. capital I noticed something interesting. The two peaks of Gauquelin high-achiever births coincide with the periods of rapid change in free electron density. (You'll find this data in appendix 4.) The first peak appears at dawn, when the rate of electron release begins to accelerate, and the second at midday, as it starts to decline. As the earth rotates on its axis, this active area of the upper atmosphere reacts like a pan of boiling water. As the sunlight hits it, enormous quantities of free electrons are boiled off like clouds of negatively charged steam in the empty spaces of the ionosphere.

Since the early days of radio, sunrise has been known to have special properties. The Radio Society of Great Britain's book *A Guide to Amateur Radio*, which was my bible when I first became a radio ham, mentions it as a good time to reflect radio waves a long way:

> *A particularly interesting "grey line" path occurs between places where dawn and dusk coincide and provide a good path from the UK to New Zealand and Australia on 3.5 MHz. Such paths may "open" for about 30 min, so that dawn and dusk are times of considerable interest.*[230]

The "grey lines" are where the earth's rotating atmosphere first starts to boil off free electrons and where it cools rapidly under the chill of darkness. Both are times of immense electrical activity in the ionosphere. Here was the first hint of how the rising of a morning star might affect the ionosphere. Could the morning star be reflecting radio pulses from the sun into these energetic regions of the ionosphere?

## Mother Earth's Daily Belly Dance

What causes the good radio paths of the "grey line"? What is going on in the ionosphere?

In the raw energy of dawn, the sun blasts the upper air with intense UV light. This onslaught smashes outer electrons from the air molecules, leaving positive ions and negative electrons to scurry around, frantically trying to recombine with each other—but they are held apart by the relentless stream of high-energy photons arriving from the sun. All this frantic activity takes place in a highly charged cloud of free-roaming electrons.

At dusk, on the other hand, as the earth's mass moves across the light of the sun, its shadow shields the atmosphere, and the rampaging hordes of disruptive UV photons move on to new areas of daylight. Now, as night falls, there is a chance for the widely scattered orphaned electrons and their bereft parent molecules to seek each other out and fall back into each other's arms. In these first moments of quiet darkness, almost every encounter is between an ionized molecule and a free electron. The meetings quickly result in the prodigal electrons being taken back into the shelter of ionized molecules. As the shadows of night lengthen, only a few wandering electrons remain to search on through the increasing ranks of neutral-restored molecules, longing for the attractive pull of an unoccupied place in an outer shell. This process continues until the light of dawn starts the whole scramble all over again.

These few moments of chaotic disruptions and reunions create the highly electrically active environment of the "grey lines" (shown in figure 19). This environment has the dramatic effect on the long-distance propagation of radio waves that has long excited amateur radio enthusiasts. But it also marks the transition between two stable states. During the day, the ionosphere is highly electrically charged, but the electrons split off into different ionic layers at dif-

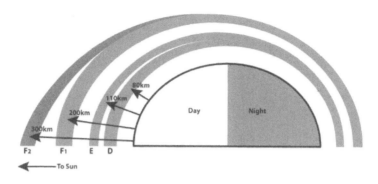

*Figure 19: Here is what the ionic layers look like when looking downwards from space above the North Pole during the northern summer [after Cole (1992)].*

ferent heights. During the night, most of the population of free electrons lie in a few tight bands. Only at the periods of splitting and recombining is there a dense group of free electrons all at roughly the same height. (A diagram of the way the electrons split during the day at various times of the year is shown in appendix 5.)

The main layers that reflect radio waves are called the E- and F-layers. But there is another layer that forms only during the day. Known as the D-layer, it is thinly spread above the daylit area of the earth and occurs in the lower atmosphere, from about 30 to 60 miles (50 to 100 km), where molecular density is high. This causes rapid re-absorption of free electrons. The D-layer, which appears every day, summer or winter, is too lightly ionized to bend radio waves, but it does weaken any radio waves that pass through it. It is denser over the equatorial regions of the earth, and towards the poles it becomes less dense and has less of a weakening effect on radio waves.

The E-layer boils above the D-layer during daylight hours, and its height remains roughly constant. It is stronger in summer than in winter, with its maximum electron density lying between 60 and 95 miles (100 and 150 km) above the earth's surface.

The F-layer stretches from about 120 to 250 miles (200 to 400 km) above the ground. During the night, there is just one F-layer about 185 miles (300 km) up. But during the day it can split into two widely separated layers known as F1 and F2. In the winter these hardly separate, but under the more intense bombardment of summer radiation, the two might be as much as 125 miles (200 km) apart. In a northern winter the F-layer will be compacted in northern latitudes, while at the same time it will be spread out into the F1- and F2-layers in the south, where it will be summer—and in the northern summer the position is reversed.

During the "grey-line" hours, dense clouds of electrons billow above the equator. Localized UV heating of the upper air creates a vast bubble of free electrons over the equatorial regions when the sun is rising and as it passes its zenith. Over the poles and the more temperate regions, there is a less dense covering. A plot of this cloud in real time looks like the wobbling of a great beer belly (see appendix 6).

It's almost as if Mother Earth has a beer belly of free electrons wobbling around her equator. As day breaks she suffers a bout of indigestion, releasing so much gas that she gurgles as the electrons pop out of the irradiated upper air like bubbles appearing in a glass of champagne. Just as the gurgling gas bubbles reach a crescendo, distending her belly into an uncomfortably wide stretch, she turns her back on the sun. Then her gassy stomach settles into a more quiescent overnight state.

While I was thinking these whimsical thoughts, it suddenly dawned on me that I already knew more about Mother Earth's dancing beer belly than I realized. I had spent many hours listening to its rumblings when I first discovered the joys of short-wave radio. Whereas an electric current is a coordinated movement of a group of electrons, the electrons in the ionospheric bulge are boiling around randomly. This means that most of their effects cancel each other out. But if a few happen to move in the same direction, then the currents they generate appear as electrical atmospheric noise. This is something that has bothered me since childhood, when I made my first hesitant ventures into radio land: the noisy crackling of atmospheric static makes it difficult to hear distant radio stations. This electrical noise is made by short, sharp pulses of radio energy. Could it perhaps be changed by the movements of planets around the sun?

## Something in the Air

When I first began to listen to short-wave stations I was often bothered by sharp crackling noises. They swamped my reception, and were sometimes so loud through my headphones that it hurt. Eventually I built a circuit called a "noise limiter," which detected the arrival of these quick-rising pulses at the aerial and shorted out the receiver before they hit my ears. In this way I managed to listen in comfort to distant stations.

There were three types of noise that hit my aerial antenna: man-made noise, atmospheric noise, and what was then called "cosmic" noise. This noise comes in two varieties, the sharp, shot-type impulse cracks that so disturbed my early listening, and a steady hissing noise, called "hash." A noise-limiter circuit does not help with hash, but it does clip and reduce impulse noise.

The study of noise is important for engineers who make radar equipment. Radar works by sending out a short pulse of radio energy and then listening for an echo. The time the echo takes to return enables the engineers to measure the distance and direction of the reflecting object. Although the output pulse of a radar installation is a high-powered signal at its source, by the time it has traveled out to a distant aircraft and returned, it is much weaker. If the echo is mixed with pulses of noise it can give a false echo. This ratio between the radar signal and the noise fixes the lower limit of sensitivity for the setup. It is Mother Earth's beer belly of bubbling free electrons that disturbs the transmission of radar signals.

The military appeal of radar expertise has made sure that a lot of research has been done on the way its signals propagate. This work has shown that there are areas of the atmosphere that regularly give odd reflection effects. These areas vary with the season and the time of day, but they are mostly to be found in the tropical latitudes, at times when electrons form high concentrations. Figure 20 (on page 228) is a map showing the areas of the world where these anomalous radar propagation occurs; it has been drawn up for the northern winter.

If the large groups of free electrons that form at dawn above the tropics all move in the same direction at the same time, like a coordinated group of microscopic line dancers, they will create current flows. And these current flows will generate pulses of radio noise that are very powerful.

Gauquelin's peaks of high-achiever morning-star births coincide with periods of chaotic change in this cloud of free electrons, when most of these electrons are clustered close together. The thought struck me that the heavy-gravity planets might be causing tidal effects in this bubbling mass of elections as their gravitational fields interacted with the sun's. These would be felt as pulses of current. If the gravity of the moon can shift the sea to and fro, what sort of movement patterns could its gravity cause in the billowing clouds of free electrons?

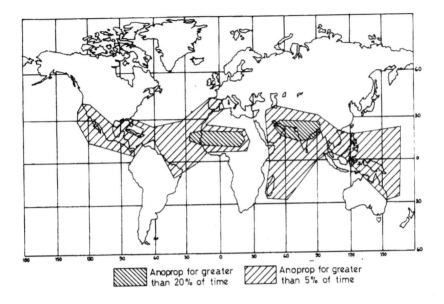

*Figure 20: Distribution of anomalous radar propagation over the globe [after Cole (1992)].*

Here at last was a possible mechanism to explain the effect of the rising of the Bright Morning Star. The tidal pull of the rising and culminating of heavy planets might be able to cause electromagnetic effects. And I already knew that radio pulses can affect the way neurons join up to form a child's brain. Now I needed to analyze the effects of interacting gravitational fields on the free electrons of the ionosphere.

## Analyzing an Interplanetary Egg Whisk

To work out how the forces of gravity act on any electron in the ionosphere when a heavy object passes close to the sun, I could use Newton's laws of motion. With them, I could work out how fast and in what direction the charged clouds of elections move. Once I knew this, I would be able to estimate the current flows, and from those, the strength of any radio waves the movements might cause.

For the first time, I began to think that George Washington may have become aware of a real physical effect when he responded to the Bright Morning Star. Perhaps there is a rational reason behind the statistical effects found by my three independent observers, McClelland, Sachs, and Gauquelin. This idea, that the tidal forces from the Bright Morning Star might cause radio pulses that trigger neurons to fire and bond, is well within the known limits of astrophysics and radio theory. It meets Stephen Hawking's demand that my theory of Masonic astrology should be "consistent with other theories which have been tested by experiment."[231]

To begin the calculation again, I decided to assume that the earth is the center of the solar system and the sun and the planets revolve around it. My reason for doing so is not that I think this is true; it's just that I want to take advantage of one of Einstein's discoveries, that there is no absolute frame of reference, and any frame is as good as any other for calculation purposes. As all frames of reference are valid, the sums I want to do are much easier if my main point of interest stands still and everything else moves around it. So, feeling a bit like a medieval pope who really believed that the sun revolved around the earth, I set up my model of the whole universe dancing round my mathematically immovable earth.

Once I knew what happened to a single electron, then I could work out the total currents in the upper air. And I could work out the frequency and strength of the radio pulses that the tidal forces created. I imagined my model to show three gravitational attractors: the earth, the sun, and a heavy planet revolving round the earth. As they traverse the sky each subjects a floating electron to a pull in a different direction. To find out how the electron moves, I used Newton's Law of Gravitational Attraction.

The electron will be dragged around by the same forces that move the sea in and out with the pattern of the tides. But, whereas the tides are damped down because of the viscosity of the liquid that makes up the sea, the electrons in the ionosphere are free to move in any direction as quickly (or as slowly) as they want, without any friction to slow them down. (I was aware that, if I wanted to refine the model, I would need to take account of the effects of such scientific complications as Colomb back-scattering, causing the electrons to repel each other if they get too close. But for the sake of this initial model, I ignored that complication.) Appendix 8 shows a diagram of the model I used for my calculation.

The three forces pulling at this single electron are all constantly moving. The pulls of the sun and the heavy planet are rotating about the center of mass of the earth. (Remember I made the earth my fixed point for ease of calculation.) The electron is in the middle of a three-way triangle of gravitational forces, all trying to tug it towards them, and two of them are moving rapidly across the sky in a complex dance that first brings them together and then moves them apart.

The easiest way to think about what is happening is to imagine the gravitational fields of the sun and the heavy planet are like the blades of an egg beater of the type that is used for making meringue or whipped cream. As the two blades approach each other, the egg white is pulled rapidly in one direction and then back again as it meets the oncoming blade. This is a much more violent mixing than will occur if only a single blade is used, since in that case, the mixture will just be pushed around in circles. The two blades trap the egg white between them, then pull it apart, beating it up into a light, frothy meringue. In the same manner, it is the beating together of the two gravitational fields, and their sudden reversal of direction during a conjunction, that will rattle and shake the electrons in the ionospheric cloud.

My calculations showed that turbulence happens at four important positions: when the planet is close to the sun, when it is culminating at its highest point in the sky as the sun rises, when it is setting as the sun rises, and when it is culminating at its lowest point as the sun sets. But only at sunrise and noon are there clouds of electrons to dance to the churning of these tidal forces. My model explains the morning-star zones. They are caused when the two gravitational fields pass across each other and cause the egg-beater effect to stir up the free electrons and generate a series of pulses of radio noise.

Another way of looking at what is happening is to imagine that electrons in the ionic cloud are all dancing together and following the directions of a caller at a square dance. But in this Alice in Wonderland dance, there are two callers, each calling separate square dances at the same time. The poor, confused electrons can't tell the difference between the two callers, so they try to dance to both sets of calls at once. They follow the last step that was called, no matter which caller shouts it out. As a result, most of the time the dancing electrons just mill around, but now and then the callers happen to call the same step at the same time, as when both the sun and the heavy planet pull almost in the same direction at the same time. However, there are times when one caller shouts "forward" just as the other shouts "back," and then the first caller shouts "back" just before the other shouts "forward." When this happens, the electrons mill about chaotically.

When the sun and the heavy planet are coming to a conjunction, in opposition or at right-angles to each other, then all the electrons jumble together in a pulsating pattern. This jiggling mass of electrons causes pulses of electric current. These currents create pulsed radio waves, which I first heard as "cosmic noise."

Fun as these mental images are, there was an easier way to find out what was happening to the current flows in the ionosphere. The mathematical model I had built could be simulated in a computer to show the sort of radio pulse it can create. The strength of the pulses will vary according to the seasonal free-electron density and the mass and distance of the heavy planet near the sun. I decided to do an order of magnitude test using numbers for the moon, and found that turbulent gravitational current flows of thousands of amps can occur over fractions of a second. This explained the sharp pulses of noise that I had so often heard when listening for distant stations. The rapidly changing current will produce a sharp, rising radio wave similar to the square-edge signal of a radar pulse.

When the heavy planet was either new or culminating, it produced tidal turbulence in the ionosphere, and my simulation showed that these flows produced both positive and negative pulses of current, and hence radio noise pulses. This happened only when the criss-crossing gravity fields beat against each other. Appendix 9 shows how I worked this out.

I decided to do more computer simulations of these pulse patterns to see how the electrons rattled around when the gravitational fields were well separated. And I found distinctive patterns of radio pulses as heavy planets moved near the sun and rose as Bright Morning Stars, or when they were at right-angles to the sun; but tidally generated radio pulses disappeared at other times. Appendix 9 shows the details of this, too.

This was a remarkable discovery. We have seen in chapter 9 how personality is formed from the building of memories, and that memories are made by neurons creating new connections. To make those connections, they must trigger and form the new synapses. The radio pulses, which occur when heavy planets rise near the sun or culminate at right-angles to it, cause a pattern of radio signals of suitable wavelengths to trigger neurons and encourage them to join up.

In a recent book about how children's brains grow, Professor Steven Pinker, Director of the Center for Cognitive Neuroscience at Massachusetts Institute of Technology, made an important point about the differences in the way even the brains of identical twins develop:

> *We still don't know whether unique experiences leave their fingerprints on our intellects and personalities. But an even earlier pin-ball game certainly could do, the one that wires up our brain in the womb and early childhood. The human genome cannot possibly specify every last connection amongst the neurons. But the environment in the sense of information encoded by the sense organs, isn't the only option . . . A cosmic ray mutates a stretch of DNA, a neurotransmitter zigs instead of zags, the growth cone of an axon goes left instead of right, and one identical twin's brain might gel into a slightly different configuration from the other's.*[232]

Both the work of Professor Giorgio Piccardi and the Stewart Report (see chapter 10) showed that a small pulse of energy from outside a delicately balanced system, such as the developing brain of a child, can nudge this pinball game in new directions. Turbulent radio pulses stirred up by heavy planets can repattern neurons as effectively as sense organs do. Here was a possible mechanism to account for differences between close siblings or even identical twins. Slight differences in neuron lengths will be triggered according to the wavelength of the noise pulse. So a long neuron will trigger to a slow pulse and a short neuron to a fast one. The neurons might act like selective radio sets, some tuning particular pulses and others remaining unaffected. A noise pulse will only affect neurons of the critical resonant length.

I decided to test this idea on somebody who really understood how brains make synapses. Fortunately Katherine Neville, who had been a great help with information about Washington, was married to just such an expert, Professor Karl H. Pribram. I knew Karl was extremely busy, finishing off a new book about the history of the study of the brain, so I asked Katherine if he could spare a little time to read through my thoughts and see if they made sense.

Soon afterwards I got an e-mail saying that he would. Here is what Katherine said:

*Karl read the brain chapter, and also read how you were thinking of incorporating the information in the later part of the book, and here are his comments. (Karl says, as a physics person, you will have no trouble with this info at all. It dovetails right into what you are doing.):*

*"Everything Robert reviews of standard neuroscience is excellent. But it won't work for what he is trying to say for cosmic influences.*

*"What **will work** is what I (Karl) have been saying for the last 50 years about fine-fibered processes (dendritic and axon branches or teledendrons)— which **do not discharge**, but rather, **oscillate between the voltages** that he (Robert) talks about. **that's** where all the modifiability and change in connectivity take place."*

And there was much more information on the way. Katherine went on to say:

*Robert, Karl will soon email you two important papers: they are somewhat overlapping in content but will be right up your alley.*

The following day I had an e-mail from Karl. After a few kind words he got down to assessing my suggestions for cosmic reshaping of the brain:

*Robert: You've done a terrific job in reviewing standard neuroscience—and coming up with excellent metaphors that make things understandable.*

*Unfortunately, the "fire together" doesn't work by itself for what you are after. There is no plasticity once the impulses have been generated. But there is a more potent mode of operation in the nervous system when it comes to modifiability: the oscillations going on in the fine-fibered web of dendrites and axon branches (teledendrons) that don't lead to complete discharge. It is in this web of fine-fibered processing that most synapses occur. The chemistry of synapses is necessary because the presynaptic voltage is so low. The all-or-none law is a part of neuromythology, a myth that is hard to get rid of. The size of a nerve impulse is proportional to the fiber-size diameter, and, as you have noted, axons branch into fine fibers before they synapse. The EEG is composed by these fine-fibered postsynaptic hyperpolarizations and depolarizations and reflects nerve impulse activity only slightly if at all.*

*I haven't done any magnetic influencing myself but have recommended it to the experimental laboratory at HeartMath where they are finding influences of heart-rate variability on the EEG, etc.—even between people a yard apart.*

Karl attached a paper called "Consciousness Reassessed" and a chapter from his book *Languages of the Brain*. Both addressed how electro-magnetic waves can create new synapses. In one key section Karl describes how he first discovered that the process of synapse formation was modulated by electromagnetic wave fronts. This was exactly the mechanism I was looking for. Here is what he says:

*The story begins in the late 1930s, working in Ralph Gerard's laboratory at the University of Chicago. Gerard showed us that a cut separating two parts of the brain cortex did not abolish transmission of an electrical stimulus across the separation as long as the parts were in some sort of contact . . .*

*By 1948 I had my own laboratory at Yale University and began a collaboration with Wolfgang Koehler who told me of his Direct Current hypothesis as the basis for cortical processing in vision . . . I set to work to test Koehler's hypothesis. We worked with monkeys and humans displaying a white cardboard in front of their eyes and recorded from their visual cortex. (It was easy in those days to do such experiments with awake humans with their permission. Surgery had been done for clinical purposes with local anesthesia of the scalp—touching the brain itself is not felt by the patient.) Indeed we found a Direct Current (DC) shift during the display.*

*In addition, I created minute epileptogenic foci in the visual cortex of monkeys and tested for their ability to distinguish very fine horizontal from vertical lines. Once electrical seizures commenced . . . I expected their ability to distinguish the lines to be impaired and even totally lost . . . Contrary to expectation, the monkeys performed the task without any deficiency.*

*Koehler exclaimed: "Now that you have disproved not only my theory of cortical function in perception but everyone else's, as well, what are you going to do?" I answered: "I'll keep my mouth shut." In fact, I refused to teach a course on brain mechanisms in sensation and perception when I transferred to Stanford University (in 1958) shortly thereafter . . .*

*This led to another series of experiments in which I imposed a DC current across the cortex from surface to depth and found that a cathodal current delayed learning while an anodal current enhanced it.*[233]

I got very excited when I realized these were the positive (anodal) and negative (cathodal) currents I shall be discussing in chapter 12, when I predict different effects between the full and new moons in the northern and southern hemispheres.

Karl's story continued.

*Some years into my tenure at Stanford, Ernest Hilgard and I were discussing an update of his introductory psychology text when he asked me about the status of our knowledge regarding brain physiology in perception. I answered that I was dissatisfied with what we knew: I and others had disproved Koehler's suggestion that perception could be ascribed to direct current brain electrical fields . . . So he asked once again to come up with some viable alternative to the ones I had so summarily dismissed.*

*I took the problem to my laboratory group . . . Lashley had proposed that interference patterns among wave fronts in brain electrical activity could serve as the substrate of perception and memory as well. This suited my earlier intuitions, but Lashley and I had discussed this alternative repeatedly, without coming up with any idea what wave fronts would look like in the brain . . . we could only examine synapses one by one, [but] presynaptic branching axons set up synaptic wave fronts. Functionally it is these wave fronts that must be taken into consideration . . . I realized that axons entering the synaptic domain from different directions would set up interference patterns.*[234]

Now it was clear that the ionic turbulence electromagnetic waves, which I had deduced from the statistical behavior patterns of the human brains and the astrophysics of gravity, were quite capable of modifying the synapse connections in the brain, and when those astro-modulated synapses were exposed to the same wave front that had originally created them in the childish brain, then they would trigger again.

I wrote back to Katherine:

*I'm enormously excited that this idea does make sense, since, if it is real, then it might explain how* Homo sapiens *made such a rapid evolutionary leap in brain function when we moved out from under the shielding of the D-layer. If we can begin to understand the interaction between our growing brain and the environment, it could well help us understand our capabilities and potentials. It certainly isn't astrology but could be something far more important.*

*Karl's explanation of the mechanism for forming neuron linkages doesn't affect my statistical and physics findings, but it makes the final linkage to the physical network of the growing brain.*

*This is exciting!! And all from wondering why George Washington took an interest in the Bright Morning Star.*

At this point, I realized that I had fulfilled Richard Dawkins' first test for astrology and shown, at least for Masonic astrology, that "the brain is the seat of personality, and, if astrology is claiming to predict personality, it must put forward a mechanism by which the positions of the stars at the moment of birth can affect the development of personality."

All right, if I'm honest, I can't claim any effect for the stars. But I have shown that planets which are rising or culminating at their highest point, with enough mass to have a tidal influence on the ionosphere, can produce patterns of radio pulses. Now Karl had explained to me how these electrical wave fronts could create new neuron linkages in a brain.

Neurons can interact with these signals from the sky and create new synapses. This is the basis for a scientific explanation for some of the statistical effects observed in Masonic astrology. But the implications of this externally triggered somatic selection process needed more thought.

With some of the slower-moving planets, such as Jupiter and Saturn, these effects will continue for many months while the child's brain is developing its early connections. The faster-moving planets might repeat the pattern of waves many times during the critical early growth stage of the child and so encourage a greater complexity of neuron links.

This is a scientific hypothesis to explain the statistical results of Sachs, Gauquelin, and McClelland. It also explains a more recent finding, published in the *British Journal of Sports Medicine* (2000;34:465-6), which noted that soccer players picked for the 1998 World Cup in France had a discernible astrological pattern to their birth dates, which centered on days when the sun and moon were in adjacent signs of the zodiac. The implication of the sun and the moon being in adjacent signs of the zodiac is that they are closing towards a conjunction, and so are generating waves of ionic turbulence pulses that are likely to affect the structure of the young players' brains.

But if I want to fully understand George Washington's decision to incorporate Masonic astrology and geomancy with the layout of the Federal City of Washington, D.C., then I must now revisit Dawkins' second test. He said that a theory of astrology should make predictions that are independently verifiable and unambiguous. Can I consistently produce predictions for Masonic astrology, now that I have a scientific hypothesis to build on?

## Conclusions

My study of radio propagation and cosmic noise showed that the rays of the sun create vast clouds of free electrons in the earth's upper atmosphere in a region called the ionosphere. I speculated that the these free electrons might be subject to tidal forces from heavy planets moving around the sun, and built a mathematical model of the effect of the crossing gravitational fields on these electrons. I found that when heavy planets rose just before the sun as Bright Morning Stars, they can cause radio pulses that are capable of changing the linking patterns of children's fast-growing brains.

The results of my computer simulations agreed with the statistical Morning-Star zone that I had used in chapter 7 to explain the results of Gauquelin, Sachs, and McClelland. Now, thanks to Karl Pribram, I knew of a physical mechanism that could modify a growing brain. I no longer had to rely on the explanation of Masonic ritual that it is the "benign rays of the Bright Morning Star" that "bring peace and tranquility to the whole human race."

But before I return to considering what inspired Brother George Washington to lay out the positions of the President's House (the White House) and the

Capitol, I need to prove my theory of Masonic astrology. Can I trust it? I must see if I can predict detectable outputs. Can I make predictions which can be tested against real-world data? That is the task I tackle in the next chapter.

# Chapter Twelve

# The Predictions of
# Masonic Astrology

## Applying the Theory of Masonic Astrology

I started on this quest thinking that Masonic astrology was just a piece of inspirational symbolism. I'd seen from George Washington's diaries that he had taken an interest in observing the rising of the Bright Morning Star. But the concept of the benign rays of the Bright Morning Star improving the lot of mankind seemed a nice image rather than something with any practical impact. Now that I had found that there could be a real beneficial effect on individual creativity and achievement, I had developed a much greater respect for the wisdom and Masonic knowledge of Brothers Christopher Wren and George Washington. When they decided to incorporate alignments towards the Bright Morning Star into city plans, they may have been implementing something that they had found to work in their own lives for the benefit of their societies.

This theory of Masonic astrology might contain scientific ideas that are important when trying to understand the success and failure of societies. But before I could be sure of this, I needed to prove that this theory is viable. That meant submitting it to Richard Dawkins' second test. He said if any astrology (and by implication that must include Masonic astrology) can pass both his tests, it must be taken seriously. I now had a scientific theory that fitted the facts. It could explain personality development in terms of astrophysics and neuronal growth. I hadn't made use of any unknown mysterious forces. But did my theory make predictions? If it had any validity, then it should predict things that were not known previously and that could be tested. But the theory of science says that nothing can be proved right. You can only show that something worked on the occasion it was tested; next time it might fail, so it would take forever to prove it was always right. The only thing science can prove with certainty is failure. If a theory fails to predict accurately, then it is incorrect and must be discarded. But, as long as it does not fail, it can be taken as a reasonable guess at reality. If I wanted to move forward I had to make predictions that could be clearly shown to be wrong—something most astrologers avoid. So I needed to make explicit predictions which I could then test against impartial observation, preferably collected by third parties. If my predictions failed, even once, then I must reject this theory; if they proved accurate, then the theory would become worthy of further investigation.

Before tackling this rather daunting task, I needed to review my reasoning and make sure I understood the steps that had taken me from curiosity about Bro. George Washington's choice of layout for his Federal City of Washington, D.C., to a general theory of the Masonic astrology that inspired him. To recap:

1. First, I found a correlation between the surges of achievement in societies (including the one founded by George Washington) as seen by McClelland, and the appearance of the Bright Morning Star that Gauquelin noted in the birth charts of successful people. The findings of Sachs lent some authority to this theory, but did not quite fit in with what McClelland and Gauquelin had found.

2. Next, I took a notion that was implicit in Gauquelin's findings and used it to make forecasts. Gauquelin's statistics showed that successful babies are born when certain Bright Morning Stars are on the eastern horizon or directly overhead. These were the planets that had the strongest gravitational pull on the earth. I used this idea that successful people are born when a heavy planet rises near, or at right-angles to, the sun to predict the fraction of high-achieving people that should be born into a society at a particular time. The predictions I made using this rule matched McClelland's observations. I called this the "morning-star-zone" technique.

3. I used the same method to check out Sachs's findings about the star-sign spread of successful people who applied to universities. I

was able to replicate the degree of variability shown in his results using the "morning-star-zone" technique.

4. Now I had a forecasting tool. It could guess the number of successful people who should be expected to be born in particular societies. But I knew of no logical reason why it should work. To try to find out why it worked, I went back to look at basic theories of personality and achievement motivation.

5. Science's collective view on personality is that it is the sum of the memories we create to remind us of our life story. Our memories are stored within our brains as neuron links. These links are formed by a series of electrical impulses through a process called long-term potentiation, a process that is started by trigger impulses, usually from our senses.

6. Children are born with lots of unlinked neurons. Babies grow self-aware brains and develop consciousness by a process called somatic selection. This is a sort of electric pruning of excess neurons, which occurs as the brain adapts to the world. In a young child there are lots of neurons but not many synapses. In an adult personality there are far fewer neurons but a lot more synapses linking them together. In a growing young brain, all the neurons are trying to link up. Those that form strong links survive, while those that don't link up don't get used and wither away. This process is summed up by the saying "neurons that fire together, wire together."

7. This selection process can be affected by outside forces. Neurons can act like simple radio sets and pick up pulses of radio energy. When they do, the radio wave front can make them oscillate and form new synapses. A radio trigger pulse of the right wavelength can set off the process of long-term potentiation, which can form new synapses so that unlinked neurons form new connections.

8. When heavy planets pass close to the sun, as viewed from the earth, the criss-crossing of the gravity fields causes abrupt movements in groups of free electrons in the ionosphere. This rattling around of clouds of free electrons creates waves of radio noise. The

pulses making up these wave fronts are similar in shape and frequency to some memory-forming pulses that occur naturally in the brain. This happens when planets with a strong gravitational pull rise as Bright Morning Stars.

These eight facts formed the basis for my theory of Masonic astrology. Now I needed to investigate their implications.

Radio-noise pulses, caused by the tidal pull of some planets on the ionosphere, can make neurons fire, and this can affect two things: the way a brain develops, and the way the brain feels when the same set of pulses later hits the fully grown brain. The original birth-star pulses affect the brain's development by encouraging neurons to make new links when the neurons are at a resonant length for the star pulses (this length could very well be shorter than the length the neurons would have grown to before linking if they had not been exposed to ionospheric radio noise). And once a neuron has made a synapse, the length from nucleus to synapse is fixed for the rest of its natural life. This trend could easily lead to a denser linking of shorter neuron axons over a period of time. The statistics suggest that the exposure to these pulses in early childhood results in a successful adult.

The second effect can occur when the pulse pattern reappears as the planet again moves across the same area of sky as it did when the brain was forming. If these neurons remain healthy, then they will be exactly the right length to be triggered again. As the Bright Morning Star recreates the pulses, it increases activity in those parts of the brain and result in some sort of emotional response. The pulse patterns that first triggered the brain's connections fire when that same planet rises in front of the sun again.

In chapter 8 I described how rats were given an emotional reward by beaming radio impulses at them. They had first been conditioned by bombarding them with radio pulses while they were given food rewards. But the experimenters found that the radio pulses alone were a sufficient reward. The food was no longer needed. The implication of this research is that people whose neuron linkages were formed in childhood by the pulses of a particular Bright Morning Star can receive emotional rewards at a subsequent appearance of their birth star.

I had arrived at this view after doing a few sums based on Newton's theory of gravity. Those calculations showed that when the gravitational fields of Bright Morning Stars criss-crossed the gravitational pull of the sun, periods of chaotic swirling occured high in the atmosphere when some planets were aligned with the sun or at right-angles to it. The resulting abrupt jiggling of loose electrons resulted in pulses of radio energy-chains of blips similar to the pulses that occur when learning and memory creation takes place in a brain—and I suspected they might be able to cause long-term-potentiation (the process which creates new neuron linkages) in an exposed brain.

Single neurons act as one-channel radio receivers, and the Stewart Report confirmed this as a possible basis for a mechanism to start spontaneous changes in the neuron connections. The statistical effects that McClelland, Gauquelin, and Sachs saw can all be explained if gravity-driven radio pulses react with babies' brains. An early surge in neuron entanglement seems to create adults who tend to achieve, and I had learned from Karl Pribram that the sort of external electro-magnetic waves that tidal forces cause in the ionosphere can create new synapses (see chapter 11). This means that economically thriving societies should contain an increased proportion of high-achieving individuals.

But these are general statements, not predictions. Is this theory strong enough to be tested by prediction and experiment? Can I answer Stephen Hawking's complaint that "the real reason most scientists don't believe in astrology is not scientific evidence or the lack of it but because it is not consistent with other theories which have been tested by experiment"?[235] To meet this requirement, I need to make predictions that might turn out to be wrong. So here goes. I am about to become a Masonic astrologer, and I'm not sure I'm happy in this role.

### The Brain Has No Firewall

When I looked at the contours of the free electron population that make up the structure of the ionosphere, I was struck by two facts.

The first was that the numbers of free electrons floating around decreases the farther away you are from the equator. In chapter 11 I explained that there are three layers of ionized molecules in the upper reaches of the atmosphere, the closest being the D-layer, with the E- and F-layers above it. The low-lying

D-layer is densest for about 30° on either side of the equator (outside this range the density drops by a factor of ten), and, since it absorbs radio signals, it lies like a radio shield over the tropics.

In my day job at Bradford University School of Management I work with vulnerable computer systems. These can be attacked by rogue programs designed to cause damage and disruption, and to protect the University's computer system, we use a piece of software called a firewall. This software looks at every message that tries to come in from the hostile outside and decides if it is dangerous or not. Potentially dangerous messages are stopped before they can do any harm.

It looked to me as if the D-layer might also act like a firewall for human brains, protecting the latitudes around the Equator from the radio pulses that are strong in the dense tropical F-layers. The thick D-layer, below the E-layer and separate from it, forms what radar engineers call "an elevated duct which traps the radar energy in a layer between the two interfaces." This duct also traps fast-rising pulses and prevents a lot of the ionospheric radio energy from reaching the ground in the tropics.[236]

The second fact that struck me was that in times of high electrical activity, the active part of the ionosphere is between 180-250 miles (300-400 kilometers) above the D-layer. This means that most of the radio pulses caused by the tidal pull of planets on the ionosphere should hit the earth at higher latitudes, where the D-layer is much less effective as a shield. Figure 21 shows a scale plot of the D- and F2-layers against latitude. From this, I worked out the average range of latitudes that would be most influenced by these ionic pulses generated by the tidal tugging of the Bright Morning Star. The area of strongest signal strength stretches from approximately 30° to 60° towards either pole.

If my theory of Masonic astrology is right, then there ought to be a correlation between the achievement motivation of a society and its latitude. Societies nearer the equator are protected by the D-layer's firewall effect and should have a smaller proportion of highly motivated people. This is a forecast that I can test.

## Prosperity and Latitude

When McClelland wanted to know what fraction of the people in a society were highly motivated, he used economic activity to assess it. I needed to find

244

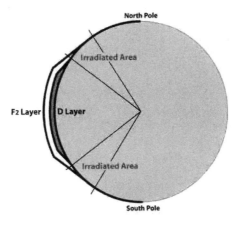

*Figure 21: Effect of the low D-layer shielding the ground from the ionic turbulence pulse signals at latitudes near the Equator.*

a similar measure for as wide a range of countries as I could. I went along to my university library and spoke to the librarian. She gave me two sources of data. One was a list of the Gross National Product (GNP) per capita for every country in the world in 1955.[237] She also found a study from 1988 that listed the GNP per capita of every country in the world.[238] These gave me two sets of data to test out the forecast. (The graphs of the data are shown in appendix 10.)

The chart for 1955 shows a much higher level of GNP per capita for societies that are between 30° and 60° of latitude from the equator. This result made me uneasy. I had begun this quest hoping I would be able to explain Masonic astrology as a simple inspirational effect and to discount any physical reality behind it. What I had found used simple science—nothing more than Newtonian mechanics combined with radio theory—but it was predicting the economic conduct of societies. Surely this has to be chance? I decided to retest the prediction on the 1988 data. The later data also showed a clear increase in average GNP per capita for societies more than 30° of latitude from the Equator.

In 1988 the average income for each person living in a country within 30° of latitude from the equator (the counties shielded from the radio pulses of the ionosphere by the D-layer) was $1,490. For countries not shielded by the D-layer the average income was $9,235—over six times greater. I did the same calculation for 1955 and found the average income to be $183 for D-layer-shielded countries, and $585 for unshielded countries. So even after the disorder of World War II, the difference in the GNP of these two areas was still a factor of three.

Now I had worked out a correlation between latitude and economic success. This result seemed to be something other than chance. It was an economic consequence I had not suspected before I made the prediction.

But perhaps I had simply stumbled across something that an economist could explain easily. So the following day, I dropped into the office of Dr. Damian Ward, a leading research economist who works with me at the Bradford School of Management. I showed him my results and correlations, and he checked my figures.

"They seem OK to me," he said.

"But have you any idea what causes it?" I asked.

"Not really," he replied. "My first guess would be that there is some sort of climate effect, because there are a lot of resource-rich counties in the list of low economic achievers. Just a minute though," he added. "I've recently read something about this in a paper from the World Bank."

Damian rummaged around on his desk for a moment and produced copies of some papers.

"Here it is," he said. He produced three papers and passed them over to me. "Borrow them and read them," he said. "But as I remember, although these writers draw attention to the correlation between distance from the equator and economic performance, even to the extent to building it into forecasting models used by the World Bank, nobody explains why it's like this." He pointed to a diagram (see appendix 10). "This shows the link Dani Rodrik found between distance from the equator and income."

The graph confirmed the results I had found for 1955 and 1988. So now I knew that this effect had been consistent over at least a couple of generations.

"Damian, are you quite sure there isn't some economic theory which explains why this happens?" I persisted.

"Not that I know," he said. "But if there is a technical reason, it will be in one of these papers, or in this." He passed me a weighty textbook on the theory of economic growth. "The only other possibility might lie in demographics. You could check if it's just an artifact of population size providing the opportunity for economic success."

I thanked Damian and went back to my own office to read. The first thing I did was to look up the populations of the countries in the 1988 data and plot them against their latitude. The correlation between latitude and number of people was +2 percent. (This means there is hardly any connection between the two factors—a correlation of plus or minus 100 percent means the two factors behave identically, whereas a correlation of 0 percent means there is no common behavior or possible linkage). I next checked the correlation between population size and GNP per capita and found it to be -4 percent. Effectively, there is no correlation (see appendix 10). But the correlation between GNP per capita and latitude averages +60 percent (which is a strong common behavior pattern). Based on this test, I could eliminate population size as the cause of the economic achievement. But I needed to be sure that there were no other simple reasons why it was happening.

Going back to look at the papers Damian had given me, I found that Robert Hall and Charles Jones of Stanford University had also noticed this latitude effect. They said:

*Finally, we include one physical measure of infrastructure: the distance of the country from the equator. A long tradition among demographers and geographers recognizes that countries with temperate climates tend to have more successful economies than those with tropical climates. However, this relationship has not been examined carefully by economists. It turns out that the relationship is powerful and robust. Distance from the equator remains an important determinant of output per worker.[239]*

They had more to say in the conclusion to their paper:

*Our results on the importance of distance from the equator calls for improved measures of climate and other aspects of geography. The role of disease in the latitude effect calls for further investigation, as well as changes that may have occurred recently as result of better understanding of public health. Singapore, located near the equator, has substantially higher output per worker, and total factor productivity than is predicted by our equation.[240]*

They highlight the fact that Singapore does not fit the usual pattern. My forecast was based on a guess that the D-layer is consistently dense for 30° on either side of the equator during the day. But this comment about Singapore made me look again at my graph of D-layer density, which shows in more detail what is happening in the air of the tropics (see appendix 5). It turns out that during the winter months the D-layer above Singapore is quite thin, and this would allow the infant population more exposure to astral radio pulses from the ionosphere. The statistics for 1988 show that Singapore was the third-best performer in the Asia Pacific group, only beaten by Hong Kong, which is also under a thin part of the D-layer, and the top earner, Brunei. (Brunei is under a thick D-layer, but it is a major exporter of oil, so the success of its economy does not depend on the motivation of its people.)

The observation of how the aggregate motivation of individuals affects the success of an economy is called the study of endogenous growth (i.e., of growth that comes from within a society). By its very nature, this growth happens only when individuals make it happen. This is the process that McClelland was looking at when he noticed the periodic patterns of peak and decline that I realized coincided with the rising of heavy planets near the sun.

It was the uneven distribution of wealth across the latitudes that first attracted McClelland's attention. This is what he said about it:

*Certain countries, primarily in northern Europe and North America, have accumulated wealth probably at a faster rate and certainly to a much higher average level than has ever been known before in the history of the world. United States per capita income in constant prices rose from 1850 to 1950, as a five-fold increase. In Great Britain average income quadrupled in the same period. At the present time, the average per capita income varies tremendously from one country to another. Thus, the average person in northern Europe or the United States has ten to twelve times as much wealth at his disposal as the average person in most of Africa or Asia. Or, to put it in its most striking fashion, approximately 7 per cent of the world's population in North America enjoy about 43 per cent of the world's wealth, while 55 per cent of the population, in Asia, have only about 16 per cent the world's wealth.*

*Even a quick glance raises some interesting questions. Why should Argentina lag so far behind the United States or Australia in per capita income? Is it so much less favored by climate and natural resources? Or compare France and Poland with the United Kingdom and Sweden. The differences here in climate and natural resources are by no means outstanding, and yet there is a marked difference in economic development to date.*[241]

Economics cannot explain the gaps that McClelland saw between levels of success. The theories assume that the proportions of motivated people is identical in all societies.

My forecast used two simple concepts, each of which arose from my theory of Masonic astrology. The first was that if lots of babies are exposed to more ionospheric radio pulses, then a greater fraction of them will grow up to be successful. This success can be measured in the same way McClelland did it, by looking at the economic success of the society these babies grow up in. The second idea was that the D-layer shields countries in the tropical latitudes from much of the radio-pulse activity. This implies that the farther from the equator a baby grows up, the more chance it has of being an economic success. Radar plots show that there are some thinner regions of the D-layer in the tropics, and countries under the thin parts should also produce more babies whose brains are pushed towards economic success.

I had now made an astrological prediction, based on Masonic theory, of how a Bright Morning Star rising just before the sun affects the way growing neurons link up. I did not really expect the forecast to be accurate, but when I checked it out using McClelland's method, I found it to fit exactly with what happens in the world. I was staggered to discover that economic theorists say that distance from the equator can be "a powerful and robust" predictor of economic achievement for a society. But nobody knows why this should be; in fact, the whole thrust of endogenous growth theory assumes that all economies are able to achieve equal economic success, and that over time other effects should even out—but the historical facts say they don't. What amazed me even more was that two countries that didn't fit the pattern, Singapore and Hong Kong, were in areas where the theory of Masonic astrology says that a larger part of the population should be successful.

I cast this economic horoscope to try to meet Richard Dawkins' criteria that predictions should be clear and testable. I have found that the proportion of successful people is not constant. It changes with the latitude where they live. The fact that economic cycles can be predicted by looking at the signal strength of radio pulses caused by Bright Morning Stars rising before the sun is an unexpected outcome. I have used only astrophysics and statistics to make this prediction. And the facts show it is accurate.

This is a strange astrological prediction, and it is unlikely to win me fame and fortune or a weekly column casting horoscopes in a newspaper. But now I need to see if there are any further prophecies I can make to test my theory of Masonic astrology. The inspiration for this next forecast popped into my head when I was relaxing reading a Sherlock Holmes story.

## Barking Mad

"Is there any point to which you would wish to draw my attention?"

"To the curious incident of the dog in the night-time."

"The dog did nothing in the night-time."

"That was the curious incident," remarked Sherlock Holmes.

Sherlock Holmes's curious exchange with Inspector Lestrade in *Silver Blaze* suggested another possible forecast I could test.

One of my early clues to how gravity might cause an electrical response in neurons came from the effect of the full moon on the brain of Pi, my wife's epileptic border collie. (I tell Pi's story in chapter 10.) He became excitable and prone to fits when the moon was full. Did any other brains respond to the full moon?

Getting excited when the moon is full is something that Pi seemed to share with many doctors working in emergency medicine. In the September 2002 edition of the *British Medical Journal*, Adam Fox and Patrick Davies wrote about the role of superstition in reducing work-related stress. They said:

*There is plenty of evidence to suggest that doctors are superstitious creatures too. Sixty four per cent of emergency physicians believe that the lunar cycle affects their workload, despite evidence to the contrary. No difference has been found between number of admissions, severity, or likelihood of trauma on such days.*[242]

Did the mismatch between the doctors' feelings and the reality of their workloads reflect a change in their degree of tolerance to stress? Or was the increase of radio pulses from the moon's gravity triggering an unsuspected emotional reaction?

Were twirling electrons in the ionosphere affecting the way both Pi's and the doctors' brains worked? Pi's brain was less complex than the doctors', but it would have developed faster than the human brains. A dog's brain may be smaller and simpler in operation, but the same principles of neuron growth still apply to it: A loosely connected bundle of neurons grows under the control of neuron growth hormone, so that the various senses are connected to the right part of the brain; the neurons form synapses when they first fire together, and they make up the same type of simple radio sets that the sub-components of the human brain do.

If a lot of growing neurons are the right length, then radio pulses created by the interaction of the gravitational fields of the sun and moon will make them fire and connect. This will leave the young dog with a high proportion of its neurons formed at the resonant length of the radio pulses caused by the moon's rising and reaching its zenith or highest point in sky. If the dog is genetically inclined towards epilepsy, it will end up with a lot of its neurons of a length that resonates with the pulses generated by the moon.

But the new moon also creates a chain of ionic turbulence pulses, so why did Pi seem to respond only to some phases of the moon and not to others? I went back to my theory of Masonic astrology to see what might be happening.

There are four critical areas where the gravity fields cross and create turbulent pulses of radio noise. These are when the moon and the sun rise together, when the moon rises 90° before the sun, when the moon rises opposite the sun, and when the moon rises 90° behind the sun.

Each of these four positions gives different patterns of alternating positive and negative pulses. The new and full moon cause the highest-amplitude pulses, as this is when the gravitational fields are acting together or against each other. The effect of this can be seen in patterns of spring and neap tides. Spring tides occur when the moon is new, and its gravitational pull aligns with that of the sun; they result in the water coming farther up the shore and receding farther out. Neap tides are lower than average, as the gravitational forces of the sun and the moon pull against each other.

The tides of ionic turbulence, however, are not quite the same as the tides of the sea. Water molecules stick together more than the ionized electrons that make up ionosphere, and they are much, much heavier. This means that water has more inertia, and once a large body of water starts to move it will tend to keep moving, even if there are short adverse tugs of gravity. Free electrons, however, have a very small mass (less than a millionth of a water molecule's) and they don't stick together at all, as their negative charges repel each other.

The effect of the gravity pulls of the sun and the moon crossing is to rattle the cloud of very light electrons to and fro. As the cloud pulsates, the chaotic dance of the electrons produces pulses of radio noise, which trigger synaptic connections.

But neurons are non-linear systems. Synapses act like one-way valves for the flow of electric current, just like the crystal rectifier in my first homemade radio set. Only pulses of negative voltage will trigger the neurons' response. Positive-voltage pulses will have no effect at all on the formation of synapses.

When the moon is new, it appears close to the sun in the sky and its gravity pulls in the same direction, but when the moon is full, its gravity pulls against the sun. When I worked through the equations (see appendix 9) I noticed that the result of these churning forces will be to create more negative pulses (and just a few positive pulses). However, when the moon is full and pulls against the sun, this position reversal will create more positive pulses (and just a few negative pulses). Whether the pulse is positive or negative depends entirely on the phase of the Cos and Sin functions.

As I was visualizing this band of pulsating current, I remembered that it is concentrated around the equator. Although this band is dense when it is in sunlight, it is far less dense when in shadow. It can be thought of as a circle of current above the equator. Looking down on this ring of current from the northern latitudes, if an east-west movement (meaning an anticlockwise rotation) caused a negative pulse, then its effect would be reversed when viewed from the southern hemisphere. If I imagined myself standing in the southern hemisphere looking up towards the rotating ring of current, then an east-west movement would be a clockwise rotation, which would cause a positive pulse. (The rule I used to calculate the sign of the pulse from the direction of the current is known as Fleming's right-hand rule.)

This led me to make another Masonic astrological prediction. Pi's epilepsy was more likely to be triggered when the moon was full, and he was not greatly affected by the new moon. I predict that if he were taken to Australia, then his pattern of response would move from the full moon to the new moon. It's a nice theory, but testing it didn't seem very practical. Was there any way I could test out this idea, short of buying Pi a crate and an air ticket?

It turned out there was a simple way to test my new prediction. I went to the library and asked Jenny, the librarian, if she knew of any studies of dog behavior and the effect of the lunar cycle. I expected her to make scathing comments about lunacy and academics, but I was wrong.

"Oh yes," she said, "some of the guys over at the School of Health did a study on the effect of the phase of the moon on dog bites not so long ago. Give me a minute and I'll find it for you."

She soon returned with a copy of the *British Medical Journal* containing an article whose authors had examined the records of 1,621 patients admitted to the Bradford Royal Infirmary for dog bites between 1997 and 1999. They analyzed the dates of first treatment and looked at the distribution of bites in relation to the phases of the moon. This is what they found:

*The incidence of animal bites rose significantly at the time of the full moon. With the period of the full moon as the reference period, the incidence rate ratio for all other periods of lunar cycle was significantly lower.*[243]

They went on:

*There were 37 full moon days and one blue moon day [the second full moon in a calendar month] from 1 January 1997 to 31 December 1999. In all, 1,621 new patients had been bitten by animals (56 cat bites (3.4%), 11 rat bites (0.7%), 13 horse bites (0.8%), and 1,541 dog bites (95.1%)). The highest numbers of bites were on or around full moon days . . . The incidence of animal bites in the time of full moon was significantly higher than the incidence in the other periods in the lunar cycle (P<0.001) . . . The rise in incidence seemed to accelerate therefore a few days before a full moon, peaking sharply on the day of the full moon before falling away rapidly to rate that was about half the rate at full moon.*[244]

So Pi is not the only animal in West Yorkshire to become over-excited at the time of the full moon. But what about my Masonic astrological prediction that if he emigrates to Australia, which is of course in the southern hemisphere, then he will become susceptible to epilepsy when the moon is new?

Jenny also found some data on this. In fact, she found an article asking just this question. This study was carried out by Australian physicians Professor Stephen Chapman and Dr. Stephen Morrell of the Department of Public Health and Community Medicine, University of Sydney. Chapman wanted to prevent dog bites to young children. He put forward an idea for an educational program for primary school children, teaching them appropriate behavior when dealing with dogs. He developed what he called "Prevent-a-Bite" and tested it in eight primary schools in Sydney. He reported in the *British Medical Journal*:

> *The Prevent-a-Bite educational intervention increased appreciably the precautionary behaviour of young children around strange dogs in the short term.*[245]

After writing this paper, Professor Chapman was approached by a local farmer who said to him, "Have you university types ever looked at whether dog bites happen more around the full moon? It's a well-known fact that they do."

Chapman thought that farmers might be storehouses of folkloric knowledge, which they say is derived from a rich tradition of watching what goes on. He cited examples such as sky color and the weather ("red sky at night, shepherd's delight; red sky in the morning, shepherd's warning") or avoiding the wrath of bulls ("red rag to a bull"). Then, reining in his natural skepticism, he investigated, and the result was another article for the *British Medical Journal* entitled "Barking mad? Another lunatic hypothesis bites the dust." This is what Chapman found:

> *We obtained from the National Injury Surveillance Unit 12 months of data on daily admissions for dog bites to all accident and emergency departments in public hospitals in Australia. We chose a year of data for analysis that would supply sufficient event numbers, both of dog bites and full moons, and would enable us to sniff out any seasonal variation in dog bite admissions . . . Altogether 1,671 accident and emergency admissions for dog bites occurred during the study period (938 males, 733 females), representing an overall mean admission rate of 4.58 per day . . . [There were] 18 peak days ( notionally >10 admissions/day), with*

*the maximum peak centring on the New Year break (the highest peak (24) occurred on New Year's Day 1998). Full moons coincided with none of these peaks. The pattern was similar for female and male admissions.*[246]

Chapman concluded:

*In Australia at least, no positive relation seems to exist between the full moon and dog bites severe enough for hospital treatment.*[247]

However, there was another pattern lurking in the data, which was spotted by Mr. A.S. Lawrence, a consultant anesthetist from Preston in the U.K. He said in a letter:

*I read with interest the two articles on frequency of dog bites related to seasonal changes, in particular the lunar cycle.*

*However, despite the humorous nature of this particular edition of the Journal, I do feel that the authors of one of the papers (Chapman & Morrell) may have thrown out the baby with the bathwater. They demonstrate that there is no association between frequency of dog bites and phase of the moon, nor day of the week, in Australia.*

*Nevertheless, there is something cyclical about the frequency of reported dog bites, although admittedly it is not in phase with lunar changes. Even if you draw a cutoff line below 10 bites per day, there are clearly 12 sharp peaks of bite frequency as high as 15 to 20 per day, lasting only a day or so, occurring on a regular basis throughout the year. Do they occur on the first day of the month, rather than the lunar cycle, as there are 12 months but 13 lunar phases in one year?*

*If I was told that the graph was actually a strip of poor quality ECG recording, I would say that the patient has clear QRS complexes, is regular enough to possibly be in sinus rhythm, but there is a lot of EMG muscle artefact noise.*

*I feel that the data should be subjected to more detailed signal analysis and other mathematical techniques which have been developed to recover information from noise to tease out further the demonstrated regular pattern of dog bite frequency. It may reveal some fascinating insight into the habits of dogs and/or humans in Australia.*[248]

There was also a comment from Dr. S. Pearce, a registrar of the Royal Southants Hospital, who said:

*Although Chapman and Morrell note the lack of peaks in admissions for dog bites at the full moon, a closer scrutiny of the data provided indicates that there are indeed peaks, but at the time of the new moon.*
*Could this be due to difficulty seeing the dogs coming?*[249]

I scanned in and digitized the wave form from the Chapman and Morrell data published in the *British Medical Journal*, and found that Dr. Pearce and Mr. Laurence were correct in what they saw. The peaks occur as the moon is in conjunction with the sun, fulfilling my second Masonic astrological prediction. This is when the gravitational turbulence equation predicts a large number of negative pulses of radio noise with frequencies which will trigger neurons of the right length. So if Pi does ever emigrate to Australia, he will need to increase the dose of his tablets around the time of the new moon.

I have now made two clear-cut and simple predictions from the theory of Masonic astrology, and both have proved to be correct when tested against reality. This means my theory has passed both of Richard Dawkins' tests of astrology. It should now be taken seriously. Now is the time to return to the original inspiration for the quest, and look at the implications of Bro. George Washington's use of Masonic astrology to found the Federal City of Washington, D.C.

## Conclusions

After reviewing the main ideas of my theory of Masonic astrology, I used it to make two unequivocal Masonic astrological forecasts.

First, I worked out that the theory of Masonic astrology predicts that the degree of economic activity of societies should increase the farther they are from the equator.

Next, I predicted that dogs' brains in the southern hemisphere should be more aroused at the new moon, rather than the full moon as Western European folklore asserts.

I made two predictions that could have been shown to be wrong by simple facts. But I found strong evidence that both were correct. This does not prove my theory, but it lets it pass on to undergo further tests of credibility. If it had failed these first tests I would have discarded it.

Here is a list of the key findings that I used to make the predictions:

1. There is a physical mechanism which, when high-gravity planets appear as Bright Morning Stars near the sun in the earth's sky, causes turbulence in the ionosphere and creates pulses of radio noise.

2. Some pulses of radio energy interact with individual neurons inside the brains of humans and animals, and when doing so cause resonant neurons to trigger.

3. The triggering of neurons can result in the formation of new neural pathways, and this is important during the development of a child's brain. The process begins in the womb about eleven weeks after conception.

4. The interconnection and regular triggering of neurons gives rise to characteristic behavior patterns and memories.

5. Societies with a larger proportion of individuals showing $n$-achievement-motivated behavior are economically more active. This means that economic activity is an indicator of where and when such groups of people live.

6. There is a link between economic achievement and distance from the equator.

7. The phase of the chains of pulses is reversed between the northern and southern hemispheres, producing different patterns of brain arousal, as measured by dog-bite data.

These facts all fit with the ideas of modern brain theory. It seems that Bro. Christopher Wren and Bro. George Washington had the good of society in mind when they drew up alignments of their capital cities to draw attention to the benign rays of the Bright Morning Star. Their knowledge of Masonic ritual predicted that its appearance should improve their societies, and in the case of Washington it did. McClelland identified the U.S., after the establishment of the Federal City of Washington, D.C., as one of his outstanding achieving societies.

I doubt forecasts of the type I have made are going to turn me into a popular astrologer, as my theory makes no predictions about individuals or their future prospects. So it's no use for casting horoscopes. But does it have any value? That is what I need to look at next.

# Chapter Thirteen

# Further Predictions
of Masonic Astrology

## Changing the World

When Niels Bohr discovered quantum theory, he changed physics forever. No longer was it possible to run a slide rule over everything in the world. Now there was a lower limit to the fineness of detail that could be measured. His theory forbids any scientist from making accurate guesses about separate particles: the best that can be done is to look at how subatomic particles behave in a crowd.

In the nineteenth century scientists thought that, if they measured how any object moved, they could recreate its every past and future move. Bohr forced them to give up this clockwork universe. Einstein, a deep thinker about space and time, was unhappy about this. He didn't think the universe should be chaotic and unpredictable. But quantum mechanics says that no events are certain, they have only a finite probability of happening—which can be calculated beforehand.

Einstein complained to Bohr, saying, "God does not play dice with the Universe."

Bohr's reply was, "Albert, it's not your job to tell God what He can and cannot do!"

What Bohr left unsaid in that rebuke was what the real job of a scientist is. In my view, it is to observe, to try to explain what is observed, and, finally, to try to create a model that enables predictions to be made. Those predictions can then be tested to confirm or deny the truth of the model.

This is the process I have tried to follow as I look at Masonic astrology. When first faced with the puzzle of why George Washington should want to influence the key alignment of the Federal City of Washington, D.C., to highlight a symbolic myth drawn from Masonic astrology, I felt as Einstein felt about God's gambling habits. I wanted to say, "Why did Washington do that? There's no way the movement of the stars can affect human behavior." But I now wondered if Bro. George felt some positive appeal at the rising of the Bright Morning Star that convinced him it had a worthwhile effect.

Masonic astrology appears to have tapped into ancient observations of natural cause and effect that science has overlooked; this is the basis of the case I make for it. Many modern Freemasons seem not to understand the spiritual insight of the Bright Morning Star and are unable to explain its effect. But Masons in George Washington's time were more aware of this heritage, as I have found from their writings. And Bro. Washington's diaries prove he took a great interest in the rising of Bright Morning Stars over Mount Vernon in the years after his Masonic Initiation.

The Craft, as Freemasons call the ritual practice of Masonry, had preserved legends which claimed that being re-born to the rays of the Bright Morning Star brought positive benefits to an individual. This idea had been incorporated into its ritual, although there was never any suggestion of real science behind it. However, various statistical studies suggested there might be some underlying cause, and I have found a scientific explanation that works independently of Freemasonry. But it was the secrets hidden in the Craft ritual that gave me clues to understanding how humanity might benefit from this effect.

If astrology was always wrong, it would have been junked long ago. Because it is sometimes more accurate than it has any sensible right to be, people feel it is telling them something useful, and there must be something in it. So they keep listening, even when astrologers talk nonsense. Masonic astrology alone has preserved some secret knowledge. It is that the benign rays of the Bright Morning Star have a beneficial effect on members of the human race. The statistical studies of Gauquelin and Sachs showed these birth-star patterns in human behavior to be more than coincidence. But nobody—astrologer, Freemason, or statistician—has managed to explain why this should be.

As we've seen, Gauquelin resorted to mystical "cosmic forces" to explain his results, while Sachs was more honest. He simply shrugged his shoulders and said that he didn't know what caused it. The astrologers I talked to were no help, as they were still living in the ruins of the clockwork world that Niels Bohr demolished. Stephen Hawking had commented on how astrologers cling to the wreckage of outdated science, saying:

> *When Copernicus and Galileo discovered that planets orbit the Sun rather than the Earth and Newton discovered the laws that governed their motion, astrology became extremely implausible.*[250]

Nothing I have found about Masonic astrology makes the casting of an individual horoscope plausible. Masonic astrology can predict only when a greater proportion of the children born will grow up to be high-achievers. It claims there is a secret key to knowledge locked inside each individual personality, and that knowledge can be freed by turning the key of Solomon's wisdom. The Masonic Temple was built to allow the light of the Bright Morning Star to shine into it as a sign of divine approval.

In Masonic ritual, Solomon holds the key to understanding the purpose of the Temple and the meaning of the Bright Morning Star that shines into it when it is complete and consecrated. His task is to continually build a new Temple as a sacred place to encourage the Divine Shekinah to shine its benign rays over all the human race. When Bro. George Washington sat in the chair of King Solomon and ritually became his humble representative, he grasped this truth and built it into the fabric of the United States. By using the tools of science to study Bro. Washington's use of this Solomon key, I have uncovered an ancient awareness of human potential that I think is worthy of further study.

There is a scientific rationale underlying Masonic astrology that can help to answer David McClelland's questions about the behavior of societies. The purpose of Freemasonry has always been to improve society and each individual's contribution to it. But Masonic astrology is not an astrology of individuals, it is an astrology of societies. And it seems to have a solid observational basis.

## The Erosion of Astrology

Science has slowly worn away the valid areas of study left open to astrology. This erosion began when Johannes Kepler set out to analyze astrology, but found the laws of planetary motion instead. In 1596, when he was Professor of Mathematics at Graz University in Austria, he published three laws that describe how planets move. They still form the basis of all the calculations we make to place satellites in the right orbits. He wrote a book called *The Cosmographic Mystery*, and turned the study of the visible movements of the stars and planets into the new science of astronomy.

Kepler is the father of modern astronomy, but he began studying the stars only because of his interest in astrology. This letter, which he wrote in 1599, three years after discovering the nature of planetary orbits, shows exactly what inspired him to study how the planets move. It also shows a remarkable insight into the mechanism which underlies Masonic astrology:

*Here is another question: how does the conformation of the heavens influence the character of a man at the moment of his birth? It influences a human being as long as he lives in no other way than that in which the peasant haphazardly ties slings around pumpkins; these do not make the pumpkin grow, but they determine its shape. So do the heavens: they do not give a man morals, experiences, happiness, children, wealth, a wife, but they shape everything with which a man has to do. And yet, from the constellation of the birth of a man, the heavens take an infinite number of forms during the course of his life. They never remain the same; so the constellation at birth is a passing one. Now how can something be active which doesn't exist?*[251]

But Kepler, and astrologers in general, have been asking the wrong questions. They are asking Newtonian questions of a system that can give only answers to questions phrased in quantum terms. A Newtonian astrologer asks "What will happen to me?" and then casts a horoscope. A Masonic astrologer asks a quantum question, "What will happen to this group of people when there is a period of gravity turbulence in the ionosphere above their heads?" and answers in terms of fractions, ratios, and averages.

Newtonian mechanics knows about indestructible particles moved by predictable forces. It claims that, given an accurate description of these fundamental particles, their interacting forces, and enough computing power, everything in the physical world can be known. The question "how does the conformation of the heavens influence the character of a man at the moment of his birth?" or the search for "a tendency for people's personalities to be predictable from their birthdays" are essentially Newtonian questions seeking to know the fate of an individual. For many applications of physics, this may be a reasonable type of question. But for the chaotic results of quantum processes it is not. This is where Gauquelin went wrong. He asked the sort of questions that astrologers do, and those questions have no answers.

The oracle of Masonic astrology hides behind a statistical veil. She will reveal herself and speak clearly only if asked a quantum question. But what sort of question can draw forth an unambiguous answer?

I believe there are two possible general questions that Masonic astrology might be able to answer. They are:

1.  What proportion of a group of people will be stimulated to act in a certain way by chains of ionospheric radio pulses?
2.  In which times and places will these pulses have their greatest effect?

Masonic astrology might conclude that George Washington should align the Capitol and the President's House (the White House) so that a Bright Morning Star will rise over the Capitol and shine its rays down Pennsylvania Avenue towards the President's House on a particular morning in February, if he wants his society to benefit.

Until astrology faces up to the challenge of meaningful questions, it will continue to wander in the wastelands of its broken clockwork universe. Only by looking at areas of behavior that science does not yet understand can it hope to progress. By studying astrology, Kepler took the study of planetary movement to a point where he discovered the laws of planetary motion. Newton seized the science of tidal flows from the superstitions of astrologers by putting forward a theory of gravity. The National Weather Service has taken responsibility for the forecasting of weather away from The Virginia Almanac, and sometimes it is even slightly more accurate.

How bright, heavy planets passing near the sun affect the behavior of groups of people remains up for grabs. But, rather than address this challenge, astrology prefers to gaze at its own navel and continue to cast horoscopes for Arians who want to seduce Leos rather than stick with the Libran who is good for them. Why not ask some hard questions that might help us all understand humanity?

I find myself in the uncomfortable position of trying to bring the unlikely predictions of Masonic astrology within the realm of science. There is a statistical link between the behavior of populations of personalities and the electromagnetic environment where their brains grow to maturity. Everything I have found so far says that this effect can be observed only in the interactions between groups. It does not seem possible to point out any single individual who will bring about future change.

So does this theory of Masonic astrology offer anything further to predict? Bro. Washington succeeded in harnessing Masonic astrology to aid the government of the young United States. But was he right in his assumption that the rising of the Bright Morning Star has a long-term civilizing influence?

## The Evolution of Star-Shaped Minds

You and I have come a long way on this journey since we set out to try to understand why George Washington laid out the focal points of the capital city of the newly created United States according to the principles of Masonic astrology.

Professor Walter Freeman's science of neurodynamics (see chapter 9) speaks of a landscape of attractors within the neural networks of the brain that form the pathways between the centers of increased neural activity that host our thoughts. In his own words:

*A cortex can be said to comprise an attractor landscape with several adjoining basins of attraction, one for each class of learned stimuli. We describe the activity of a sensory cortex in a waking animal as an itinerant trajectory over its landscape . . . a succession of momentary pauses in the basins of attractors, to which the cortex travels once a learned stimulus has arrived. The attractors are not shaped by the stimuli directly, but by previous experience with modulators as well as sensory input.*[252]

Edelman and Tononi agree with this idea that highly active clusters of inter-connected neurons are an important focus for consciousness, and that they affect the way we think. They worded it slightly differently:

*Consciousness . . . can be explained only by a distributed neural process, rather than by specific local properties of neurons . . . we formulate a hypothesis that explicitly states what is special about the subsets of neuronal groups that sustain conscious experience and how they can be identified. The hypothesis states:*

  1. *A group of neurons can contribute directly to conscious experience only if it is part of a distributed functional cluster . . .*
  2. *To sustain conscious experience, it is essential that this functional cluster be highly differentiated, as indicated by high values of complexity.*

*We call such a cluster . . . a "dynamic core," to emphasize both its integration and its constantly changing composition.*[253]

Professor Freeman's theory of how the brain works, with neuronal activity moving between a series of attractive landmarks in landscape, together with Edelman and Tononi's dynamic core hypothesis helped me put together a theory of why Masonic astrological influences change human behavior, and this theory is "consistent with other theories which have been tested by experiment."[254] But I still have another problem in the back of my mind. And that is the remarkable evolutionary development of our species over the last few millennia. Masonic ritual claims to preserve knowledge passed down from "Time Immemorial."

I recalled a comment from the great anthropologist Richard Leakey about innovation in early human history. He suggests that human creativity is a relatively recent evolutionary change:

*The overall pattern is simple: a technological innovation occurred around 200,000 years ago; it became the central part of a new, more sophisticated tool assemblage. Stability then prevailed once again, with no more significant innovations for at least another 100,000 years. Again, we see here an unimaginable—to us—period of lack of innovation. When innovation did come, it ignited a fire that burned with a recognizably human flame.*[255]

I decided to look again at Leakey's work on the evolution of humanness. He was puzzled by something that was now interesting me. He thought there was an uncoupling of the evolution of the modern human form and the development of new technologies. In other words, our species became human long before it became creative:

> In Western Europe the appearance of modern tool technologies—the Upper Pale-olithic—coincides with the appearance of modern humans, some forty thousand years ago. But almost certainly this represents the arrival of those people in that region . . . We see the early development of the blade technology, which comes to define modern human technology, appearing in Africa close to 100,000 years ago. But it is a slow development, not a full efflorescence . . . And in the Middle East we have modern people and a complete absence of modern tool technologies.[256]

Leakey makes an important point about the evolution of human creativity, saying that only a small advantage is needed for modern humans to grow rapidly and for earlier bipedal ape species to become extinct.[257] Does the theory of Masonic astrology offer an explanation for what this advantage might be? It might, because, as Leakey explains, a modest advantage in creativity has a major effect over long time periods:

> It seems counterintuitive to believe that a modest difference in subsistence skills—amounting to about a 2 percent margin in mortality per generation—could lead one population to success and the other to extinction. But often in biology our perceptions are rooted in present experience, and we have little grasp of what a long time dimension can do. In this case, a slim margin in mortality over a millennium translates into a big difference in ultimate survival.[258]

Could an environmental change such as exposure to the radio pulses of the ionosphere give modern humans this survival advantage? Richard Dawkins said of the effects of environment on evolution:

> After many generations of cumulative selection in a particular place, the local ani-mals and plants become well fitted to the conditions . . . If the conditions in which a lineage of animals lives remain constant—say it is dry and hot and has been so

*without a break for 100 generations—evolution in that lineage is likely to come to a halt, at least as far as adaptations to temperature and humidity are concerned. The animals will become as well fitted as they can be to the local conditions. This doesn't mean that they couldn't be completely redesigned to be even better. It does mean that they can't improve themselves by any small (and therefore likely) evolutionary step . . . Evolution will come to a standstill until something in the conditions changes: the onset of an ice age, a change in the average rainfall of the area, a shift in the prevailing wind. Such changes do happen when we are dealing with a timescale as long as the evolutionary one. As a consequence, evolution normally does not come to a halt, but constantly "tracks" the changing environment.*[259]

I was struck by the idea that such an environmental change had occurred 70,000 years ago, the time when our ancestors carved the first diamond patterns on the pieces of red ochre at Blombos Cave on the southern-most tip of South Africa. This group of *Homo sapiens* moved outside the protection of the D-layer (that blanket of ionized air that lies over the tropics and acts as a firewall against many ionospheric signals), and they exposed their children's growing brains to ionospheric radio pulses for the first time in human history. The result was that their high-achieving children drew the first written symbols. The latitude of Blombos Cave is 34° South.

Dr. Christopher Stringer, a researcher into modern human origins based at the Natural History Museum in London, and Dr. Clive Gamble, Reader in Archeology at Southampton University, said this about the sudden growth of human creativity:

*The source of modern behaviour will remain conjectural until we have a better understanding of which evolutionary forces and mechanisms actually shaped modern behaviour. What is quite clear, however, is that wherever new developments took place they did so rapidly (the flick of a switch), adapting to the anatomy of modern humans that had been around for perhaps 70,000 years. Such behaviour, based on the structural principles of symbolically organized culture, spread rather like a virus among the host population, and then spread further as the host itself now expanded. The rapidity of the process, which took place so many thousands of years ago, makes it difficult for archaeologists to study. But we believe that the global expansion of humans began some 60,000-40,000 years ago.*[260]

267

This leads me to make another prediction from the theory of Masonic astrology: All major advances in human creativity took place in groups of *Homo sapiens* that moved outside the cover of the D-layer.

To test this prediction, I needed to see if the major advances in civilization began at latitudes greater than 30° North or South of the Equator. Fortunately, Stringer and Gamble listed a table of the key changes in creative behavior and the dates they occurred, marking the path from the ancient Stone Age to modern man.[261] I tracked back through the locations of their examples for each event, and added the latitude from the equator into their list. Here is the result:

| Event | Years Before Present | Latitude |
|---|---|---|
| Storage pits | 40,000 | 55 |
| Quarries | 40,000 | 55 |
| Social storage | 40,000 | 55 |
| Artifact styles | 55,000 | 52 |
| Regional art | 40,000 | 50 |
| Long-term occupation of harsh environments | 40,000 | 50 |
| Ceramic technology | 25,000 | 50 |
| Long-distance trade | 58,000 | 48 |
| Art | 40,000 | 48 |
| Bone tools | 40,000 | 48 |
| Open site burials | 40,000 | 48 |
| Colonization of high mountains | 20,000 | 48 |
| Structured living space | 65,000 | 46 |
| Huts | 48,000 | 46 |
| Chains of connection | 40,000 | 45 |
| Built hearths | 52,000 | 38 |
| Colonization of boreal forest | 38,000 | 37 |
| Spoken language | 80,000 | 34 |
| Microliths | 70,000 | 33 |
| Body ornament | 40,000 | 32 |
| Blade technology | 80,000 | 31 |
| First evidence of planning for the future | 60,000 | 31 |

*Figure 22: The diamond-shaped images of Blombos Cave,* c. 70,000 BCE, *and (inset) the modern Masonic Square and Compasses.*

Once again, a prediction from the theory of Masonic astrology fits the facts. The earliest archaeological evidence of human creativity happened in societies that were living outside the shielding of the D-layer.

Let me sum up how I arrived at this evolutionary theory.

The species *Homo sapiens*, with its flexible brain and long-drawn-out infancy (to allow learning experiences to create useful structures within the brain[262]), emerged as a result of genetically driven evolution about 180,000 years ago in central Africa.[263] The brain our species possessed then was extremely flexible and relied on environmental learning in the first few years of life to give its owner genetic advantages and tune in to the place it lived.[264] For the next 80,000 years, these new humans did not move far from central Africa, and they didn't create any civilizations. They, and their flexible but vulnerable brains, stayed inside the Faraday cage of the D-layer.

Then, about 70,000 years ago, a sizable group established themselves at the edge of South Africa, near Blombos Cave.[265] They are the first modern humans on record to have moved outside the earth's natural firewall and the first *Homo sapiens* to leave a written record of their symbols. And they created symbols that Freemasonry still makes use of today. (See figure 22.)

When the Bright Morning Star rose close to the sun, this group's embryos and growing children were exposed to the radio pulses that churning gravitational fields induced in the ionosphere. It is no coincidence that they invented the first known symbolic system of notation. But how did this radically different environment affect the flexible wiring of their malleable brains, no longer protected by the D-layer firewall? The theories of brain science explain how it might have happened.

The operation of these dynamic cores, or point attractors, as a focus for thoughts is important in understanding neuron behavior. To explain how they work, here's a story about a visit to one of my postgraduate students, who worked at a large motor vehicle testing center. After I had finished the formal business of my visit, he offered to take me for a spin around the high-speed test track, which was used for endurance testing of prototype cars.

### Riding the Walls of Death
The track was a perfect banked circle, built inside a natural hollow and, as we had it to ourselves, he took the powerful car around it at high speed. We were driving at a steady 100 mph, high up the banking of the track, when he asked me if I would like a candy. It seemed a strange request to make as we roared round the circuit, and I wondered why he asked. Expecting some sort of humorous retort, I said I would like one. At that point he took both his hands off the wheel, took a toffee from the bag on the dashboard, and proceeded to use both hands to unwrap it. He then turned towards me, handed it to me, and winked. The car continued on its track at a steady 100 mph.

My student burst out laughing as he put his hands back on the wheel.

"If you could have seen your face when I let go of the wheel," he said.

"I'll send you the cleaning bill for my underwear," I replied.

He went on to explain that track was built with a number of lanes, each of which had a characteristic speed. If you drove a car at just that speed, it would stay in the lane. Increase or reduce the speed and the car would move up the bank for an increase, and down for a decrease. It is the same effect that is exploited in circuses by wall-of-death motorcycle riders, who ride around the inside of a wooden cylinder. The crowds looking down marvel at the daring of the riders, who seem to defy gravity by riding around with "no hands."

For our purposes, each of the speed lanes on that test track represents a stable state in Freeman's landscape of attractors, or a dynamic core in Edelman and Tononi's theories. The shape of the track represents one of the neuron communities that is hosting a thought pattern, while the speed of the car selects which thought is activated.

For the car to hold its line on the track, the shape must be a perfect banked circle. There are two possible ways in which this shape can be formed. You can take a flat piece of land and build a banking upwards, in the same way a circus will erect a wooden track to carry the wall-of-death rider, or you can take advantage of natural hollows in the ground and dig them out a little bit more, then lay your track in the shape of the landscape, as was done at my student's test track. The learning process is like building the circus's wall of death, while the resonant linking of neural synapses when the brain is exposed to ionic radio pulses is like the natural forces that create a hollow. One involves a lot of human effort to build from flat nothingness, the other takes advantage of what is there. When a hollow already exists, it is much quicker and easier to build a stable track. A brain filled with these ready-made attractors is more open to new ideas, making it more creative and high-achieving.

The earth's electromagnetic environment outside the tropics gave rise to a process of somatic selection favoring brains capable of developing language, writing, and civilization. At that point, Darwinian evolution took over, and an arms race began between the cultural imitation of ideas and genetic transmission of neural growth patterns. This idea led to my prediction that our species developed its creative brain structure and started to build achieving societies when *Homo sapiens* moved far enough away from the equator for the growing brains of their children to be exposed the radio pulses of the ionosphere.

In evolutionary terms, we *Homo sapiens*, with our over-large brains, appeared only in the last 180,000 years, and only in the last ten thousand years or so did we develop complicated societies that have a sufficiently elaborate economic structure to be able to record evidence of any astral effects on economic success. The time scales seem far too brief for evolution to work. And yet during the last few thousand years, humankind has blossomed into the accomplished species it is today.

There has long been a debate about why humanity evolved into the most successful species on the planet. The theory of Masonic astrology suggests that civilization was kick-started when our species moved outside the shelter of the D-layer (beyond latitudes 30° north or south of the equator).

My third prediction from Masonic astrology had been confirmed by the latitudinal table of key events. Exposure to the "benign rays" of the Bright Morning Star in the higher latitudes coincided with the evolution and development of human civilization. My theory says that ionic radio pulses provided an environmental variable that launched the evolution of modern man's thinking capacity.

To stretch the wall-of-death metaphor a little further, picture the human brainscape as it first evolved. It looked like a vast flat plain where hard-working individuals laboriously set up wooden tracks to let their learned-behavior patterns roar around on high-powered motorcycles. The gravity-defying track of each bike represented a dynamic center constructed from hard-won experience, and had to be arduously taught to the next generation. Each of these cylindrical tracks was separate and distinct, and to move from one track to another, thoughts had to slow down, come out of one wooden structure, drive across the flatlands to another place, and then build a new track. In a brainscape without imitation or natural aptitude, every behavioral action had to be learned the hard way: by discovering and doing it yourself. This was why the rate of innovation was so slow.

Then pioneers of our species moved out from under the shelter of the D-layer. Pulses of energy rained down from the sky, pitting the smooth surface of their brainscapes with a peppering of conical craters, all of differing slopes and depths.

Now there was a wide choice of gravity-defying tracks for thought patterns to race around. Each smoothly sloped crater had stable tracks for many different speeds. If a thought went too fast to maintain its stability in a shallow crater, it could fly off the top rim and have a very good chance of landing in a deeper cone where it could be stable at its chosen speed. (Perhaps my earlier metaphor of a marble thrown into a wok makes this easier to imagine.) In these circumstances, imitation and innovation were not just possible—they became inevitable. Instead of laboring to build a new track, in the much more complex brainscape, a thought pattern could easily find a track that was already there. The astral influences of Bright Morning Stars, making tidal waves in the ionosphere as they passed close to the sun, created these useful hollows in our brainscapes. Once growing human brains were exposed to the synapse-shaping possibilities of ionic turbulence, our species surged forward.

The increasing complexity of the human brainscape made it possible to imitate useful traits rapidly. Farming, building, writing, and the ability to live together in larger communities developed. Those individuals whose genetic makeup enabled them to take best advantage of this effect became desirable mates, and passed on their genetic advantage to their offspring. And in the background was the ongoing effect of the earth's environment. As *Homo sapiens* moved farther away from the shelter of the equatorial D-layer, they became more exposed to the neuron-linking pulses of electromagnetic force raining down from the ionosphere.

This is why I could find a link between economic activity and distance from the equator. The theory of Masonic astrology says that the earth's electromagnetic environment causes changes in the brain structure of some individuals, and this enabled *Homo sapiens* to exploit an inherent evolutionary advantage. Once this process of high-speed copying of useful survival tricks, such as language, was established, then Darwinian processes took over and the rapid rise in the human population became inevitable. What a strange conclusion to arrive at from a consideration of the "superstition" of Masonic astrology! But, as a Freemason, perhaps I shouldn't be surprised: the Craft has always claimed to hold secrets of great worth.

## Identifying Individuals

This line of thinking suggests another prediction for me to test. It should be possible to identify people with high levels of $n$-achievement by the presence of areas of dense neural activity in their brains. These would be caused by the increased clusters of linkages burned into their developing brains by exposure to the pulse chains of the ionosphere.

I ran a literature search on brain scans and creativity. Up popped a paper published by a group of neuroscientists led by Professor Jeremy Gray of Washington University in St. Louis, MO. He and colleagues from Harvard had carried out just the sort of trial that could test my prediction. They took a group of 48 volunteers, gave them various reasoning exercises, and scanned their brain process as they carried them out. They found "bright spots of high neural activity": the natural hollows in the brainscape that my theory of Masonic astrology predicts should be present in the brains of high-achieving individuals.

They developed a measure called a general fluid intelligence (*gF*) test that assessed reasoning and problem-solving ability. As their subjects took the tests, their brains were scanned by functional-magnetic-resonance imaging (fMRI), a technique that showed the areas of the brain with the most neural activity. They found "a remarkable correlation between high *gF* scores and a distinctive clustering patterns of brain stimulation." There were distinct neuron structures in the pre-frontal cortex which showed greater activity in those who performed well.[266]

Washington University reported this work in a press release, which said:

*Human intelligence is like a mental juggling act in which the smartest perform-*
*ers use specific brain regions to resist distraction and keep attention focused on*
*critical pieces of information, according to a new brain imaging study from Wash-*
*ington University in St. Louis . . .*

*Curious about the specific cognitive and neural mechanisms that underlie indi-*
*vidual differences in intelligence, Gray and colleagues devised a study to explore*
*the inner workings of one important aspect of human intelligence. The study*
*sought to better understand the process through which the mind reasons and solves*
*novel problems, an ability known among psychologists as "fluid intelligence." . . .*
*Describing the study as "impressive" in part because of its relatively large number*
*of participants, the journal (*Nature Neuroscience*) suggests the findings "will*
*help to constrain theories of the neural mechanisms underlying differences in gen-*
*eral intelligence." . . .*

*A key finding of the study was that participants with higher fluid intelligence*
*were better able to respond correctly despite the interference from the "lure" items*
*and they appeared to do so by engaging several key brain regions more strongly,*
*including the prefrontal and parietal cortex.*[267]

Interviewed for the Washington University Web site, Gray's coauthor, Professor Todd Braver, said:

*"I find this study exciting in part because it opens a door to doing many further studies that capitalize on differences in psychological functions among individuals,"* added Braver. *"Individuals differ in cognitive abilities and in many other ways as well, such as personality. We can use this same type of approach to understand how these psychological differences are reflected in brain function."*[268]

I suggest that using these fMRI techniques to study the brain development of children born into different electromagnetic environments would help our understanding of how some humans become much higher achievers than others. It could also test why Michel Gauquelin's limited version of Bright Morning Star astrology was able to identify those who grew up to become high-achievers.

In *Turning the Hiram Key*, I carried out a study of how Freemasonry works to encourage spiritual intelligence and motivate achievement. Masonic astrology underpins and extends this work with a theory of why some high-achieving individuals react so positively to the methods of Masonic teaching encoded in the rituals. If high-achieving individuals have distinct neuron structures in their pre-frontal cortex, and these were formed by radio pulses from the ionosphere during their early childhood, then I should be able to take any high-achieving individual and find the Bright Morning Stars in their childhood skies. My study of brain research suggests that this must be between six months before and twelve months after their birth—not at the moment of cutting the cord, as claimed by traditional astrology.

My fourth testable prediction from the theory of Masonic astrology is that high-achieving individuals should have Bright Morning Stars in the skies during the months when their brains were forming.

To test this prediction, I decided to look at the skies above the births of three of the high-achieving players who figured in the story of the birth of the United States of America; their birth dates are spread throughout the first half of the eighteenth century. The three are William Blake, George Washington, and Benjamin Franklin. Blake was born on November 28, 1757; Washington on February 22, 1732; and Franklin on January 17, 1706.

**William Blake** was born with Jupiter five degrees in front of the sun and rising as a Bright Morning Star. When he was two months old Saturn passed the sun and became a Bright Morning Star in his childhood skies. When Blake was four months old, Venus was close to the sun, and then also began to rise in the morning sky.

For three months before **George Washington** was born Venus was a Bright Morning Star sinking towards the rising sun. On his birthday, Mars was at its zenith as the sun rose, and so was at right-angles to the sun. By the time Washington was three months old, Saturn had passed the sun to rise as a Bright Morning Star, and when he was eight months old Jupiter appeared in the dawn sky. Washington had all four planets that Gauquelin had identified as important appearing in his birth skies while his brain was forming.

**Ben Franklin** had both Venus and Mars rising as morning stars as he was born. Saturn appeared when he was four months old, and by the time he was six months old, Jupiter appeared in his birth-star zone. Franklin had all four of the important planets rising before the sun in his childhood skies.

This was three out of three for another Masonic astrological prediction. Gauquelin had already shown that if you look at the birth skies of non-high-achievers, you do not find these planets anywhere near their critical birth-star zones.[269]

I decided to run a second check on this prediction by looking at another three high-achievers who lived in three different centuries. I took the great scientists Albert Einstein and Sir Isaac Newton, and threw a Masonic musician into the mix, Bro. Wolfgang Amadeus Mozart. Einstein was born March 14, 1879; Newton on January 4, 1643; and Mozart on January 27, 1756.

The month before **Albert Einstein** was born, Jupiter and Mars were a pair of Bright Morning Stars. Within two weeks of his birth, Saturn appeared in the birth-star zone. And when he was six months old, Venus popped up in the pre-dawn sky.

Venus was crossing the sun as **Sir Isaac Newton** was born, to appear as a Bright Morning Star by the time he was a month old. It was closely followed by Saturn and Jupiter by the time he was four months old. By the time Newton was ten months old, Mars had joined the array of Bright Morning Stars in his birth skies.

Saturn was a Bright Morning Star when **Wolfgang Amadeus Mozart** was born. By the time he was seven months old, Venus appeared, and when he was nine months old, Jupiter appeared. Mars appeared when he was eleven months old.

These three high-achievers from three different centuries all have Bright Morning Stars shining "benign rays" down over the formation of their brain structures, just as Masonic astrology predicts they should.

Although I have been looking at horoscopes, this type of prediction is not fortune-telling in any way at all. The theory of Masonic astrology suggests that a larger proportion of high-achievers should be born when these planets are rising just before the sun. I have selected known high-achievers and checked to see if the important planets appear in their birth-star zones. For each of the six individuals I checked, they did. I suppose I should not be surprised, as the brain research I have surveyed gives a strong theoretical basis to the statistical analysis of Masonic astrology.

Scientific working tools to investigate the ancient art of Masonic astrology are now available. I hope the scientific establishment will start to use them to investigate the ancient wisdom that Freemasonry has preserved. Brother George Washington encoded a hidden message about the importance of Masonic astrology and its potential role in creating a high-achieving society in his Federal City of Washington, D.C. Now is the time to read and use it.

Richard Dawkins said:

*If the methods of Astrologers were really shown to be valid it would be a fact of signal importance for science. Under such circumstances astrology should be taken seriously indeed.*[270]

Bro. George Washington took Masonic astrology seriously, and left us his Solomon Key to decode its validity. Now is the time for the scientific establishment to take Masonic astrology very seriously indeed.

## Conclusions

Masonic astrology is a quantum discipline, it can make only statistical predictions for large groups, it cannot make predictions about the future of individuals. Hence it is able to answer only about whole societies. However, the theory does predict that creative individuals should have hot spots (or banked racing tracks for thoughts) in their brains, which will be activated when their owners try to solve problems. The brain-scan work of Professors Grey and Braver shows that this is exactly what happens.

The theory of Masonic astrology suggests that *Homo sapiens* evolved creative intelligence only when we moved outside of the shielding of the D-layer, a prediction that is supported by archaeological evidence. The theory envisages that high-achievers should have the either Venus, Mars, Jupiter, or Saturn appearing as Bright Morning Stars in their childhood skies. I tested this prediction on six high-achieving individuals and failed to prove it wrong. Michel Gauquelin had previously found that these planets did not figure in the birth charts of people who were not high-achievers.

I submit there is now a strong enough case to warrant serious scientific investigation into the potential benefits of understanding the processes of the Bright Morning Star.

The last question left to address in my quest to understand Bro. George Washington and his application of Masonic principles to creating the United States is the one I began with: What are the Masonic principles which inspired George Washington? In the last chapter, we'll finally find the answer.

# Chapter Fourteen

# Understanding the Solomon Key

### Do These Findings Validate Astrology?

Does my analysis of George Washington's use of Masonic astrology show that the methods of all astrologers are valid? I don't think so. But the patterns of cultural behavior that inspired Masonic astrology are real. They can be explained in scientific terms, and have met the two tests set out by Professor Richard Dawkins of Oxford University, the author of a number of books on the science of evolution. In what is perhaps his best-known book, *The Blind Watchmaker*,[271] Dawkins likens the process of natural selection to an unconscious, automatic, blind, yet essentially non-random process that Darwin discovered. He also proposed a set of rules to validate any form of astrology, and I have used these rules in my researches.

In the course of our quest, I have made four unambiguous predictions. From the theory of Masonic astrology, I deduced from Bro. Washington's writing and actions:

1. Societies outside the shielding effect of the D-layer (outside a latitude of 30° North or South of the Equator) will be economically higher-achieving than those under the dense parts of the D-layer.
2. Animals will be more excitable and more likely to bite humans at the full moon in the northern hemisphere and at the new moon in the southern hemisphere.
3. The key creative advances in human civilization will have happened in societies outside the shielding effect of the D-layer.
4. High-achieving individuals will have one or more of the planets Venus, Mars, Jupiter, or Saturn, appearing as Bright Morning Stars in the skies while their brains were forming.

I tested each of these predictions using independent data, and in each case I failed to disprove them, so the theory remains plausible.

Masonic astrology says that the rising of the Bright Morning Star has a beneficial effect on Masons who are symbolically reborn under the light of its benign rays. I have since found statistical evidence and a physical mechanism of gravitational turbulence in the ionosphere, which suggests that children born when there is a bright planet near the sun are more likely to become creative high-achievers when they grow up and have based my predictions on this theory. I am sure that there are many other tests that I have not thought of to further investigate the theory of Masonic astrology. If the theory is wrong, its predictions will fail. But it has passed every test I have applied to it.

The selfish genes that connived to make up the DNA coalition that is *Homo sapiens* stumbled on a way of making the brain of their new creation more flexible. There is a clearly laid out path—what an accountant would call an audit trail—linking simple minds to the later development of complex mind types. It can be revealed just by asking the question, What evolutionary purpose does a brain have?

We were not the first bipedal apes to venture out of Africa. *Homo habilis* and Neanderthal Man were in the higher latitudes long before modern humans. But we were the first species with a loosely structured, adaptive brain to move outside the shelter of the D-layer. The earlier species did not have the flexibility of brain development to allow their children's neurons to respond to the signals of the Bright Morning Star. *Homo sapiens* did and, as a direct result, we developed into symbologists, invented language and writing, and became farmers and builders. The rest is our history. Early humans seem to have noticed the astral lights that heralded the birth of high-achievers and created myths, which the Freemasons encapsulated into the ritual message of the Bright Morning Star. Masons do indeed have "many and valuable secrets!"

The oysters that danced in time with the moon, even when Frank Brown moved them hundreds of miles from the sea, didn't need a complex brain for the neurons of their nervous systems to respond to the pulses of the moon's passage. If ever the sea returns to cover Evanston, Illinois, Frank's oysters will be ready for it. But they don't talk about secrets, they just react to the electrical trigger of the passing moon.

If Richard Dawkins is right, then Mother Nature is blind,[272] but she is not random. She cannot guess the future but she is a good watchmaker, and a super-hoarder. When she first made oysters that worked well enough to survive, she used the radio reception properties of a general-purpose neuron that was lying at the back of her tool box to sense the movements of the Moon. This selection made sure that her oysters opened and closed with the tide. But she never throws anything away. Her blindness often takes her up dead-end alleys, but now and again, she stumbles on a good idea.

The evolution of the neuron might just have been a quick fix to link muscles to sensors, but it also had the useful additional property of being able to hear the footfalls of heavy objects moving round the sun. In her usual miserly way, the old blind watchmaker kept using and reusing neurons to improve the way her creatures reacted to their environment. She added more and more layers of tangled interconnections as she bolted on neuron units to aid her creations' chances of survival. Most of our brain's activity is unconscious, and consists of the pulses of these free-standing modules. Our heart rate, blood pressure, even our balance sensors and the opening and closing of the irises of our eyes, are not under our conscious control. Self-consciousness is a new evolutionary idea, and we do not yet understand all its mysteries.

Our quest to understand George Washington's motives is almost over. But what about my original queries? Why was Bro. George inspired by Masonic astrology? And why did he hide the key to Masonic astrology in an alignment that could be spotted by a Freemason? I needed to reassess the Masonic geomancy of the city of Washington, D.C., in the light of what I had learned about the scientific basis of Masonic astrology.

As I explained in *Turning the Hiram Key*, I believe that the whole ritual structure of Freemasonry evolved to capitalize on creative possibilities in the brain. It is a way of developing spiritual intelligence to take advantage of the properties of consciousness. Bro. George knew this and used it.

It does seem that the rising of the Bright Morning Star is important to mankind, and that George Washington was truly inspired when he incorporated ideas from this Masonic astrology into the layout of his Federal City of Washington, D.C. Astrologer David Ovason said:

*The designer [of Washington] intended this union of earth and skies to remain a secret. He knew how mysteries work. He recognized that it did not matter a great deal whether anyone who lived in his city discovered the meaning of his mystery: it was sufficient that he had bridged the material with the spiritual.*[273]

Bro. George Washington, in his Masonic role, occupied the chair of King Solomon and was entrusted by the Craft with the secrets of the Solomon Key. He encoded this Masonic secret of the union of the earth and skies into the layout of the White House and the Capitol. Time has now revealed his secret of the Solomon Key at a period of history when scientific tools exist that can utilize its enormous potential for understanding humanity.

## Washington's Motive

During the 1770s, George Washington bought land near Mount Vernon and along the Ohio Valley. He spread his risks into different types of farming, growing wheat as well as tobacco. He also expanded and remodeled Mount Vernon.[274] During the whole of this period of his life, while he was living and surveying the site where the Federal City of Washington, D.C., would one day be built, his diaries show that he took a great interest in the rising of the Bright Morning Stars. He knew the landscape and the skyscape that arched over it. As the planets appeared in the dawn sky, they generated radio pulses that the neurons of George Washington's brain were primed to respond to. He may not have known why, but he must have felt the inspirational power that the rising of his birth-stars evoked in the depths of his brain.

When Bro. Washington came to build the new Federal City, the center of the fledgling United States, he laid out the key focal points to provide the Masonic inspiration he had felt for his successors. He made sure that at least once during every Presidential term, a key Bright Morning Star would be seen in an inspirational tableau. Here is the exciting and stimulating series of cosmological events that George Washington's choice of the site for the President's House (the White House) arranged for each of his successors to see:

In the pre-dawn of that special day in February, around the fifth day of the month, the Bright Morning Star of Venus rises from the apex of the Capitol dome. As the sun rises, the shadow of the dome falls exactly along the ceremonial avenue that leads to the President's House (the White House). That same evening, when the President looks out from his official home towards the Washington Monument, he sees the Zodiac, the Holy Royal Arch of Freemasonry, exactly as it appeared on the date of the consecration of King Solomon's Temple. Later Freemasons have made sure this inspiring view will be centered above the monument to the First Masonic President of the United States. In Masonic terms, this geomancy will be inviting the five-pointed Masonic Bright Morning Star to shine down to aid the affairs of the United States.

William Preston's Third degree ritual lecture, first delivered at the time that Washington was in his second term, explains the Masonic purpose of the morning star:

*Listen to the voice of nature, which bears witness that, even in this perishable frame, resides a vital and immortal principle, which inspires a holy confidence that the Lord of life will enable us to trample the king of terrors beneath our feet, and lift our eyes to that Bright Morning Star, whose rising brings peace and salvation to the faithful and obedient of the human race.*

Bro. Washington created a powerful and enduring symbol by his choice of site for the President's House. But is there some deeper reason why he decided to do this? Masonic ritual might give us a clue. This is how Freemasonry defines itself:

*Q: What is Freemasonry?*
*A: A peculiar system of morality, veiled in allegory, and illustrated by symbols.*

What Masonic symbol can best illustrate the Solomon Key?

## The Symbol of the Solomon Key

Does Masonic ritual suggest what form the Solomon Key might take? In *Turning the Hiram Key*, I combined Masonic symbols to illustrate the Hiram Key (see figure 23).

*Figure 23: The symbol of the Hiram Key.*

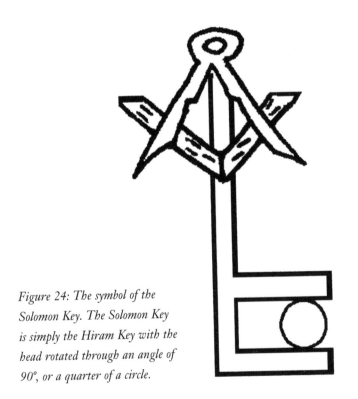

*Figure 24: The symbol of the Solomon Key. The Solomon Key is simply the Hiram Key with the head rotated through an angle of 90°, or a quarter of a circle.*

284

Masonic truths are traditionally illuminated by symbols, so I drew a symbol of the Hiram Key that represents my truth and feelings about Masonry. (I will describe it from my scientist's viewpoint, although you may choose to interpret it differently.) The symbol is threefold. The head of the key—the part I hold to turn it—is made up of the mystic sign (as Freemasons call the combination of the Square and Compasses): the square representing the independence of the brain's autonomous systems of arousal and quiescence, and the compasses symbolizing a tool to measure, control, and understand their responses. Together, the square and compasses combine to form the lozenge-shaped handle for the key. This is linked by a square-section shaft to the symbol of the center, the shape that engages with and unlocks the Glory there. It is a circle bounded by two pillars, and represents the balance between light and darkness, good and bad, arousal and quiescence, the center and the periphery. At the middle of the circle is the point from which you can no longer err.[275]

This is the key that is traditionally held by Hiram Abif, who in Masonic myth is the widow's son who was murdered before the Temple was completed. To make sure you remember, I will repeat what I said in chapter 1 about the three keys to Freemasonry:

*Traditionally there are three Grand Masters who conduct the rituals of the Temple, and each knows a different part of the secret of Freemasonry. They are Hiram, King of Tyre; Hiram Abif; and Solomon, King of Israel. Each holds one of three keys to the mystery. Hiram of Tyre holds the key to the secrets of where and what to build, Hiram Abif holds the key to the secrets of death and rebirth, but Solomon holds the key to understanding the purpose of the Temple and the import of the Bright Morning Star that shines into it when it is consecrated. His task is to continually build the New Jerusalem as a sacred place for the Divine Shekinah to shine its benign rays over all the human race.*

The Solomon Key is the key to creative behavior and the source of Masonic inspiration. It is the key that inspired Bro. Washington to view the Bright Morning Star at dawn and then to turn from the brightness of the East, which in Freemasonry represents spiritual inspiration, through an angle of 90°, or a quarter of a circle, to face the South. The South signifies light and knowledge, and, on the evening after the rising of the Bright Morning Star above the Capitol, the Holy Royal Arch of the Zodiac as it was at the founding of the Temple of Solomon will appear in the night sky to the South. So my symbol of the Solomon Key will be similar to the Hiram Key with the head rotated through a right-angle, to show that it represents not a quest but an inspiration drawn from Masonic principles of spiritual intelligence and knowledge. This symbol captures the symbolic importance of the points of the compass, but to understand them fully, we must return to the ritual.

## The Ritual Directions of Washington, D.C.

As we learned at the beginning of this book, Masonry consists of three degrees, each with its own peculiar lessons, and its ritual takes place at a particular compass point within the lodge. The First degree teaches control of the emotions and is conducted where the East meets the North. The Second degree teaches development of the intellect and is conferred at the point where the East meets the South. The Third degree teaches the Master Mason to subdue his own ego in the interests of his society and is carried out on an East-West line.

Candidates for Masonic initiation are ritually brought from darkness to light during the ceremony. They are brought into the illuminated lodge blindfolded to symbolize this state of ignorance. The lodge welcomes the candidate where the dark North meets the light of dawn in the East.

In the Second degree of Freemasonry, the apprentice work of mastering the emotions is supposed to have been achieved, and the Craftsman has satisfied some tests of progress. Only then is the Apprentice Mason permitted to extend his research into the more hidden paths of the nature and the science of humanity. The work now is no longer upon the outer sensuous nature, but upon the mind and the subtle and subjective faculties it contains.

In Freemasonry, the mind—the cognitive, discriminative, intellectual principle within each of us—is symbolized by the Junior Warden. The role of the Junior Warden within the lodge is to encourage all the members to control and purify their minds, to strengthen their understanding, and to educate their intellect to discriminate between illusion and reality.

In Masonic ritual, the Junior Warden is called upon to declare by what method the mental efficiency for the Second-degree work of a Fellowcraft (the name given to a Freemason who has been passed to the Second degree) will be demonstrated. The reply is cryptic, and uses a square or the geometrical figure of 90° representing the fourth part of a circle.

In most modern lodges, a Junior Warden would unlikely be able to explain what the symbol of the circle means, or what proof can be given by one-fourth of it. What becomes of the other three-fourths? An enlightened Junior Warden, a Mason of the level of understanding of George Washington, would know that the ritual is drawing on geometrical symbolism inherited from the mysteries of Greece and Egypt, which has traditionally been employed as a mathematical symbol of self-knowledge. His ritual answer would have been:

*The circle is the totality of my being in a perfect state. The complete, rounded whole has lapsed from perfection into disorder, into confusion and incompleteness. But, with the help of Great Architect and my own industry in Masonic science, I can restore its original circular perfection. The fourth part of that circle, which I am now trying to perfect, is my intelligent principle, my mind, my understanding. This I continually labor to purify and rectify, converting it from an irregular figure and a mass of confused, undisciplined notions into a true square or right angle. The square is a symbol of a rectified mind. Therefore, it is by the square or angle of 90 degrees, as, that I wish to be proved to have attained Second degree rank.*

The ritual explains the remaining three-fourths of the circle as follows:

*The spiritual geometricians of old divided the circle of the human individual into four equal parts and gave to them the names of the four elements, of progressive density, Earth, Water, Air, Fire; all four of them, in due balance and synthesis, are necessary to compose a perfect being. One fourth part, the earthy bodily form is wholly irrational and so much gross matter and dead weight, yet it is important in providing the requisite form and body for the rest. Another fourth part, the airy mind, is rational and therefore meant to counterpoise and control the irrational body. Blended with these two quarters is the emotional or watery nature, which savors of both the rational and irrational elements and is influenced by whichever of these is allowed to predominate. Lastly, beyond these three resides the fire of the spirit, the supra-rational principle which is higher than the mind, which when awakened, supplies the dynamic driving-power of the spiritual will.*

*The circle is divided by a cross into four equal parts or right-angles meeting at the center. This is the symbol of a rectified Mason, made perfect in all four parts and working from that center of being from which all originated and which ought to control and equilibrate us all.*

Brother Washington built the spiritual insight of this Masonic ritual into the positioning of the President's House (the White House) and the Capitol in Washington, D.C. On that key day in February, he arranged an inspirational sight from the President's House along the great avenue leading to the Seat of Government. It was a view of the Bright Morning Star rising from the circular dome of the Capitol, now with the statute atop it positioned to face its sublime light. (This is the view that Washington would have seen from the East of the lodge as he was first made a Master Mason.) That same evening, if the President turns through an angle of 90°, or the fourth part of circle, he will see the Holy Royal Arch of the Zodiac positioned to the south of the city in the form that Masonic lore says it once stood over the consecration of King Solomon's Temple.

The ritual of Freemasonry contains teaching about the meaning of directions. Each of the four quarters of the lodge, signified in the tracing boards (see pages 37–38) as points of the compass, have meanings attached to them. Here is a summary of these meanings:

**The North** is the side of unenlightenment, the place of darkness. It calls for exertion in the teeth of opposition. It presents darkness and difficulty to call forth the energy of the spirit. The North is associated with mental darkness and signifies the place of imperfection and undevelopment. Junior members of the Craft are seated in the North of the Lodge, for, symbolically, it represents the condition of the spiritually unenlightened, the novice whose spiritual latent light has not yet risen above the horizon of consciousness to disperse the clouds of material interests and the impulses of the sensual life. It is a sphere of benightedness and ignorance, controlled by sense-reactions and impressions received by our lowest and least reliable mode of perception, our physical senses.

**The East** of the Lodge represents spirituality, the highest and most spiritual mode of consciousness. Often this is little developed, but is still latent to become active in moments of stress or deep emotion.

**The West,** the polar opposite of the East, represents normal rational understanding, the consciousness we employ in everyday affairs. It is material-mindedness or common sense.

**The South** is the meeting place of spiritual intuition and rational understanding. It is a point denoting abstract thought and intellectual power at its highest.

Thus the four sides of the Lodge point to four different, yet progressive, modes of consciousness: sense-impression (North), spiritual intuition (East), reasoning (West), and intellectual understanding (South), making up four possible ways of knowing.

Geographically, Bro. Washington placed the Capitol in the southeast and the President's House in the northwest. Symbolically, therefore, the Capitol, which houses the elected representatives of the people, is in the spiritual East, and the President's House, the residence of the executive who must take decisions on behalf of the nation, in the rational West. But the Capitol is also in the intellectual South, to denote that it must exercise its combined intellect to discuss and improve the government of the nation, and the President's House in the sense-impression North, to show how the role of that office is to understand the pressures of the physical senses that drive so many state actions.

Whenever the President leaves the White House to speak in the Capitol, the Head of State travels on two symbolic journeys. The first journey is from West to East, from the political reasoning of the mind to the democratic intuition of the spirit. The second journey is from North to South, from the buffeting of the physical onslaught of managing the day-to-day affairs of the nation to the place where all the views of the people are discussed and considered. These two symbolic journeys are perhaps best summed up in the formality of the State of the Union Address.

The Masonic ritual that conveyed the secrets of Grand Master Solomon to Bro. George Washington helped develop the strength, clarity, and illumination of his mind. When remembering his achievement I like to imagine Bro. Washington holding in his right hand the Masonic Solomon Key which symbolizes the inspiration to be drawn from the works of the Grand Geometrician of the Universe, as manifested in the glorious stars of the heavens. As his outer senses and his mind were purified and disciplined, the hidden spiritual Fire, the light of the Bright Morning Star of his personal system, emerged into his consciousness. In the ritual of closing the Second degree, the Junior Warden makes a symbolic declaration that a striking discovery of a great light or "blazing star" has been found at the center of the temple. This told Bro. George that if he worked at building the temple of his own mind, he would glimpse a great and supernatural light shining in his heart and center. Following this light would lead him to the most potent symbol in Masonry, that of the Holy Royal Arch of the Heavens, marking the celestial realms of the Grand Geometrician of the Universe.

When Bro. George personally aligned the stake that marked out the foundation of the President's House (the White House), he turned his internal Masonic inspiration into a new Temple of the Republic.

Freemasonry taught him that the New City and the New Temple can be constructed only within the human consciousness. Bro. George Washington set out to create a state of being wherein there was a perfect balance between every component part of the nation. His monument and message is the Federal City of Washington, D.C. But does its symbolism also appeal to something deep in the collective soul of the nation? Another scientist has already looked at this aspect of symbolism.

## The Collective Symbols of Humanity

The ideas of Dr. Carl Gustav Jung infuse modern psychology. He coined such familiar terms as extrovert, introvert, and archetype. But his main contribution to the study of the human mind was his work on the unconscious mind. He put forward the idea that parts of our brain are not directly under the control of our consciousness, and sometimes not even easily accessible to it, but remain a vital part of the life any individual.

Jung said there is a collective unconscious that is shared by all humans and that this contains archetypes and mental predispositions that are universal. He thought that these archetypes exist independently of the world and can be known directly only by the unconscious mind. And he added that archetypes arise spontaneously in our minds at times of crisis. He thought that times of stress could make large numbers of people access the collective unconscious and release archetypal symbols to show a deep truth hidden from ordinary consciousness.

Before he died in 1961 Jung edited a final book. He contributed an introductory section to it in which he said:

> *When all available energy is spent in the investigation of nature, very little attention is paid to the essence of man, which is his psyche, although many researches are made into its conscious functions. But the really complex and unfamiliar part of the mind, from which symbols are produced, is still virtually unexplored. It seems almost incredible that though we receive signals from it every night, deciphering these communications seems too tedious for any but a very few people to be bothered with it. Man's greatest instrument, his psyche, is little thought of, and it is often directly mistrusted and despised . . . Our actual knowledge of the unconscious shows that it is a natural phenomenon . . . The study of symbolism is an enormous task, and one that has not yet been mastered. But a beginning has been made at last. The early results are encouraging.[276]*

The theory of Masonic astrology, I have deduced from studying the work, life, and writings of George Washington, suggests a mechanism by which Jung's collective unconscious could work. Planets move across the sky in predictable ways. When the same bright birth-star that nurtured a baby's brain as it was forming moves back near the sun, then that person's neurons will be resonantly tickled by the repeat performance of the pattern of ionospheric radio pulses that formed his or her brain.

Jung said that his archetypes correspond to shared experiences, such as confronting death or choosing a mate. They manifest themselves symbolically in religions, myths, fairy tales, and fantasies. But they could be triggered by the neurodynamics of the brain, settling on a point attractor in the brainscape.[277] If

291

the memory of a particular symbol happens to be attracted to one of the astro-logically formed hot spots of synaptic connections, who knows how many other people will have similar point attractors in their mindscapes? Does this mean they might all be triggered to have similar types of thoughts and feelings when their birth-star rises just before the sun, or reaches its zenith at dawn?

Is this why similar ideas emerge from the collective unconscious in different people at the same time? Our minds grow up listening to the silent footfalls of the planets that walked across the childhood skies of our forming brains. As Karl H. Pribram pointed out, revisiting past haunts often releases floods of memories you do not realize you had.[278] When the gravity pulses of the Bright Morning Star lightly shake the grains of your dreams, shaping them into new patterns, what memories does it evoke in your mind?

### Washington's City, Masonic Astrology and Aspiration

George Washington was born on February 22, 1732. As I have already men-tioned, when he was born Mars was at the zenith of the dawn sky, making it at right-angles to the sun. The first year of his life, the period when he was rap-idly forming neurological connections in his brain, was the beginning of a new Venus cycle. Around his first birthday Venus was a Bright Morning Star rising just before the sun over Jenkins Heights.

The theory of Masonic astrology not only suggests that Washington was a prime candidate to become a high-achiever, but it also suggests that he should have been sensitive to the pattern of ionospheric pulses that helped shape his brain as a child. The theory says he would have been inspired to new creative heights when the Bright Morning Star of Venus appeared in the dawn sky, simply because he was stimulated by its resonant electrical pulses from the ion-osphere. He would not necessarily have known why he felt inspired and creative, but he was able to link his feelings to the recurrent appearance of the Bright Morning Star. And his knowledge of the Key of Solomon gave him a ritual reason to explain his spiritual uplift. Is it any wonder that he set out to share this source of inspiration with his newly founded country?

This idea from Masonic astrology also offers an explanation for a well-known creative process, the "library or literary angels." This is a metaphor for the cre-ative muse that guides the hands of struggling writers towards inspirational books and ideas as they seek to clarify their thoughts. It is the name writers and artists give to their mysterious process of inspiration. How might this new theory help understand them? Best-selling thriller-writer Stephen King, no stranger to being creative, describes how a visit from a "library angel" feels for him:

*Let's just get one thing clear right away shall we? There is no Idea Dump, no Story Central, no Island of Buried Bestsellers; good story ideas seem to come quite literally from nowhere, sailing at you right out of the empty sky: two previously unrelated ideas come together and make something new under the sun. Your job isn't to find these ideas but to recognize them when they show up.*[279]

When this happens, has his brain been resonated by a chain of ionospheric pulses that steer his thoughts into a new creative direction? This is just the way George Washington would have been inspired by the recurrence of the Bright Morning Star, stimulating the resonant neurons created by its passage through his childhood.

Might these ideas mean that astrologers could use the positions of the planets to tell us about our future? I very much doubt it. But there might be shared neural resonances, triggered by the patterns of ionospheric pulses that change with the astrological season. This might be how the more successful astrologers latch onto this collective mood. Some do seem to be able to tap the collective mood of modern people. Perhaps astrologer Robin Heath is right in describing what he does as:

*quite similar to the act of prayer. The cosmos (sky, God, gods, the 'above', heaven) is being contacted, knows that this is happening, and responds accordingly to the circumstances prevailing at the time and the consciousness of the astrologer.*[280]

His description of what happens in his brain when he does astrology is similar to Stephen King's description of how his ideas arise.

But is this astrological prediction, or just ionospherically triggered inspiration? Whatever it is, the Masonic myth that inspired Brother George Washington to lay out the hypotenuse of the great Federal Triangle of Washington, D.C., to highlight the rising of the Bright Morning Star on a day of the year when the Holy Royal Arch of Jerusalem appears as it did above Solomon's Temple, has been perpetuated by successive generations of his Masonic brethren. They have extended his vision to build an inspirational center for a whole nation.

The builder of Washington, D.C., knew a great secret about the human condition: the rising of the Bright Morning Star above a newborn child increases that individual's chance of growing up to become a high-achiever, and any high-achiever born under the light of the Bright Morning Star will receive new inspiration when it rises again in the same place.

Did George Washington, and his brother Masons who have continued to enhance the city of Washington, know this and deliberately set out to harness it to ensure the success and continuation of the democratic republic they all loved? I will let Michel Gauquelin have the last word on this:

*Astrology has always remained enigmatic and, to the perfectly proper question, "Should one believe it?," I can only answer by rejecting both the unconditional opponents and the confirmed upholders. Of course, I am aware that . . . the truth, the whole truth and nothing but the truth, does not exist in astrology—not yet, anyway.*[281]

Perhaps it does now.

# APPENDIXES

## Appendix 1

### Gravitational Pull of the Sun and Planets on the Earth

The following table shows the main objects in the solar system, their mass, the closest they get to the earth (in millions of miles), the farthest they move away from the earth (also in millions of miles), and the strongest and weakest gravitational force they can exert on the surface of the earth. (Appropriately, the unit used to measure gravitational force is the Newton.)

| Object | Mass | Nearest | Farthest | Field Strong | Field Weak |
|---|---|---|---|---|---|
| Moon | 0.07349 | 0.23 | 0.25 | 0.556798 | 0.446937 |
| Sun | 1900000 | 91.40 | 94.51 | 87.81876 | 82.12874 |
| Mercury | 0.3302 | 48.01 | 137.89 | 5.53E-05 | 6.71E-06 |
| Venus | 4.8685 | 23.71 | 162.20 | 0.003345 | 7.15E-05 |
| Mars | 0.64185 | 36.99 | 234.46 | 0.000181 | 4.51E-06 |
| Jupiter | 1898.6 | 365.63 | 601.93 | 0.005484 | 0.002023 |
| Saturn | 586.46 | 745.93 | 1035.61 | 0.000407 | 0.000211 |
| Uranus | 86.832 | 1608.85 | 1960.86 | 1.30E-05 | 8.72E-06 |
| Neptune | 102.43 | 2667.14 | 2919.06 | 5.56E-06 | 4.64E-06 |
| Pluto | 0.0125 | 2661.26 | 4633.21 | 6.81E-10 | 2.25E-10 |

# Appendix 2

### Effect of Height on Free Electron Density

Ultraviolet (UV) radiation from the sun ionizes the upper atmosphere. The stripped molecules become ions, and the separated electrons become free particles. Ions and electrons recombine into electrically neutral molecules if they can.

Nearer the earth's surface there is a greater density of molecules, so the free electrons quickly recombine, but in the upper atmosphere, where there is less molecular density, there is a much smaller chance of a free electron finding and rejoining an ionized molecule. Also, the recombination rate is slower at higher atmospheric levels. Moreover, in the higher regions, the strength of the UV radiation is stronger, so more ions are formed. But UV radiation is absorbed as it passes through the atmosphere, and its ionizing power is reduced as it gets close to the ground.

These two factors cause a peak of ionized molecules and a cloud of free electrons at the height where they overlap, as shown in this diagram.

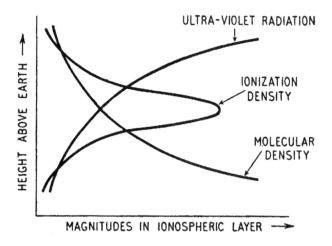

*Figure 25: This shows the interaction of UV strength and molecular density causing the formation of ionized layers in the atmosphere. The magnitudes plotted are the quantities of free electrons in the various height levels, or strata, of the ionosphere.*

# Appendix 3

## Free Electron Density Above Washington, D.C., Over a Day

The critical frequency (that at which the full energy of a test signal is reflected back to Earth—a direct measure of the free electron density in the ionosphere) is measured minute-by-minute by tracking stations around the world, and the plots of the data can be accessed via the Web. Using this data, I worked out the change in electron density over Washington, D.C., during a typical day, and the result is shown below.

The diagram shows a vast surge in the number of free electrons as sunlight blasts the night-cooled air at about 6 a.m. As the sun comes over the horizon and its energy hits the upper atmosphere, the free electron density increases rapidly. The concentration of free electrons increases by at least two or three orders of magnitude, i.e., by about a thousand times.

A surplus of free electrons begins to form from early morning until about midday, when the sun is at its zenith. Thereafter the rate of recombination exceeds the rate of creation, and the population of free electrons continues to diminish until 10 p.m., when it stabilizes at the nighttime level. It remains at this level until the arrival of the sun's rays the following morning starts the whole cycle off again.

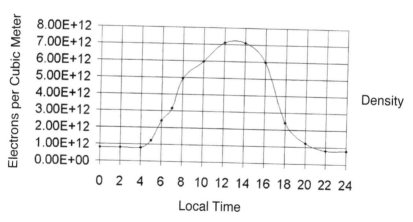

*Figure 26: Variation of free electron density in the ionosphere above Washington, D.C., over a twenty-four-hour period. At the peak, each cubic foot of ionospheric space contains about 700 billion free electrons.*

# Appendix 4

**Relationship Between Gauquelin's High-Achiever Births and Changes in Ionospheric Free Electron Activity**

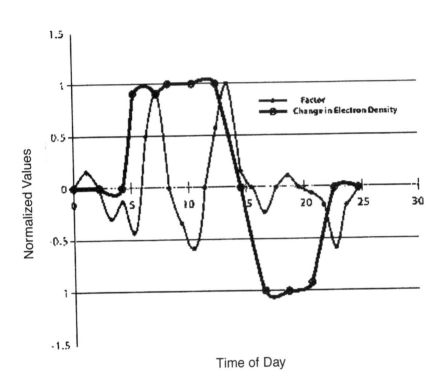

*Figure 27: This shows the rate of change in the density of free electrons plotted on the same axis as Gauquelin's birth peaks of high-achievers (plotted as the "Morning-Star factor").*

# Appendix 5

## How the Ionosphere Splits into Layers at Different Seasons

The structure of layers in the ionosphere varies between the northern and southern hemispheres, but the pattern for summer and winter is the same in both hemispheres. This shows some typical measurements of ionized layers at different times and seasons.

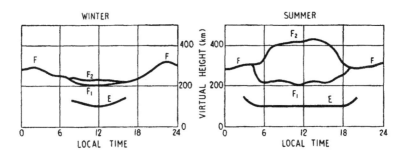

*Figure 28: Typical heights of ionospheric layers at various times and seasons.*

The layers change under the strength of the sun's radiation, and the angle at which it hits them. The positions and intensity alter, with a steady daily pattern imposed onto a longer seasonal pattern. During the summer months, when the radiation is stronger, the F-layer splits into two separated strips, as the graphs below show.

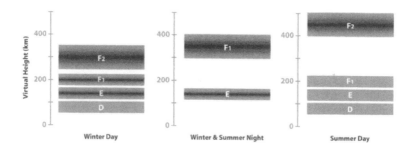

*Figure 29: Typical seasonal variation of the ionospheric layer structure over twenty-four hours.*

# Appendix 6

### Density of the Electron Clouds Above the Earth

Looking down from above the Equator, this contoured graph of electron density with respect to time of day and latitude shows how dense clouds of electrons billow above the equator and then thin out towards the poles. It also shows how there is a rapid rise in free electron numbers from 6 a.m. at all latitudes, with a decline after about 6 p.m. The density remains low overnight. The effect of this localized heating of the upper air creates a vast bubble of free electrons over the equatorial regions when the sun is at its zenith. Over the Poles and the more temperate regions, there is a less dense covering, which thins out even more during the night. Seeing these sequences in enhanced colors and speeded-up time as a Webcast gives the impression of watching a living, moving, pulsating being. It looks like the wobbling of a great beer belly.

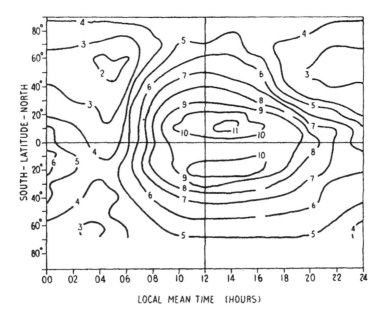

*Figure 30: Typical electron density plot of latitude versus time of day for the northern hemisphere in winer.*

Another way to chart the cloud of free electrons that we live under, is to look sideways at the atmosphere. The outer edge of the atmosphere extends to about 1,100 km (about 700 miles) before the free electron density drops to zero. But this free electron density varies greatly in height and between day and night, as the graph below shows. As discussed in chapter 11, the D-layer is the closest to the ground and absorbs radio signals during the day. The E- and F-layers are much higher and act as reflectors for radio waves during the night. At some times the F-layer splits in to separate F1 and F2 layers as shown in the diagram.

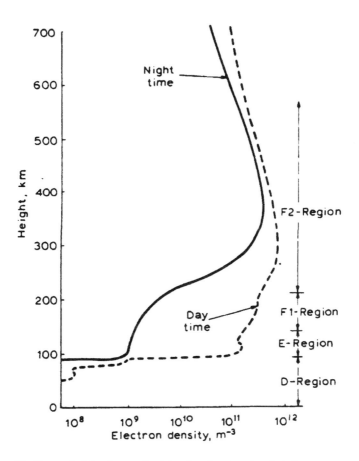

*Figure 31: Day and night electron densities plotted against height [after Mazda (1983)].*

There is one final view that might help us understand the shape of these invisible electron clouds that continually swarm around the atmosphere of the earth. This is a plot of the variation in free electron density according to latitude.

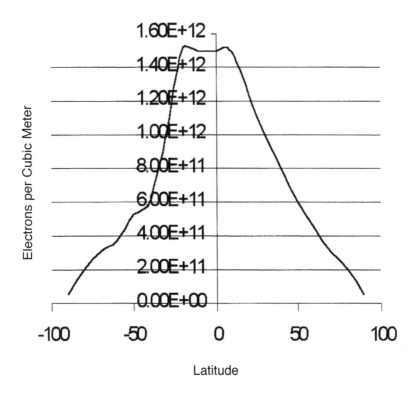

*Figure 32: The variation of free electron density by latitude, showing a peak at the equator.*

# Appendix 7

## The Spectrum of Radio Noise

Environmental noise signals have been extensively studied, so the strength of signals and the frequency at which they appear is well known. This graph shows how the main sources of noise vary with frequency.

Line A shows that in temperate zones, the daytime noise is mainly human-generated below 12 Mhz (megahertz). This is because the D-layer masks atmospheric and cosmic noise. At night, when the D-layer disperses, more atmospheric noise is heard at lower frequencies. At night in equatorial latitudes, the atmospheric noise is much higher at frequencies below 12 Mhz. Above 12 Mhz, there is a steady level of background noise coming from the outer ranges of the atmosphere and beyond.

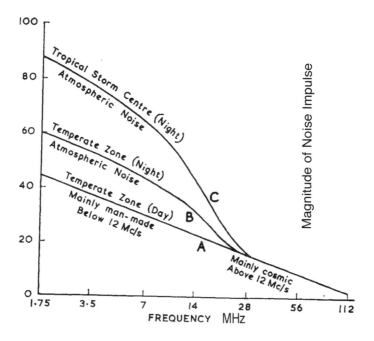

*Figure 33: External noise signals at various times and frequencies [source: Radio Society of Great Britain (1963)]. 1 Mc/s (megacycle per second) = 1 MHz, or a million oscillations per second.*

# Appendix 8

**Gravitational Effects on a Free Electron**

My model shows three gravitational attractors, the earth, the sun, and a heavy planet revolving round the earth. They pull a floating electron in different directions as they traverse the sky.

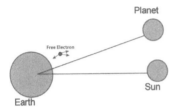

*Figure 34: The effect of three different gravitational fields on a free electron in the ionosphere.*

*Calculating the movement of a free electron subject to three moving gravitational fields*

In order to make this calculation, I first had to define some variables to use:

Let $m_e$ = the mass of the earth

Let $m_p$ = the mass of the planet

Let $m_s$ = the mass of the sun

Let $m_0$ = the mass of the free electron

Let $d_1$ = the distance between the free electron and the planet

Let $d_2$ = the distance between the free electron and the sun

Let h = the height of the ionized layer which contains the free electron

Let $f_1$ = the gravitational force of the earth on the electron

Let $f_2$ = the gravitational force of the sun on the electron

Let $f_3$ = the gravitational force of the planet on the electron

Let G = Newton's general gravitational constant

My first step was to calculate these three forces in terms of the known parameters:

1. First, the gravitational pull of the earth on the electron.

$$f_1 = G\frac{m_0\, m_e}{h^2}$$

2. Next, the pull of the sun on the same electron.

$$f_2 = G\frac{m_0\, m_s}{d_2^2}$$

3. Finally, the pull of the planet on that poor, much-tugged electron.

$$f_3 = G\frac{m_0\, m_p}{d_1^2}$$

To work out how these forces moved the electron, I needed to know how they were acting over time, and to do that I had to have some line to measure from. I decided to define a line between the centers of mass of the sun and the earth at midnight GMT (Greenwich Mean Time) as my reference line. The angle that the sun makes with this line is represented by θ. The angle the planet makes with this same reference line is φ. Both these angles change continuously, but both the angles and their rates of change can easily be measured by standard astronomical techniques.

Using these time-varying angles, and their relationship to the gravitational forces, I could now work out the cumulative force on the electron along the line between the centers of mass of the sun and the earth ($f_v$) and also at right angles to this line ($f_h$), which is the force parallel to the surface of the earth. These two forces turned out to be a very interesting function of the θ and φ as I have shown below.

$$f_v = G\frac{m_0 m_e}{h^2}Cos\phi - G\frac{m_0 m_s}{d_2^2}\cdot\frac{hSin\phi}{\sqrt{h^2 + d_2^2 - 2hd_2Cos\phi}}$$
$$- G\frac{m_0 m_p}{d_1^2}\cdot\frac{d_1 Sin\theta - hSin\phi}{\sqrt{d_1^2 + h^2 - 2hd_1(Sin\theta Sin\phi + Cos\theta Cos\phi)}}$$

I found the combination of these perpendicular and vertical forces by adding the two vectors to find the resultant or combined forces which I've called $f_r$.

$$f_h = G\frac{m_0 m_e}{h^2}Sin\phi - G\frac{m_0 m_s}{d_2^2}\cdot\frac{d_2 - hCos\phi}{\sqrt{h^2 + d_2^2 - 2hd_2Cos\phi}}$$
$$- G\frac{m_0 m_p}{d_1^2}\cdot\frac{d_1 Sin\theta - hSin\phi}{\sqrt{d_1^2 + h^2 - 2hd_1(Sin\theta Sin\phi + Cos\theta Cos\phi)}}$$

At first sight, this function looks a little complicated, but it has some very clear features that indicate that it is going to cause turbulent behavior. The interaction between the Sin and Cos functions is going to be very unstable around the points when either angle approaches 0°, 90°, 180°, or 270°. At this point, one of the functions is rapidly approaching 1, while the other is approaching 0. When the number one is divided by zero, the function tries to become infinitely large. This means that when the gravitation fields of the sun and planet occupy approximately the same angle in the sky, when they are opposite each other, or when they are at right angles to each other, the criss-crossing forces are really going to churn up the electron cloud and seriously rattle individual electrons around.

### Calculating current flow in the ionosphere

I calculated the size of a current flow using the standard formula, shown below. Where I is the current density, e is the charge on a single electron, N is the free electron density, x is the direction of movement, and t is time.

$$I = -Ne\frac{dx}{dt}$$

# Appendix 9

## Modeling a Planet Close to the Sun in the Sky, Appearing as a Bright Morning Star

Having calculated that the electromagnetic effect of the gravitational pull of a planet near the sun was large enough to be visible as significant current flows in the ionosphere, I simulated how it pulsed over time, using a standardized set of values for the masses and distances. I did so by entering the equations for the combined force into my computer, and working out what happens to the varying function (Function fr in appendix 8) as the sun and the planet move in relation to each other. I was then able to plot a series of points showing the timing and shape of the waveforms that the function generated for any planet which was rising or at its zenith as the sun rose. The graph below shows the results of this calculation.

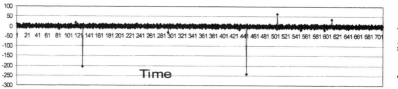

*Figure 35: The turbulent current flows produced over an evening/morning cycle, as the planet rises as a Bright Morning Star, close before the sun.*

When the planet was either new or full it produced tidal turbulence in the ionosphere. My simulation showed that these flows produced both positive and negative pulses of current, and hence radio noise-pulses. This happened when the criss-crossing gravity fields beat against each other.

I decided to do more detailed simulations of these pulse patterns to see how the electrons rattled around when the gravitational fields were widely separated. First, I looked in more detail at the normal current flow patterns when there were no critical angles in the function (Function fr in appendix 8), i.e., when the planet was well away from the sun, and so not a Bright Morning Star. There were none of the massive short-duration radio pulses I had seen occurring when a heavy planet was near the sun. The tidal forces on the ionospheric electrons are shown in the diagram below.

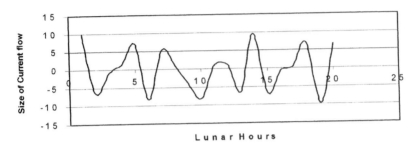

*Figure 36: The current flow caused by "normal" tidal interactions between a planet and the sun.*

Next, I looked at what happens to the radio noise pattern when the planet is close to the sun, either rising just before it or just after. The graph below is the result, showing the pulse pattern as a planet moves from an evening to a morning star, in the process crossing sun's gravitational field with its own. I had to use a much larger vertical scale to show the size of the peaks that occurred at this time. This is the basic planetary position that Gauquelin identified as statistically significant for the birth of high-achieving individuals.

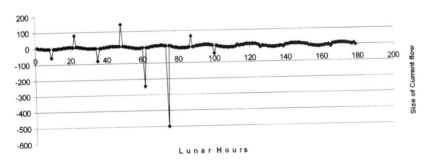

*Figure 37: The much larger pulses that occur when the planet is close to the sun and rising as a Bright Morning Star.*

# Appendix 10

### Economic Activity and Latitude

Here is a plot of GNP per capita against the latitude for the capital cities of each society in the world of 1955. This work confirms the results for 1955 and 1988 and shows that this effect has been consistent for at least two generations.

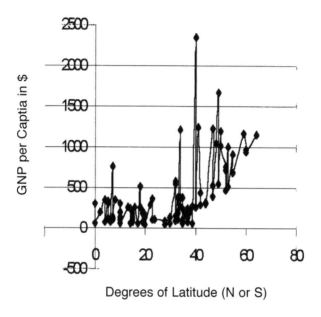

*Figure 38: GNP per capita in 1955 versus degrees of latitude from the equator.*

Societies between 30° and 60° from the equator had a much higher level of GNP, just as predicted by my new theory of astrology.

I decided to retest the prediction on the 1988 data for GNP per capita against latitude. The result is shown in figure 39.

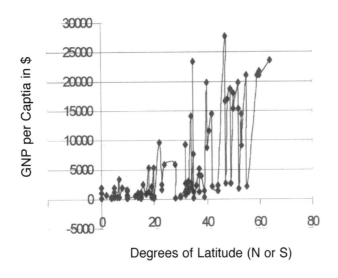

*Figure 39: GNP per capita in 1988 versus degree of latitude from the equator.*

Here is the World Bank Data showing the same relationship in 2002:

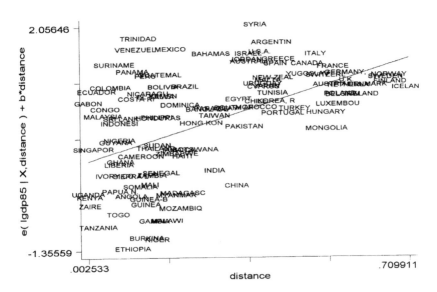

*Figure 40: Correlation between average income in 2002 and distance from the equator [after Rodrik (2002)].*

## Population Levels

I checked the populations of the countries in the 1988 data and plotted them against their latitude.

The correlation between latitude and number of people is +2 percent, and the correlation between population size and GNP per capita is −4 percent, whereas the correlation between GNP per capita and latitude averages +60 percent.

This test eliminates population size as a cause of economic success.

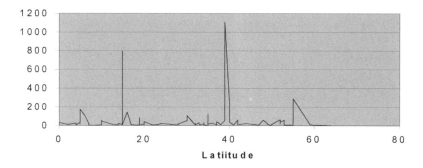

*Figure 41: Plot of the population of the countries shown in figure 39 versus their latitude.*

# Bibliography

Abell G.O. (1979). "Recent Advances," *Zetetic Scholar*, April.

American Institute of Architects, Committee of the Washington-Metropolitan Chapter (1957). *Washington Architecture 1791-1957*, Reinhold, New York.

Aronson, J. (1997), Letter, *BMJ*, p. 314 (29 March).

Ashmole, E. (1652). *Theatrum Chemicum Brittanicum*, London.

Atkinson, J.W. (1958). *Motives in Fantasy, Action and Society*, Van Nostrand, London, p. 56.

Aubrey, J. (1685). *Naturall Historie of Wiltshire*, copy with additional notes in Aubrey's hand, 1691 [Bodleian Library, MS Aubrey 2. f.72v.].

Bate, R.R., D.D. Mueller, and J.E. White (1971). *Fundamentals of Astrodynamics*, Dover, New York.

Bhagwati, J. (1966). *The Economics of Underdeveloped Countries*, Weidenfeld and Nicolson, London.

Bhattacharjee, C., P. Bradley, M. Smith, A. Scally and B.J. Wilson (2000). "Do Animals Bite More During a Full Moon? Retrospective Observational Analysis," *BMJ*, 321, December, 1559-61.

Bliss, T.V.P. and T. Lomo (1973). "Long-lasting Potentiation of Synaptic Transmission in the Dentate Area of the Anaesthetised Rabbit Following Stimulation of the Perforant Path," *Journal of Physiology*, 232, 331-56.

Bowling, K.R. (2002). *Peter Charles L'Enfant: Vision, Honor and Male Friendship in the Early American Republic*, printed for the Friends of the George Washington University Libraries.

Brown, F.A., Jr. (1954). "Persistent Activity Rhythms in the Oyster," *American Journal of Physiology*, 178, p. 510.

— (1962). *Biological Clocks*, Heath, Boston, MA.

— (1965). "Propensity for Lunar Periodicity in Hamsters," *Proceedings of the Society of Experimental Biological Medicine*, 120, p. 792.

— (1966). "Living Clocks," *Science*, 130, p. 1535.

Brown, F.A., Jr. and E. Terracini (1959). "Exogenous Timing of Rat Spontaneous Activity Periods," *Proceedings of the Society of Experimental Biological Medicine*, 102, p. 457.

Brown, R. (1958). *Words and Things*, Macmillan, London.

Brown, R.S. (1892). *Stellar Theology and Masonic Astronomy Explained*, Appleton, Boston MA.

Campion, N. (1989). "Mundane Astrology," in A. Kitson (ed.) *History and Astrology*, Unwin Paperbacks, London, p. 56.

Carlile, R. (1825). *Manual of Freemasonry*, William Reeves, London.

Carlson, N.R. (1986). *Physiology of Behavior*, Allyn and Bacon, Boston, MA.

Chapman, S., J. Cornwall , J. Righetti and L. Sung (2000). "Preventing Dog Bites in Children: Randomised Controlled Trial of an Educational Intervention," *BMJ*, 320, June, 1512-13.

Chapman, S., and S. Morrell (2000). "Barking Mad? Another Lunatic Hypothesis Bites the Dust," *BMJ*, 321, December, 1561-3.

Cole, H. (1992). *Understanding Radar*, Blackwell Scientific, Oxford.

Cole, L.C. (1957). "Biological Clock in the Unicorn," *Science*, 130, p. 874.

Conel, J. (1939). *The Post-Natal Development of the Human Cerebral Cortex*, Harvard University Press, Harvard, MA, vol. I.

Dawkins, R. (1995). "The Real Romance of the Stars," *The Independent on Sunday*, December 31.

— (1988). *The Blind Watchmaker*, Penguin Books, London.

Dennett, D.C. (1984). *Elbow Room: The Varieties of Free Will Worth Wanting*, MIT Press, Cambridge, MA.

Dyer, C. (1987). *William Preston and his Work*, Lewis Masonic, Shepperton.

Eccles, J.C. (1973). *The Understanding of the Brain*, McGraw Hill, New York.

— (1982). "The Synapse: From electrical to chemical transmission," *Annual Review of Neuroscience*, vol. 5, pp. 325-39.

Edelman, G.M. (1989). *Neural Darwinism: The Theory of Neuronal Group Selection*, Basic Books, London.

Edelman, G., and G. Tononi (2000). *Consciousness: How Matter Becomes Imagination*, Penguin, London.

Ertel, S. (1989). "Purifying Gauquelin's Grain of Gold," *Correlation*, 9, 1.

Eysenck, H.J., and D.K. Nias (1982). *Astrology, Science or Superstition?*, Maurice Temple Smith, London

Fox, A. and P. Davies (2002). "Can Superstitious Behaviour Reduce Work Stress?," in supplement with *BMJ*, 2002:325:S83 (14 September).

Freeman, D.S. (1970). *Washington*, Eyre and Spottiswoode, London.

Freeman, W.J. (2000). *How Brains Make Up Their Minds*, Phoenix, London.

Frohlich, H. (1968). "Long-range Coherence and Energy Storage in Biological Systems," *Int. J. Quantum Chem.*, II, 641.

—(1980). "The Biological Effects of Microwaves and Related Questions," *Adv. Electronics Electron. Phys*, 53, 85.

Gauquelin, M. (1969). *The Cosmic Clocks*, Paladin, London.

— (1983). *The Truth about Astrology*, Blackwell, Oxford.

— (1988). *Planetary Heredity*, ACS Publications, El Cajon, CA.

— (1994). *Cosmic Influences on Human Behavior*, Aurora Press, Santa Fe.

Gauquelin, M. and F. (1967). "A Possible Hereditary Effect on Time of Birth in Relation to the Diurnal Movement of the Moon and the Nearest Planets: Its Relationship With Geomagnetic Activity," *Int. J. Biometeorol.*, 11:341.

Gilbert, R. A. (1996). "Notes on the Lodge of Antiquity," *Ars Quatuor Coronatorum*, vol. 109, p. 188.

Gleitman, H. (1992). *Basic Psychology*, Norton, London.

Gopnik, A., A. Meltzoff and P. Kuhl (1999). *How Babies Think*, Phoenix, London.

Gray, J.R., et al. (2003). "Neural Mechanisms of General Fluid Intelligence," *Nature Neuroscience*, 6 (2) February.

Greenfield, S. (1997). *The Human Brain-A Guided Tour*, Weidenfeld and Nicolson, London.

— (2000). *The Private Life of the Brain*, Penguin, London.

Hall, R.E., and C.I. Jones (1997). "Levels of Economic Activity Across Countries," *Papers and Proceedings of the 109th Annual Meeting of American Economic Association*, Stanford University Press, Berkeley, CA.

Hancock, G., and R. Bauval (2004), *Talisman*, Michael Joseph, London.

Hawker, P. (1980). *A Guide to Amateur Radio*, Radio Society of Great Britain, London.

Hawking, S. (2001). *The Universe in a Nutshell*, Transworld, London.

Heath, R. (1996), Editorial, *The Astrological Journal*, vol. 28, no. 3.

— (2005). *Powerpoints, Secret Rulers and Hidden Forces in the Landscape.* Blue Stone Press, Llandysul.

Henderson, M. (2002). "Scratches that Trace the Ascent of Man," *The Times*, January 11, p. 5.

Hobson, J.A. (1989). *Sleep*, Scientific American Library, New York.

Houlding, D: ( 1997). *The Traditional Astrologer Magazine*, Issue 14, May.

315

Hutchinson, H. F. (1976). *Sir Christopher Wren, a biography*, Reader's Union, Newton Abbot.

Jung, C.G. (ed.) (1943). *Man and His Symbols*, Arkana, Penguin Books, 1990, pp. 102-3 (first published Aldus Books, 1964).

Kandel, E.R., J.H. Schwartz and T.M. Jessel (2000). *Principles of Neural Science* (4th ed.) McGraw Hill, New York.

King, S. (2000). *On Writing: A Memoir*, Hodder and Stoughton, London.

Laurence, A.S. (2001), Letter, *BMJ*, January 18.

Law, S.P. (1986). "The Regulation of Menstrual Cycle and Its Relationship to the Moon," *Acta Obstet. Gynecol. Scand.* 65 (1), pp. 45-8.

Leakey, R., and R. Lewin (1992). *Origins Reconsidered: In Search of What Made Us Human*, Little Brown, London.

Lenneberg, E.H. (1967). *Biological Foundations of Language*, Wiley, New York.

Lomas, R. (2003). *Freemasonry and the Birth of Modern Science*, Fair Winds Press, Gloucester MA.

— (2005). *Turning the Hiram Key*, Fair Winds Press, Gloucester, MA.

Lomas, R., and C. Knight (1996). *The Hiram Key*, Fair Winds Press, Gloucester MA.

— (1997). *The Second Messiah*, Fair Winds Press, Gloucester MA.

— (2000). *Uriel's Machine*, Fair Winds Press, Gloucester MA.

— (2002). *The Book of Hiram*, Century, London.

McClelland, D.C. (1961). *The Achieving Society*, Free Press, New York.

Mason, R. and S.P.R. Rose (1987). "Lasting Changes in Spontaneous Multiunit Activity in the Chick Forebrain Following Passive Avoidance Training," *Neuroscience*, 21, pp. 931-41.

Mathies, H.J. (1986). *Learning and Memory: Mechanisms of information storage in the nervous system*, Pergamon, London.

Mazda, F. (1983). *Electronic Engineer's Reference Book*, 5th ed., Butterworth, London.

Michel, G.E. and C.I. Moore (1995). *Developmental Psychobiology: An Interdisciplinary Science*, MIT Press, Cambridge, MA.

Montaigne, K. and W.F. Pickard (1984). "Offset of the vacuolar potential of Characean cells in response electromagnetic radiation over the range 250 Hz-250 Khz," *Bioelectromagnetics*, 5, 31.

Moser, C. (1992). *Book of Vital World Statistics*, Hutchinson, London.

Newton, I. (1952). *Mathematical Principles of Natural Philosophy*, University of Chicago Press, Chicago IL.

Oliver, G. (1867). *Origin of the Royal Arch: English Royal Arch Degree*, William Reeves, London.

Ovason, D. (1999). *The Secret Zodiacs of Washington D.C.*, Century, London.

Paradine, C.G., and B.H. Rivett (1964). *Statistical Methods for Technologists*, English Universities Press, London.

Pearce, S., Letter (2000). *BMJ*, December 24.

Piccardi, G. (1960). "Exposé Introductif," Symposium Intern. sur les Rel. Phen. Sol et Terre, Brussels: Presses Académiques Européennes.

Pincus, J.H., and G.J. Tucker (1978). *Behavioral Neurology*, Oxford University Press, Oxford and New York.

Pinker, S. (1994). *The Language Instinct*, Penguin, London.

— (2003). *The Blank Slate*, Penguin, London.

Plath, S. (1966). *The Bell Jar*, Faber and Faber, London.

Playfair, G.L., and S. Hill (1978). *The Cycles of Heaven*, Pan, London.

Pople, J. (1950). "A Theory of the Structure of Water," *Proceedings of the Royal Society*, A, ccii, p. 323.

Prescott, A. (2000). "The Devil's Freemason: Richard Carlile and his Manual of Freemasonry," paper presented at the Sheffield Masonic Study Circle, November 30.

Preston, W. (1795). *Illustrations of Masonry*, G. and T. Wilkie, London.

Pribram, K.H. (1971). *Languages of the Brain: Experimental Paradoxes and Principles in Neuropsychology*, Englewood Cliffs, N.J., Prentice-Hall.

Pribram, K.H. (ed.) (1969). *On the Biology of Learning*, Harcourt, Brace and World, New York..

Radio Society of Great Britain (1963). *The Amateur Radio Handbook*, RSGB, London.

Repacholi, M.H. (1998). "Low Level Exposure to Radio-Frequency Electromagnetic Fields: Health Effects and Research Needs," *Bioelectromagnetics*, 19, 1.

Rodrik, D. (2002). *In Search of Deep Determinants of Economic Growth*, World Bank. Washington.

Rose, S. (1992). *The Making of Memory: From Molecules to Mind*, Bantam Press, London.

Ross, J.B., and M.M. McLaughlin (eds.) (1968). *The Portable Renaissance Reader*, Penguin, London.

Sachs, G. (1998). *The Astrology File*, Orion, London.

Seale, W. (1997). "The Design of Lafayette Park," *White House History*, White House Historical Association, Washington, vol. 2, no.1, p 6.

Seymour, P. (1997). *The Scientific Basis of Astrology*, Quantum, London.

Stevenson, D. (1988). *The Origins of Freemasonry: Scotland's Century 1590-1710*, Cambridge University Press, Cambridge.

Stringer, C., and C. Gamble (1993). *In Search of the Neanderthals*, Thames and Hudson, London.

Sykes, B. (2001). *The Seven Daughters of Eve*, Bantam, London.

Thomas, A., S. Chess, and H.G. Birch (1970). "The Origin of Personality," *Scientific American*, 223, pp. 102-9.

Van Buren, E. (1983). *The Secret of the Illuminati*, Spearman, London.

Washington, G.: George Washington Papers at the Library of Congress, 1741-1799.

Watkins, A. (1925). *The Old Straight Track* (reprinted Abacus, London, 1974).

Whitfield, P. (2001). *Astrology: A History*, British Library, London.

Wills, C. (1993). *The Runaway Brain, The Evolution of Human Uniqueness*, Flamingo, London.

Wilson, C. (2001). "Why I Now Believe Astrology Is a Science," *Daily Mail*, March 22.

Wren, C. (1750). *Parentalia or Memoirs of the Family of the Wrens . . . but chiefly of Sir C. Wren . . . Compiled by his son Christopher*, S. Wren and J. Ames, London.

# Footnotes

1 McClelland, D. C. (1961). *The Achieving Society*, Free Press, New York, p. 150.

2 20 days before or after the winter solstice, the Sun sets behind Ward Hill on Hoy, and then 30 minutes later reappears in the Dwarfie Gap, so seeming to rise in the West.

3 Heath, R. (2005). *Powerpoints, Secret Rulers and Hidden Forces in the Landscape*. Blue Stone Press, Llandysul, p. 7.

4 Ibid., p. 7.

5 Hutchinson, H. F. (1976). *Sir Christopher Wren, a biography*, Reader's Union, Newton Abbot, p. 65.

6 Wren, C. (1750). Quoted in: Wren, S., *Parentalia or Memoirs of the Family of the Wrens*, London.

7 Preston, W. (1795). *Illustrations of Masonry*, G. and T. Wilkie, London, book 4, section 3.

8 Heath (2005), pp. 17-18.

9 Ibid., p. 106.

10 Carlile, R. (1825). *Manual of Freemasonry*, William Reeves, London, p. vii.

11 Ibid., p. xiii.

12 http://www.blakearchive.org.

13 Heath (2005), p. 113.

14 http://memory.loc.gov/ammem/gwhtml/gwtime.html (accessed 15 Sept 2005).

15 Freeman, D. S. (1970). *Washington*, Eyre & Spottiswoode, London, p. 575.

16 Ibid., p. 583.

17 Van Buren, E. (1983). *The Secret of the Illuminati*, Spearman, London, pp. 142-4.

18 Prescott, A. (2000). "The Devil's Freemason: Richard Carlile and his Manual of Freemasonry," paper presented at the Sheffield Masonic Study Circle, 30 November: http://freemasonry.dept.shef.ac.uk/?q=papers_8.

19 Stevenson, D. (1988). *The Origins of Freemasonry*, Cambridge University Press, Cambridge, p. xii.

20 Ibid., p. xii.

21 Ashmole, E. (1652). *Theatrum Chemicum Brittanicum*, London, http://oldsite.library.upenn.edu/etext/collections/science/ashmole/index.html#TOC.

22 Campion, N. (1989) in A. Kitson (ed.) *History and Astrology*, Unwin Paperbacks, London, p. 56.

23 Houlding, D. (1997). "Judicial Astrology," *The Traditional Astrologer Magazine*, issue 14, May.

24 Dyer, C. (1987). *William Preston and his Work*, Lewis Masonic, Hersham, p 1.

25 The full text of the 1795 Edition can be found at: http://www.robertlomas.com/preston/padlock/index.html.

26 Dyer (1987), pp. 2-3.

27 Preston (1795), Introduction.

28 Lomas, R. (2005). *Turning the Hiram Key*, Fair Winds Press, Gloucester MA, p. 239.

29 Preston, W. (1772). *Illustrations of Masonry*, G. and T. Wilkie, London, book 2, section

4.
[30] http://www.freemasonrywatch.org/washington.html (accessed 14 Sept 2005).
[31] Ibid. (accessed 16 Sept 2005).
[32] http://www.cr.nps.gov (accessed Sept 2005).
[33] http://memory.loc.gov/ammem/gwhtml/gwintro.html (accessed 16 Sept 2005).
[34] George Washington Papers at the Library of Congress, 1741-1799.
[35] Ibid.
[36] Ibid.
[37] Ibid.
[38] Jusserand, Jean Jules (1916). *With Americans of Past and Present Days*, Random House, New York, part II, chapter III.
[39] Ibid.
[40] L'Enfant's "Observations Explanatory of the Plan," inscribed on it.
[41] Ibid.
[42] Washington Papers 1741-1799, letter to L'Enfant 2 Dec 1791.
[43] Ibid., letter to L'Enfant 26 Feb 1792.
[44] Ibid.
[45] Ibid.
[46] Ibid.
[47] Ibid.
[48] http://www.freemasonrywatch.org/washington.html (accessed 18 Sept 2005).
[49] Bowling, K. R. (2002). *Peter Charles L'Enfant: Vision, Honor and Male Friendship in the Early American Republic*, printed for the Friends of the George Washington University Libraries.
[50] Washington Papers 1741-1799: series 4, General Correspondence, 1697-1799. Peter Charles L'Enfant to George Washington, September 4, 1778.
[51] Ibid.: George Washington to Capt L'Enfant, March 1, 1782.
[52] Washington Papers 1741-1799: George Washington to Continental Congress, March 7, 1783.
[53] Ibid.: George Washington to Pierre Charles L'Enfant, January 1, 1787.
[54] *Washington Architecture 1791-1957*. Prepared by a Committee of the Washington-Metropolitan Chapter American Institute of Architects, Reinhold, New York, 1957, p. 5.
[55] http://www.gwmemorial.org (accessed 18 Sept 2005).
[56] Seale, W. (1997). "The Design of Lafayette Park," *White House History*, White House Historical Association, Washington, vol. 2, no.1, p 6.
[57] Washington Papers 1741-1799: George Washington to Alexandria, Virginia, Lodge Number 39 (Masons), December 28, 1783.
[58] Ibid.: George Washington to Georgetown, South Carolina, Masons, April 30, 1791.
[59] Ibid.: George Washington to Pennsylvania Grand Lodge Masons, January, 1797.
[60] http://freemasonry.bcy.ca (accessed 18 Sept 2005).
[61] Ovason, D. (1999). *The Secret Zodiacs of Washington D.C.*, Century, London. pp. 348-9.
[62] *Freemasonry Today*, 16, 2000, quoted in G. Hancock and R. Bauval (2004), *Talisman*,

Michael Joseph, London, p. 436.

[63] Ovason (1999), p. 76.

[64] Ibid., p. 171.

[65] Ibid., p. 118.

[66] Hancock, G. and R. Bauval (2004). *Talisman*, Michael Joseph, London, plate 46.

[67] http://memory.loc.gov/cgi-bin/ampage?collId=mgw1&fileName=mgw1b/gwpage741.db&recNum=0

[68] Watkins, A. (1925). *The Old Straight Track*, reprinted Abacus, London, 1974, p. 132.

[69] Carlile (1825), p xiii.

[70] http://internet.lodge.org.uk/library/research/prescott-devil.pdf.

[71] Ibid., p viii.

[72] Ibid., p xiv.

[73] Brown, R. S. (1892). *Stellar Theology and Masonic Astronomy Explained*, Appleton, Boston MA, p. 38.

[74] Oliver, Rev. G. (1867). *Origin of the Royal Arch: English Royal Arch Degree*, William Reeves, London.

[75] Brown (1892), pp. 78-9.

[76] Ibid., p. 35.

[77] Ibid., p 36.

[78] Ibid., p 36.

[79] Aubrey, J. (1685). *Naturall Historie of Wiltshire*, copy with additional notes in Aubrey's hand, 1691 [Bodleian Library, MS Aubrey 2. f.72v.].

[80] Gilbert, R. A. (1996). *Ars Quatuor Coronatorum*, vol. 109, London, p. 188.

[81] Hutchison, H. F. (1976), pp. 59-60.

[82] Preston (1772). *Illustration of Masonry*, G. and T. Wilkie, London, pp. 216-19.

[83] Lomas, R. (2003). *Freemasonry and the Birth of Modern Science*, Fair Winds Press, Gloucester MA.

[84] Stevenson (1988), p. 24.

[85] Ibid., p. 15.

[86] Ovason (1999), p. 350.

[87] Lomas, R, and C. Knight (2002). *The Book of Hiram*, Century, London.

[88] McClelland (1961), p. 60.

[89] Ibid., p. 86.

[90] Atkinson, J. W. (1958). *Motives in Fantasy, Action and Society*, Van Nostrand, London, p. 56.

[91] McClelland (1961), p. 364.

[92] Dawkins, R. (1995). "The Real Romance of the Stars," *The Independent* December 31.

[93] Heath, R. (1996). Editorial, *The Astrological Journal*, vol. 28, no. 3.

[94] Dawkins (1995).

[95] http://www.simonyi.ox.ac.uk/dawkins/WorldOfDawkin-archive/Dawkin/Work/Articles/1995-12romance_in_stars.shtml (accessed 21 Sept 2005).

[96] Heath, R. Private communication.

[97] Dictionary of National Biography (1903) (ed. Sidney Lee), Smith, Elder, London.

⁹⁸ Whitfield, P. (2001.) *Astrology: A History*, British Library, London, p. 172.

⁹⁹ Wilson, C. (2001). *Daily Mail*, March 22.

¹⁰⁰ Ibid.

¹⁰¹ Wilson, C. Private communication.

¹⁰² Hawking, S. (2001).*The Universe in a Nutshell*, Transworld, London, p. 103.

¹⁰³ McClelland (1961), p. 150.

¹⁰⁴ Ibid., p. 151.

¹⁰⁵ Dawkins (1995).

¹⁰⁶ Ibid.

¹⁰⁷ Thomas, A., S. Chess, and H. G. Birch (1970). "The Origin of Personality," *Scientific American*, 223, pp. 102-9.

¹⁰⁸ Bate, R.R., D. D. Mueller, and J. E. White (1971). *Fundamentals of Astrodynamics*, Dover, New York.

¹⁰⁹ Newton, I. (1952). *Mathematical Principles of Natural Philosophy*, University of Chicago Press, Chicago IL.

¹¹⁰ Eysenck, H.J., and D.K. Nias (1982). *Astrology, Science or Superstition?*, Maurice Temple Smith, London, p. 219.

¹¹¹ Gauquelin, M. (1969). *The Cosmic Clocks*, Paladin, London, pp. 156-71.

¹¹² Ibid., p. 157.

¹¹³ Gauquelin, M. (1994). *Cosmic Influences on Human Behavior*, Aurora Press, Santa Fe, p. 301.

¹¹⁴ Gauquelin (1969), p. 164.

¹¹⁵ Gauquelin, M. and F. (1967) "A Possible Hereditary Effect on Time of Birth in Relation to the Diurnal Movement of the Moon and the Nearest Planets: Its Relationship With Geomagnetic Activity," *Int. J. Biometeorol.*, 11:341.

¹¹⁶ Gauquelin (1969), p. 164.

¹¹⁷ Ibid., p. 184.

¹¹⁸ Seymour, P. (1997). *The Scientific Basis of Astrology*, Quantum, London, p. 58.

¹¹⁹ Ertel, S. (1989). "Purifying Gauquelin's Grain of Gold," *Correlation*, 9, 1.

¹²⁰ Gauquelin (1994), pp. 189-92.

¹²¹ Eysenck and Nias (1982), p. 193.

¹²² Gauquelin, M. (1988). *Planetary Heredity*, ACS Publications, El Cajon, CA.

¹²³ Seymour (1997), pp. 225-30.

¹²⁴ Eysenck and Nias (1982), p. 208.

¹²⁵ Gauquelin (1994), pp. 263-9.

¹²⁶ Ibid., pp. 206-11.

¹²⁷ Eysenck and Nias (1982), p. 206.

¹²⁸ Ibid., p. 208.

¹²⁹ Abell G.O. (1979). "Recent Advances," *Zetetic Scholar*, April.

¹³⁰ Gauquelin (1994), p. 301.

¹³¹ Sachs, G. (1998). *The Astrology File*, Orion, London, p. 10.

¹³² Ibid., pp. 49-61.

¹³³ Ibid., pp. 68-9.

[134] Ibid., p. 203.

[135] Ibid., p. 223.

[136] Ibid., p. 205.

[137] Lomas. R. and C. Knight (2003). *The Book of Hiram*, Century, London.

[138] Ibid., pp. 318-29.

[139] Gauquelin (1994), p. 124.

[140] Ibid., p. 127.

[141] Ibid., p. 111.

[142] Ibid., p. 90.

[143] McClelland (1961), p. 58.

[144] Eysenck and Nias (1982), p. viii.

[145] Ibid., p. viii.

[146] Ibid., p. 218.

[147] Ibid., p. 218.

[148] Ibid., p. 218.

[149] McClelland (1961).

[150] Newton (1952).

[151] McClelland (1961).

[152] Paradine, C.G., and B.H. Rivett (1964). *Statistical Methods for Technologists*, English Universities Press, London, p. 77.

[153] Gauquelin (1994).

[154] Rose, S. (1992). *The Making of Memory: From Molecules to Mind*, Bantam Press, London, p. 112.

[155] Pribram, K.H. (ed.) (1969). *On the Biology of Learning*, Harcourt, Brace and World, New York, p. 86.

[156] Rose (1992), p. 119.

[157] Greenfield, S. (1997). *The Human Brain—A Guided Tour*, Weidenfeld and Nicolson, London, p. 130.

[158] Ibid., pp. 138-9.

[159] Conel, J. (1939). *The Post-Natal Development of the Human Cerebral Cortex*, vol. I, Harvard University Press, Harvard, MA, p. 156.

[160] Edelman, G., and G. Tononi (2000). *Consciousness: How Matter Becomes Imagination*, Penguin, London, pp. 143-54.

[161] Ibid., p. 108.

[162] Rose (1992), p. 102.

[163] Greenfield, S. (2000). *The Private Life of the Brain*, Penguin, London, p. 62.

[164] Pinker, S. (1994). *The Language Instinct*, Penguin, London.

[165] Brown, R. (1958). *Words and Things*, Macmillan, London, p. 46.

[166] Gleitman, H. (1992). *Basic Psychology*, Norton, London.

[167] Lenneberg, E.H. (1967). *Biological Foundations of Language*, Wiley, New York.

[168] Greenfield (2000), p. 60.

[169] Rose (1992).

[170] Edelman and Tononi (2000), p.82.

[171] Greenfield (2000), p. 54.

[172] Gleitman (1992), p. 126.

[173] Carlson, N.R. (1986). *Physiology of Behavior*, Allyn and Bacon, Boston, MA.

[174] Eccles, J.C. (1982). "The Synapse: From electrical to chemical transmission," *Annual Review of Neuroscience*, vol. 5, pp. 325-39.

[175] Eccles, J.C. (1973). *The Understanding of the Brain*, McGraw Hill, New York.

[176] Bliss, T.V.P. and T. Lomo (1973). "Long-lasting Potentiation of Synaptic Transmission in the Dentate Area of the Anaesthetised Rabbit Following Stimulation of the Perforant Path," *Journal of Physiology*, 232, 331-56.

[177] Rose (1992), pp. 227-40.

[178] Mathies, H.J. (1986). *Learning and Memory: Mechanisms of information storage in the nervous system*, Pergamon, London, p. 86.

[179] Rose (1992), p. 247.

[180] Mason, R. and S.P.R. Rose (1987). "Lasting Changes in Spontaneous Multiunit Activity in the Chick Forebrain Following Passive Avoidance Training," *Neuroscience*, 21, pp. 931-41.

[181] Rose (1992), p.271.

[182] Ibid., p.178.

[183] *Sunday Times*, December 9, 2001.

[184] Plath, S. (1966). *The Bell Jar*, Faber and Faber, London, p. 138.

[185] Reynolds, M. (2000). *Hemingway: The Final Years*, Norton, London, p. 28.

[186] *Sunday Times*, December 9, 2001.

[187] Freeman, W.J. (2000). *How Brains Make Up Their Minds*, Phoenix, London, p. 52.

[188] Ibid., p. 55.

[189] Gauquelin (1994), p. 189.

[190] Freeman (2000), p. 46.

[191] Pincus, J.H., and G.J. Tucker (1978). *Behavioral Neurology*, Oxford University Press, Oxford and New York, p. xiii.

[192] Dennett, D.C. (1984). *Elbow Room: The Varieties of Free Will Worth Wanting*, MIT Press, Cambridge, MA, p. 5.

[193] Edelman, G.M. (1989). *Neural Darwinism: The Theory of Neuronal Group Selection*, Basic Books, London, p. 3.

[194] Michel, G.E. and C.I. Moore (1995). *Developmental Psychobiology: An Interdisciplinary Science*, MIT Press, Cambridge, MA, p. 8.

[195] Greenfield (2000), p. 167.

[196] Ibid., p. 22.

[197] Ibid., p. 168.

[198] Hobson, J.A. (1989). *Sleep*, Scientific American Library, New York, p. 58.

[199] Gopnik, A., A. Meltzoff and P. Kuhl (1999). *How Babies Think*, Phoenix, London, p. 183.

[200] Ibid., pp. 184-5.

[201] Edelman and Tononi (2000), p. 86.

[202] Pincus and Tucker (1978), pp. 9-22.

[203] Ibid., p. 20.

[204] Ibid., p. 12.

[205] Piccardi, G. (1960). "Exposé Introductif," Symposium Intern. sur les Rel. Phen. Sol et Terre, Brussels: Presses Académiques Européennes. It can be seen in translation at: http://www.springerlink.com/(br4n4245ie5kim45rxl0k0jl)/app/home/search-articles-results.asp?referrer=searchmainxml&backto=contribution,1,1;issue,9,9;journal,42,180; linkingpublicationresults,1:100429,1 (accessed June 5, 2006).

[206] Pople, J. (1950). "A Theory of the Structure of Water," *Proceedings of the Royal Society*, A, ccii, p. 323.

[207] Piccardi (1960).

[208] Brown, F.A., Jr. (1954). "Persistent Activity Rhythms in the Oyster," *American Journal of Physiology*, 178, p. 510.

[209] Brown, F.A., Jr. and E. Terracini (1959). "Exogenous Timing of Rat Spontaneous Activity Periods," *Proceedings of the Society of Experimental Biological Medicine*, 102, p. 457.

[210] Brown, F.A., Jr. (1965). "Propensity for Lunar Periodicity in Hamsters," *Proceedings of the Society of Experimental Biological Medicine*, 120, p. 792.

[211] Brown, F.A., Jr. (1966). "Living Clocks," *Science*, 130, p. 1535.

[212] Cole, L.C. (1957). "Biological Clock in the Unicorn," *Science*, 130, p. 874.

[213] Brown, F.A., Jr. (1962). *Biological Clocks*, Heath, Boston, MA, p. 62.

[214] Law, S.P. (1986). "The Regulation of Menstrual Cycle and Its Relationship to the Moon," *Acta Obstet. Gynecol. Scand.* 65 (1), pp. 45-8.

[215] Aronson, J. (1997). Letter, *BMJ*, p. 314 (29 March).

[216] Playfair, G.L., and S. Hill (1978). *The Cycles of Heaven*, Pan, London, p. 233.

[217] Independent Expert Group on Mobile Phones (2000). *Mobile phones and health*, IEGMP; also available on http://www.iegmp.org.uk (accessed May 28, 2006).

[218] Ibid., 5.13.

[219] Montaigne, K. and W.F. Pickard (1984). "Offset of the vacuolar potential of Characean cells in response electromagnetic radiation over the range 250 Hz-250 Khz," *Bioelectromagnetics*, 5, 31.

[220] Independent Expert Group on Mobile Phones (2000), 5.16.

[221] Frohlich, H. (1968). "Long-range Coherence and Energy Storage in Biological Systems," *Int. J. Quantum Chem.*, II, 641.

[222] Frohlich, H. (1980). "The Biological Effects of Microwaves and Related Questions," *Adv. Electronics Electron. Phys*, 53, 85.

[223] Independent Expert Group on Mobile Phones (2000), 5.17-5.18.

[224] Kandel, E.R., J.H. Schwartz and T.M. Jessel (2000). *Principles of Neural Science* (4th ed.), McGraw Hill, New York.

[225] Repacholi, M.H. (1998). "Low Level Exposure to Radio-Frequency Electromagnetic Fields: Health Effects and Research Needs," *Bioelectromagnetics*, 19, 1.

[226] Independent Expert Group on Mobile Phones (2000), 5.47-5.48.

[227] Gopnik, Meltzoff and Kuhl (1999), pp. 185-6.

[228] Edelman and Tononi (2000), p. 88.

[229] Rose (1992), p. 272.

[230] Hawker, P. (1980). *A Guide to Amateur Radio*, Radio Society of Great Britain, London, p. 10.

[231] Hawking (2001), p. 103.

[232] Pinker, S. (2003). *The Blank Slate*, Penguin, London, p. 26.

[233] Pribram, K.H. (1971). *Languages of the Brain: Experimental Paradoxes and Principles in Neuropsychology*, Englewood Cliffs, N.J., Prentice-Hall.

[234] Ibid. (see figs 1-14).

[235] Hawking (2001), p. 103.

[236] Cole, H. (1992). *Understanding Radar*, Blackwell Scientific, Oxford, pp. 42-6.

[237] Bhagwati, J. (1966). *The Economics of Underdeveloped Countries*, Weidenfeld and Nicolson, London.

[238] Moser, C. (1992). *Book of Vital World Statistics*, Hutchinson, London.

[239] Hall, R.E., and C.I. Jones (1997). "Levels of Economic Activity Across Countries," *Papers and Proceedings of the 109th Annual Meeting of American Economic Association*, Stanford University Press, Berkeley, CA.

[240] Ibid.

[241] McClelland (1961), pp. 1-2.

[242] Fox, A. and P. Davies (2002). "Can Superstitious Behaviour Reduce Work Stress?," in supplement with *BMJ* 2002:325:S83 (14 September); see full text at http://careerfocus.bmjjournals.com/cgi/content/full/325/7364/S83 (accessed June 5, 2006), quoting survey by D.F. Danzl, "Lunacy" *J Emerg Med* 1987, 5, pp. 91-5.

[243] Bhattacharjee, C., P. Bradley, M. Smith, A. Scally and B.J. Wilson (2000). "Do Animals Bite More During a Full Moon? Retrospective Observational Analysis," *BMJ*, 321, December, 1559-61.

[244] Ibid.

[245] Chapman, S., J. Cornwall , J. Righetti and L. Sung (2000). "Preventing Dog Bites in Children: Randomised Controlled Trial of an Educational Intervention," *BMJ*, 320, June, 1512-13.

[246] Chapman, S., and S. Morrell (2000). "Barking Mad? Another Lunatic Hypothesis Bites the Dust," *BMJ*, 321, December, 1561-3.

[247] Ibid.

[248] Laurence, A.S. (2001). Letter, *BMJ*, January 18.

[249] Pearce, S., Letter, (2000). *BMJ*, December 24.

[250] Hawking (2001), p. 103.

[251] Quoted in Ross, J.B., and M.M. McLaughlin (eds.) (1968). *The Portable Renaissance Reader*, Penguin, London.

[252] Freeman (2000), p. 107.

[253] Edelman and Tononi (2000), p. 257.

[254] Hawking (2001), p. 103.

[255] Leakey, R., and R. Lewin (1992). *Origins Reconsidered: In Search of What Made Us Human*, Little Brown, London, p. 227.

[256] Ibid., pp. 228-9.

[257] Ibid., p. 234.

[258] Ibid., p. 235.

[259] Dawkins, R. (1988). *The Blind Watchmaker*, Penguin Books, London, p. 305.

[260] Stringer, C., and C. Gamble (1993). *In Search of the Neanderthals*, Thames and Hudson, London, p. 218.

[261] Ibid., p. 119.

[262] Gopnik, Meltzoff and Kuhl (1999).

[263] Sykes, B. (2001). *The Seven Daughters of Eve*, Bantam, London.

[264] Wills, C. (1993). *The Runaway Brain, The Evolution of Human Uniqueness*, Flamingo, London.

[265] Henderson, M. (2002). "Scratches that trace the ascent of man," *The Times*, January 11, p. 5.

[266] Gray, J.R., et al. (2003). "Neural mechanisms of general fluid intelligence," *Nature Neuroscience*, 6 (2) February.

[267] http://news-info.wustl.edu/News/2003/fluid.htm (accessed June 5, 2006).

[268] Ibid.

[269] Gauquelin (1994), pp. 55-8.

[270] Dawkins (1995).

[271] Dawkins (1988).

[272] Ibid.

[273] Overson, D. (1999). *The Secret Zodiacs of Washington*, Century, London, p. 350.

[274] http://memory.loc.gov/ammem/gwhtml/gwtime.html (accessed Sept 15, 2005).

[275] Lomas (2005), pp. 374-5.

[276] Jung, C.G. (ed.) (1943). *Man and His Symbols*, Arkana, Penguin Books, 1990, pp. 102-3 (first published Aldus Books, 1964).

[277] Freeman (2000).

[278] Pribram (1969).

[279] King, S. (2000). *On Writing: A Memoir*, Hodder and Stoughton, London, p. 20.

[280] Heath, R., Private Communication.

[281] Gauquelin, M. (1983). *The Truth about Astrology*, Blackwell, Oxford, p. 181.

# Index

Abell, George, 138
Aberdeen, 91, 92
Adams, John, 49
Africa, 248, 265, 266, 268, 279
Aholiab, 97
Albion, 30
Alexandria, 20, 64, 74
Alexandria Lodge, 20, 74
Algebraic subterfuge, 209
*Alice in Wonderland*, 230
All or None Law, 180
Allegheny River, 19
Allegory, 14, 35, 282
Allensbach, 141, 147
Alzheimer's disease, 168
Amala, 177
Amateur radio, 223, 224, 302
America, 14-17, 20, 30, 32, 33, 49, 50, 53, 55, 63, 70, 72-74, 76, 84, 85, 114, 116, 248, 274
*America, A Prophecy*, 30, 32, 33
American Constitution, 15
Ancient and Accepted Scottish Rite, 99
Anticonvulsant tablets, 203, 205
Apollo, 121-123, 168
Aquarius, 123, 143, 144, 162, 163
Archeoastronomy, 24
Architecture, 27, 39, 88
Argentina, 248
Aries, 86, 131, 143, 144, 147
Arizona, 62
Ark of the Covenant, 98
Aronson, Jeff, 210
Ashmole, Elias, 52, 53, 111
Asia, 248
Astrological journal, 108, 112
Astrology, 15, 33, 52-55, 60, 62, 77, 82, 85, 96, 97, 103, 104, 107-117, 119, 120, 124-129, 131, 132, 135-138, 140, 141, 147-149, 153-155, 157, 159, 160, 162-166, 171, 176, 183, 200, 219, 220, 236, 237, 239, 240, 243, 245,

256, 259-263, 274, 276-278, 291-293, 308
Astronomy, 15, 28, 55, 88, 111, 120, 125, 261
Astrophysics, 229, 235, 239, 250
Attorney General, 67
Aubrey, John, 87
Australia, 220, 223, 248, 252, 254-256
Autumnal Equinox, 93
AWA, 147
Axons, 173, 179, 180, 187, 188, 190, 191, 194, 232, 233, 235, 242

Babies, 109, 140, 160, 161, 163-165, 167, 169-171, 173-176, 183, 189, 193, 194, 197, 210, 218, 240, 241, 243, 249, 255, 290
Babylon, 27, 54
Bacon, Francis, 49, 54
Baigent, Michael, 76
Banneker, Ben, 64, 65
Barbados, 19
Bauval, Robert, 77, 78
Bazeleel, 97, 98
Beautiful Virgin, 78
Beauty, 51
Beer belly, 226, 227, 299
Belgium, 133
Bell Jar, 185
Belly Dance, 224
Beowulf cluster, 197
Berkeley University, 197
Birth, 59, 82, 107, 112, 127, 129, 131-141, 146-150, 153, 156-159, 162-166, 171, 173, 174, 176, 177, 192, 194, 195, 198, 200, 210, 236, 237, 240, 242, 259, 261, 262, 274-277, 279, 281, 290, 291, 307
Birth-star, 242, 259, 275, 276, 290, 291
Blake, William, 29, 30, 32, 33, 55, 274
Blastocyst, 172
Bliss, Tim, 180
Blombos Cave, 266, 268
Bodleian Library, 87

Bohr, Niels, 258, 260
Border collie, 201, 219, 250
Bowling, Kenneth R, 70
Bradford Royal Infirmary, 253
Bradford University School of Management, 244, 246
Brain, 8, 36, 124-126, 128, 165-183, 185-200, 202, 204, 205, 210-216, 218-220, 228, 232-237, 241-243, 250, 251, 257, 263, 264, 268-270, 272-277, 279-281, 284, 289-292
Brain City, 189
Brainscape, 191, 271-273, 290
Braver, Todd, 273
Bright Morning Star, 14, 15, 17, 21, 32, 33, 35, 39, 41, 46, 50-53, 57, 59, 60, 78, 94-104, 107, 112, 114, 117, 119, 120, 129, 137, 140, 148, 149, 157, 160, 161, 163, 164, 166, 176, 183, 187, 189, 196, 199, 200, 215, 216, 218, 228, 229, 231, 236, 237, 239, 240, 242-244, 249, 250, 257, 259, 260, 262, 263, 269, 271, 272, 274-282, 284, 285, 287, 289, 291-293, 306, 307
Bristol, 157
Britain, 23, 24, 30, 32, 50, 159, 220, 248
*British Medical Journal*, 210, 250, 253, 254, 256
Brocq, Louis, 150
Brodgar, 23, 24
Brotherly Love, 14, 17
Brown, Frank, 207-209, 211, 279
Brown, Roger, 177
Bruce, Sir William, 27
Brunei, 248
Brussels, 206
Bursting activity, 182, 219
Butterfly, 193

Campion, Nicholas, 54